THE MODERN POETS

THE MODERN POETS

AN AMERICAN-BRITISH ANTHOLOGY

edited by JOHN MALCOLM BRINNIN, *University of Connecticut*

and BILL READ, *Boston University*

with photographs by ROLLIE McKENNA

McGraw-Hill Book Company, Inc.
NEW YORK   SAN FRANCISCO   TORONTO

The photographs reproduced herein are used by permission of the copyright holder, Rollie McKenna.

The following poems originally appeared in *The New Yorker:* "The Prodigal" (1951), "A Cold Spring" (1952), and "Florida" (1962), by Elizabeth Bishop; "Ego" (1956), by Philip Booth; "Hotel Paradiso e Commerciale" (1960), by John Malcolm Brinnin; "Calm Winter Sleep" (1961) and "The Choice" (1961), by Hilary Corke; "The Sleeping Giant" (1955), by Donald Hall; "The Great Bear" (1958), by John Hollander; "In the Night" (1955), by Elizabeth Jennings; "Voices from the Other World" (1957), by James Merrill; "Underwood" (1954), "The Gift to Be Simple" (1955), and "Water Island" (1960), by Howard Moss; "Pigeons" (1954), by Alastair Reid; "The Glass Blower" and "Midsummer" (1962), by James Scully; "Letter Written on a Ferry Crossing Long Island Sound" (1961), by Anne Sexton; "The Green Shepherd" (1956) and "My Father in the Night Commanding No" (1961), by Louis Simpson; "Bone Thoughts on a Dry Day"

PREFACE

AMONG THE WORKS OF MODERN POETS, poems that give pleasure are far more common, we believe, than poems that present problems. To make an anthology that would confirm this belief, we have looked into the weighty collected poems of recognized masters and the modest first volumes of apprentices. Confining ourselves to the contemporary, we have nevertheless been able to choose from a range spanning five or six generations of American and British verse. Our aim has been to pick, from the works of the finest living poets, poems of representative substance and power that can travel freely in any English-speaking country without an interpreter. Having found these in abundance, we present them in confidence that they will move, delight, and beguile even those readers who encounter them for the first time. Instead of the usual notes, we have informal commentaries and brief biographies. The photographic portraits have a documentary interest in themselves. In a determination to avoid the sort of well-meaning apparatus which is designed to initiate and instruct but which, too often, only alienates and befuddles, we have otherwise allowed the poems to speak for themselves.

Contrary to rumor, modern poetry is not an obstacle course or an occult science. Such notions, infectious as the common cold and just as hard to shake, have tended to put a curse on poetry—a form of art that, above everything else, is a communication to be shared. The poems in this volume invite congenial acquaintance. They give proof, page by page, that before they are puzzles to be solved or substances to be analyzed, they are human documents waiting to be claimed.

Where we have provided commentary, our aim has been merely to set a perspective, identify an allusion, turn a key that may help to make a first reading a comparatively full and easy one. Commentary cannot account for the ultimate values of any poem, but, by supplying points of information and by suggesting interpretations, we can perhaps provide the bases on which these values may be discovered. We trust that most of the poems are self-contained and self-explanatory.

Ezra Pound was unavailable to be photographed by Rollie McKenna. The only other poet not represented by a portrait is E. E. Cummings, whose death occurred while this volume was being prepared.

JOHN MALCOLM BRINNIN

BILL READ

CONTENTS

THE MODERN POETS

DANNIE ABSE, *born September, 1923, in Wales, lives in Golders Green, London, with his wife and two children. His early life as a member of a socially conscious Jewish family in Wales is recorded in his autobiographical novel* Ash on a Young Man's Sleeve. *Like his father, he is a physician and during World War II served with the Medical Corps of the Royal Air Force. He was one of the founders of a mid-fifties movement in poetry whose members were known as "mavericks" and whom critics tended to categorize as "neo-Georgian."*

*The person to whom this poem is addressed is, like
the author, both a physician and a poet. Ehrlich was
the German scientist who discovered salvarsan after
606 experiments; Koch was another German, who
devised a method of staining bacteria with aniline
dyes, leading to his discovery of the bacterial causes of
many infectious diseases; "that Greek" is Archi-
medes, whose cry, translated back to its
original, was "Eureka!"*

LETTER TO ALEX COMFORT

Alex, perhaps a colour of which neither of us had dreamt
may appear in the test-tube with God knows what admonition.
Ehrlich certainly was one who broke down the mental doors,
yet only after his six hundred and sixth attempt.

Koch also, painfully and with true German thoroughness
eliminated the impossible, and proved that too many of us
are dying from the same disease. Yet was his green dream,
like yours, fired to burn away an ancient distress.

Still I, myself, don't like Germans, but prefer the unkempt
voyagers, who, like butterflies drunk with suns,
can only totter crookedly in the dazed air
to reach charmingly their destination, as if by accident.

That Greek one then is my hero, who watched the bath water
rise above his navel and rushed out naked, 'I found it,
I found it' into the street in all his shining, and forgot
that others would only stare at his genitals. What laughter!

Or Newton, leaning in Woolsthorpe against the garden wall
forgot his indigestion and all such trivialities,
but gaped up at heaven in just surprise, and with
true gravity, witnessed the vertical apple fall.

O what a marvellous observation! Who would have reckoned
that such a pedestrian miracle could alter history,
that henceforward everyone must fall, whatever
their rank, at thirty-two feet per second, per second?

You too, I know, have waited for doors to fly open and played
with your cold chemicals and written long letters
to the Press; listened to the truth afraid and dug deep
into the wriggling earth for a rainbow, with an honest spade.

But nothing rises. Neither spectres, nor oil, nor love.
And the old professor must think you mad, Alex, as you rehearse
poems in the laboratory like vows, and curse those clever scientists
who dissect away the wings and the haggard heart from the dove.

In a century when nearly all times seem to be periods
between wars, poets have often attempted to render
the general fears of whole nations in specific, personal, and therefore more emotional terms. Here the
author uses unusual words like metaphrast (one who
alters the sense of something) and preterites (words
or tenses that belong to the past) as he relates a
small incident in relation to the bad dream of the
past and the appalling prospect of the future.

VERSES AT NIGHT

SLEEPLESS, by the windowpane I stare—
    black aeroplanes disturb the air.
    The ticking moon glares down aghast.
        The seven branched tree is bare.

Oh how much like Europe's gothic Past!
    This scene my nightmare's metaphrast:
    glow of the radioactive worm,
        the preterites of the Blast.

Unreal? East and West fat Neros yearn
       for other fiddled Romes to burn,
       and so dogma cancels dogma
              and heretics in their turn.

By my wife now I lie quiet as a
       thought of how moon and stars might blur,
       and miles of smoke squirm overhead
              rising to Man's arbiter;

the grey skin shrivelling from the head,
       our two skulls in the double bed,
       leukaemia in the soul of all
              flowing through the blood instead.

'No', I shout, as by her side I sprawl,
       'No', again, as I hear my small
       dear daughter whimper in her cot
              and across the darkness call.

CONRAD AIKEN, *born August 5, 1889,*
in Savannah, Georgia, has recently returned
with his wife to live in his native city after
having for many years lived variously
in the village of Brewster on Cape Cod,
an apartment in New York, and several
houses in Rye, on the Sussex coast of
England. He went to Harvard as a member
of the famous class of 1911, which included
T. S. Eliot, Heywood Broun, Robert Benchley,
and Walter Lippmann, and has subsequently
published scores of works including novels,
short stories, plays, criticism, and the auto-
biography Ushant, *in which he recounts the*
story of his equal but divided loyalty to his
own culture and that of England. He was
Consultant in Poetry at the Library of Con-
gress for two years but has otherwise de-
clined public positions and avoided public
appearances.

*By showing how the springtime of Cape Cod, the
landfall of Pilgrims who crossed on the* Mayflower,
*repeats the springtime of the Elizabethan poets William
Shakespeare, Ben Jonson, and William Drummond
—who are here designated as "Will," "Ben," and "the
crab-apple sage at Hawthornden," respectively—the
poet reflects on the continuity of history, the
echoes of lost language, and the persistence
of human aspiration.*

MAYFLOWER

LISTEN: the ancient voices hail us from the farther shore:
now, more than ever, in the New England spring,
we hear from the sea once more
the ghostly leave-takings, the hawser falling, the anchor weighing,
cries and farewells, the weeping on the quayside, and the praying:
and the devout fathers, with no thought to fail,
westward to unknown waters set joyless sail,
and at length, 'by God's providence,' 'by break of day espied
land, which we deemed to be Cape Cod.'
'It cause us to rejoice together and praise God,
seeing so goodly a land, and wooded to the brink of the sea.'
And still we share that providential tide,
the pleasant bay, wooded on every side
with 'oaks, pines, juniper, sassafras,' and the wild fowl rising
in clouds and numbers past surmising.
Yes: the ancient voices speak once more,
as spring, praised then by Will and Ben,
winds up our country clock again:
their spring, still living, now
when caterpillars tent the bough,
and seagulls speak
over the ale-wives running in Payne Creek.
The lyre-tree, seven-branched, the ancient plum, has cast

her sterile bloom, and the soft skin is cast
to glisten on the broken wall,
where the new snake sleeps in altered light;
and before sun-up, and late at night,
the pinkwinks shrill, the pinkwinks trill,
crying from the bog's edge to lost Sheepfold Hill.
Spring, spring, spring, spring, they cry,
water voice and reed voice,
spring, spring, spring, spring, they rejoice,
we who never die, never die!
But already the mayflower on the side hill is brown and dry,
Dry Hill is dry, the bog is drained,
and although for weeks it has not rained,
and the quick plough breaks dust,
yet towards summer the golden-rod and wormwood thrust.
The woodchuck is in the peas. And on his log,
the whip-poor-will shrieks and thumps in the bright May-morning fog.

Three hundred years from Will and Ben,
and the crab-apple sage at Hawthornden;
and now they wind our country clock again,
themselves, whose will it was that wound it then.
Three hundred years of snow and change,
the Mermaid voices growing lost and strange;
heard at first clearly on this yellow sand,
ghost voices, shadow of ghost and whisper of ghost,
haunting us briefly in the bright and savage land,
heard in the sea-roar, then sunk in silence, lost.
Yet not lost wholly:
in deed, in charter, and in covenant sweetly kept,
in laws and ordinances, in the Quaker's Thee and Thou,
in the grave rites of birth and death, the marriage vow,
and the ballad's melancholy.
Sung by the driftwood fire or behind the plough,
in the summer-kitchen to the warm cricket-song,

sung at maying, sung at haying,
shouted at husking to the fiddle's playing,
murmured to the cradle's rocking,
and the wheel humming, the treadle knocking.
And in the names kept too: sorrel and purslane,
ground-ivy, catnip, elecampane,
burdock and spurge, and sultry tansy,
woad-waxen, and the johnny-jump-up pansy.
Yet even so, though in the observance kept,
here most of all where first our fathers stept,
was something of the spirit that became idle, and at last
lost all that love; and heard no more
the voices singing from a distant shore.
Intricately, into the present, sank the past:
or, dreaming only of the future, slept.

II

God's Acres once were plenty, the harvest good:
five churchyards, six, in this sparse neighbourhood,
each with its huddled parish of straight stones,
green rows of sod above neat rows of bones.
The weeping willow grieves above the urn,
the hour-glass with wings awaits its immortal turn:
on every slab a story and a glory,
the death's head grinning his memento mori.
All face the sunset, too: all face the west.
What dream was this of a more perfect rest—?
One would have thought the east, that the first ray
might touch them out of darkness into day.
Or were they sceptics, and perforce, in doubt,
wistful to watch the last of light go out?
And in the sunset the names look westward, names like eyes:
the sweet-sounding and still watchful names. Here lies
Mercy or Thankful, here Amanda Clark,
the wife of Rufus; nor do they dread the dark,

but gaily now step down the road past Stony Brook,
call from the pasture as from the pages of a book,
their own book, but their own lives written,
each look and laugh and heartache, nothing forgotten.
Rufus it was who cleared of bullbriar the Long Field,
walled it with fieldstone, and brought to fabulous yield
the clay-damp corner plot, where wild grape twines.
Amanda planted the cedars, the trumpet-vines,
mint-beds, and matrimony vine, and columbines.
Each child set out and tended his own tree,
to each his name was given. Thus, they still live, still see:
Mercy, Deborah, Thankful, Rufus and Amanda Clark,
trees that praise sunlight, voices that praise the dark.
The houses are gone, the little shops are gone,
squirrels preach in the chapel. A row of stone
all now that's left of the cobbler's, or in tall grass
a scrap of harness where once the tannery was.
And the blue lilacs, the grey laylocks, take possession
round every haunted cellar-hole, like an obsession:
keep watch in the dead houses, on vanished stairs,
where Ephraim or Ahira mended chairs:
sneak up the slope where once the smoke-house stood
and herrings bronzed in smoke of sweet fernwood.
Lost, lost, lost, lost—the bells from Quivett Neck
sing through the Sabbath fog over ruin and wreck,
roofs sinking, walls falling, ploughland grown up to wood.
Five churchyards, six, in this sparse neighbourhood:
God's Acres once were plenty, the harvest good.

III

Three hundred years: in time's eye only a moment.
Time only for the catbird's wail,
from one June to another, flaunting his tail,
the joyful celebrant with his own mournful comment.
Time only for the single dream,

as, in this misty morning, all our generations seem,
seem only one, one face, one hope, one name:
those who first crossed the sea, first came,
and the newborn grandchild, crying, one and the same.
Yes now, now most of all, in the fateful glare
of mankind's hatred everywhere,
time yields its place, with its own bell
uncharms and then recharms its spell:
and time is gone, but everything else is here,
all is clear, all is one day, one year,
the many generations seem,
and are, one single purpose, one single name and dream.
Three hundred years from Will and Ben
our country clock's wound up again.
And as it chimes we hear ourselves still saying
the living words which they said then—
words for haying, words for maying,
love of earth, love of love, love of God,
but most the strong-rooted and sweet-smelling love of sod,
earth natural and native in the clay-red heart,
ourselves like pines in the sand growing, part
of the deep water underground,
the wild rose in the mouth, the sound
of leaves in surf and surf in leaves,
wind suffering in the chimney and round the eaves,
forgetfulness in the chattering brook, sleepiness in the sand,
forget-me-nots in the eyes, moonlight in the palm of the hand.

All's here, all's kept, for now
spring brings back the selfsame apple bough
that braved the sea three hundred years ago.
It is our heart, our love, which we had lost,
our very ghost,
forgotten in trouble on an alien coast.
Now, in the many-voiced country lane

which parts the fields of poverty grass and clover,
as the loud quail repeats twice over
Bob White, not quite, not quite, Bob White,
see it again and say it again,
world without end to love and have it,
bee-blossom heart to love and live it,
this holy land, our faith itself, to share again
with our godfathers, Will and Ben.

KINGSLEY AMIS, *born April 16, 1922, in London, lives with his wife and three children in Oxford, where he is a lecturer at the university, which he earlier attended as a student. He is best known as a writer of fiction, especially for his comic*

character has become one of the most widely discussed figures in recent British literature. He is an authority on jazz and science fiction, about which he contributes articles to a number of magazines. In 1958–1959, he was visiting lecturer at Princeton and, until his recent appointment to Oxford, taught in Wales at University College, Swansea.

THE door still swinging to, and girls revive,
Aeronauts in the utmost altitudes
      Of boredom fainting, dive
In the bright oxygen of my nod;
Angels as well, a squadron of draped nudes,
      They roar towards their god.

Militant all, they fight to take my hat,
No more as yet; the other men retire
      Insulted, gestured at;
Each girl presses on me her share of what
Makes up the barn-door target of desire:
      And I am a crack shot.

Speech fails them, amorous, but each one's look,
Endorsed in other ways, begs me to sign
      Her body's autograph-book;
"Me first, Kingsley; I'm cleverest" each declares,
But no gourmet races downstairs to dine,
      Nor will I race upstairs.

Feigning aplomb, perhaps for half an hour,
I hover, and am shown by each princess
      The entrance to her tower;
Open, in that its tenant throws the key
At once to anyone, but not unless
      The anyone is me.

Now from the corridor their fathers cheer,
Their brothers, their young men; the cheers increase
      As soon as I appear;
From each I win a handshake and sincere
Congratulations; from the chief of police
      A nod, a wink, a leer.

This over, all delay is over too;
The first eight girls (the roster now agreed)
      Leap on me, and undo . . .
But honesty impels me to confess
That this is 'all a dream', which was, indeed,
      Not difficult to guess.

But wait; not 'just a dream', because, though good
And beautiful, it is also true, and hence
      Is rarely understood;
Who would choose any feasible ideal
In here and now's giant circumference,
      If that small room were real?

Only the best; the others find, have found
Love's ordinary distances too great,
      And eager, stand their ground;
Map-drunk explorers, dry-land sailors, they
See no arrival that can compensate
      For boredom on the way;

And, seeming doctrinaire, but really weak,
Limelighted dolls guttering in their brain,
      They come with me, to seek
The halls of theoretical delight,
The women of that ever-fresh terrain,
      The night after to-night.

W. H. AUDEN, *born February 21, 1907, in York, England, lives in New York City and in Kirchstetten, Austria. He was educated at Oxford, where he began to publish the poems that were to set the tone and climate for what later became known as the "Auden generation" of poets. After a short period of participation in the Spanish Civil War as a civilian on the Loyalist side, and marriage to Erika, the daughter of Thomas Mann, he came to the United States in 1939 and, a few years later, became an American citizen. He has taught for short periods at the University of Michigan, Swarthmore, Smith, and at the New School for Social Research, in New York, where his course in Shakespeare drew such crowds of students that a secretary was moved to remark, "You'd think Shakespeare was giving a course in Auden." Besides many volumes of poetry, a volume of essays, and two travel books,* Letters from Iceland *and* Journey to a War, *on which he collaborated with Louis MacNeice and the novelist Christopher Isherwood, respectively, he has collaborated with Isherwood on three plays and with Chester Kallman on the librettos of two operas.*

St. Cecilia, who lived in second- or third-century Rome, is the virgin martyr who came to be regarded as the patroness of music. In literature and art she is usually represented at the organ. The vision of Aphrodite (Venus), goddess of love, invoked here, recalls Botticelli's painting The Birth of Venus.

SONG FOR ST. CECILIA'S DAY

IN a garden shady this holy lady
With reverent cadence and subtle psalm,
Like a black swan as death came on
Poured forth her song in perfect calm:
And by ocean's margin this innocent virgin
Constructed an organ to enlarge her prayer,
And notes tremendous from her great engine
Thundered out on the Roman air.

Blonde Aphrodite rose up excited,
Moved to delight by the melody,
White as an orchid she rode quite naked
In an oyster shell on top of the sea;
At sounds so entrancing the angels dancing
Came out of their trance into time again,
And around the wicked in Hell's abysses
The huge flame flickered and eased their pain.

*Blessed Cecilia, appear in visions
To all musicians, appear and inspire:
Translated Daughter, come down and startle
Composing mortals with immortal fire.*

MUSÉE DES BEAUX ARTS

ABOUT suffering they were never wrong,
The Old Masters: how well they understood
Its human position; how it takes place
While someone else is eating or opening a window or just walking
    dully along;
How, when the aged are reverently, passionately waiting
For the miraculous birth, there always must be
Children who did not specially want it to happen, skating
On a pond at the edge of the wood:
They never forgot
That even the dreadful martyrdom must run its course
Anyhow in a corner, some untidy spot
Where the dogs go on with their doggy life, and the torturer's horse
Scratches its innocent behind on a tree.
In Breughel's *Icarus*, for instance: how everything turns away
Quite leisurely from the disaster; the ploughman may
Have heard the splash, the forsaken cry,
But for him it was not an important failure; the sun shone
As it had to on the white legs disappearing into the green
Water; and the expensive delicate ship that must have seen
Something amazing, a boy falling out of the sky,
Had somewhere to get to and sailed calmly on.

As I walked out one evening,
    Walking down Bristol Street,
The crowds upon the pavement
    Were fields of harvest wheat.

And down by the brimming river
    I heard a lover sing
Under an arch of the railway:
    "Love has no ending.

I'll love you, dear, I'll love you
    Till China and Africa meet,
And the river jumps over the mountain
    And the salmon sing in the street.

I'll love you till the ocean
    Is folded and hung up to dry,
And the seven stars go squawking
    Like geese about the sky.

The years shall run like rabbits,
    For in my arms I hold
The Flower of the Ages,
    And the first love of the world."

But all the clocks in the city
    Began to whirr and chime:
"O let not Time deceive you,
    You cannot conquer Time.

In the burrows of the Nightmare
    Where Justice naked is,
Time watches from the shadow
    And coughs when you would kiss.

In headaches and in worry
   Vaguely life leaks away,
And Time will have his fancy
   Tomorrow or today.

Into many a green valley
   Drifts the appalling snow;
Time breaks the threaded dances
   And the diver's brilliant bow.

O plunge your hands in water,
   Plunge them in up to the wrist;
Stare, stare in the basin
   And wonder what you've missed.

The glacier knocks in the cupboard,
   The desert sighs in the bed,
And the crack in the tea-cup opens
   A lane to the land of the dead.

Where the beggars raffle the banknotes
   And the Giant is enchanting to Jack,
And the Lily-white Boy is a Roarer,
   And Jill goes down on her back.

O look, look in the mirror,
   O look in your distress;
Life remains a blessing
   Although you cannot bless.

O stand, stand at the window
   As the tears scald and start;
You shall love your crooked neighbor
   With your crooked heart."

It was late, late in the evening,
   The lovers they were gone;
The clocks had ceased their chiming,
   And the deep river ran on.

ROBERT BAGG, *born September 21, 1935, in Orange, New Jersey, lives with his wife and their four children in Chaplin, Connecticut. He was graduated from Amherst College in 1957 and then spent a year in Cap d'Antibes, France, and another in Italy as winner of the* Prix de Rome *before entering upon graduate work at the University of Connecticut. He is the adaptor and narrator of a short film,* Siege of the Summerhouse, *based on his poem of the same title.*

INSCRIPTIONS on Greek tombstones intrigued him,
The way stones spoke to the dead with sure words.
'This little stone, good Sabinus, records
Our great friendship, which I still need. Leave the numb
Waters of Lethe alone, and remember me.'
Sometimes the dead answer, 'Please don't worry
Long over me. Do your work, be happy. At nineteen
Cancer killed me, and I leave the sweet sun.'

We both had strong Platonic appetites.
Three-pound symposiums of grapes and plums
Gnawed bare to their Aristotelian pits
He pocketed. 'Logic thrives on a peach blossom's
Troubles,' he said, and when a calm mirror
Lake reflected us, we dove underwater,
Blew out mouthfuls, and swam until the honey
Of exhaustion filled every cell in the body.

From a frame normally tense and careless
A tennis ball exacted gracefulness
By skipping on the tip of the net's tongue.
The dust kicked from our reflexes in long-
Winded rallies. Sharp satisfying plocks,
Both of us bent on keeping play alive,
We'd silence with a winning forehand drive,
Let sweat cool, and drink harsh gulps from our Cokes.

His death ten seconds in my ears, I shook
Off sorrow, walked out in a cool downpour
And drank rain from my palms. I had no power,
So thirsty for his slippery life, to make
Anything but absurdity of that bath.
I wandered Amherst in drenched shame

Because I had let weather drive the same
Wonder from my feelings as a man's death.

This Spring, at Epidaurus, dying of poems,
I stood tired and sweaty in a great cloudburst.
Only for honest, singleminded thirst
Will sense be made from the skies by cupped palms,
Said the acoustics in this theater, where
Greek speech lives cupped in the worn marble's care.
I shall drink many palmfuls of my friend's life
In your presence, laurel and myrtle leaf;

Then set these stones speaking to each other.
'I am Ron Wyn, promising philosopher,
I pledged myself to music, calculus
And Greek, but mastered none, since my last promise,
To death, was the one I fulfilled first.'
'Rest easy, Ron. Although our friendship was killed
To metaphor by the illiterate world
I grave these rocks with love, in which you are versed.'

GEORGE BARKER, *born February 26, 1913, in Loughton, Essex, lives on a farm in Haslemere, Surrey, with his wife and six children. He attended no university, his sketchy formal education having been undertaken in short periods of study at the Marlborough Road School, in Chelsea, and the Regent Street Polytechnic. When he left school at the age of fourteen, he tried his hand at many jobs and was at one time a designer of wallpaper and at another a garage mechanic. Having made an impressive early reputation as a poet, he was appointed visiting professor of English literature at the Imperial Tohoku University in Japan in 1939, after which he came to the United States, remaining for four years before returning to England and ground service with the Royal Air Force. He has published three novels:* Alanna Autumnal; Janus; The Dead Seagull.

In the first sense, this sonnet is a completely personal poem; in a second, the poet's portrait of his mother is a statement in which the endurance and resurgent vitality of civilians during the bombing of London are regarded as monumental virtues.

TO MY MOTHER

Most near, most dear, most loved and most far,
Under the window where I often found her
Sitting as huge as Asia, seismic with laughter,
Gin and chicken helpless in her Irish hand,
Irresistible as Rabelais, but most tender for
The lame dogs and hurt birds that surround her,—
She is a procession no one can follow after
But be like a little dog following a brass band.

She will not glance up at the bomber, or condescend
To drop her gin and scuttle to a cellar,
But lean on the mahogany table like a mountain
Whom only faith can move, and so I send
O all my faith, and all my love to tell her
That she will move from mourning into morning.

from TO MY SON

Part I

My darkling child the stars have obeyed
In your deliverance and laid
You cold on the doorstep of a house
Where few are happy and times get worse.
I will not gild your nativity

With a desirable lie, nor pity
The birth that invests me with a second
Heart on which I had not reckoned:
No less than I do you will drink
Cold comfort at a loveless brink,
And when the wheel of mischance grazes
You as you play I shall know pauses
Of the skipping heart. Let the day, bending
A bright hand about you, attend you
Into the fatherless night when we
Are each of us alone and at sea
Without a North Star—but may
The night seem safer the next day.
The best of all is not to be born,
But how can we tell this to the morning
That, as we groan, comes up over the hill
Of our midnight grief? I see you, still,
An unbroken daybreak in my darkest
Heart, destined to illuminate the stark
Day of necessity in proper season.
Why were you born? I love. This is the reason.
But do not ask me why or whom—
Does it much matter what prefix doom
Wears to her name? She and I
Shall always meet when all wishes
Under a dazzle of unpropitious
But irresistible ascendencies
Clasp each other because they freeze.
I saw her face. Saw fate had taught her
That she was an elected daughter
And in obedience to the pull
Of that which knows it is beautiful
I moved towards her in the cold
And fell into a moon. The golden

Undergrowth of her sex enmeshed
The dying fugitive it refreshed
For henceforward daily dying.
Sucking blood a Venus, sighing,
Toys her prey back into life:
He rules her with the sexual knife
That kills him. But all this
Comes later, my dear son, and is
Knowledge of a kind that seems
Too bitter for the simple schemes
Of a world in which the killer
Neither hates nor loves the killed.
Your bed is a kingdom where
Tears pacify the dogs of despair
And the cold sheets, getting warm,
Protect you all night long from harm.
My bed is made. I lie on love
Like dynamos. The rub and shove
Turn generations on their way.
We weep as we embrace and die.
When the normal day begins
We, rising, step out of our sins
Not even smiling. The monsters settle
Back into their sleeping metal.
My dear son, you rode down on
The spinal throes of a mastodon
One quiet night in May. I bare
That hour because I do not dare
Let flesh grow over it. Your own
Heartburst, one day, like a cyst,
Will fester so, if you desist
From speech. The tongue is a bird
Where the worm, in the heart interred,
Can be caught by no other. Let him, ringing

Lark of the bloodiest field, bring
The overworn heart relief. I write
These lines in a train on a night
You sleep away in Ireland. Do not stir.
I would not have my unpleasanter
Thoughts disturb you. It is late.
The moon stares down, dispassionate
As the world stares up at her.
All things are lost in genera.
The train crawls on. The coast creeps near.
The rain has started. And the year
Is almost ended. I have been
Too long away from my domain:
Too much pursued my own will o'
The whips against a stranger pillow,
Too many seas of wounds sailed over
To think that destinations cover
The running sore of separation.
I, like the train, must learn my station
And stop a while there. Let me hide
My restlessness at your bedside,
Where, my dear son, you keep
Four better guardians of your sleep.

JOHN BERRYMAN, *born October 25, 1914, in McAlester, Oklahoma, lives in Minneapolis, where he teaches in the English department of the University of Minnesota. He was educated at Columbia and at Clare College, Cambridge, and has taught at Wayne University and at Princeton. He is the author of a critical biography of Stephen Crane and of one of the few highly regarded long poems recently written in America,* Homage to Mistress Bradstreet.

The pictorial subject of this poem is the
painting Hunters in the Snow, *by Breughel.*
Every image in the poem is a transcription of
its counterpart in the painting.

WINTER LANDSCAPE

THE three men coming down the winter hill
In brown, with tall poles and a pack of hounds
At heel, through the arrangement of the trees,
Past the five figures at the burning straw,
Returning cold and silent to their town,

Returning to the drifted snow, the rink
Lively with children, to the older men,
The long companions they can never reach,
The blue light, men with ladders, by the church
The sledge and shadow in the twilit street,

Are not aware that in the sandy time
To come, the evil waste of history
Outstretched, they will be seen upon the brow
Of that same hill: when all their company
Will have been irrecoverably lost,

These men, this particular three in brown
Witnessed by birds will keep the scene and say
By their configuration with the trees,
The small bridge, the red houses and the fire,
What place, what time, what morning occasion

Sent them into the wood, a pack of hounds
At heel and the tall poles upon their shoulders,
Thence to return as now we see them and
Ankle-deep in snow down the winter hill
Descend, while three birds watch and the fourth flies.

JOHN BETJEMAN, *born 1906, in England, lives in the Smithfield market district of London and in Wantage, Berkshire. He is married and has a son and a daughter. Educated at Marlborough and at Oxford, he was British Press Attaché in Dublin from 1941 to 1943 and, in 1944, held a post in the British Admiralty. Although he has for many years written poems and is well known as an expert on architecture, particularly Victorian, his wide fame in England did not arrive until the publication of his* Collected Poems, *which became one of the best selling volumes of verse since Byron. In recent years he has gained a wide popular reputation through appearances on British television channels. He is pictured here dressed in clothes that once belonged to Henry James.*

Miss J. Hunter Dunn, Miss J. Hunter Dunn,
Furnish'd and burnish'd by Aldershot sun,
What strenuous singles we played after tea,
We in the tournament—you against me!

Love-thirty, love-forty, oh! weakness of joy,
The speed of a swallow, the grace of a boy,
With carefullest carelessness, gaily you won,
I am weak from your loveliness, Joan Hunter Dunn.

Miss Joan Hunter Dunn, Miss Joan Hunter Dunn,
How mad I am, sad I am, glad that you won.
The warm-handled racket is back in its press,
But my shock-headed victor, she loves me no less.

Her father's euonymus shines as we walk,
And swing past the summer-house, buried in talk,
And cool the verandah that welcomes us in
To the six-o'clock news and a lime-juice and gin.

The scent of the conifers, sound of the bath,
The view from my bedroom of moss-dappled path,
As I struggle with double-end evening tie,
For we dance at the Golf Club, my victor and I.

On the floor of her bedroom lie blazer and shorts
And the cream-coloured walls are be-trophied with sports,
And westering, questioning settles the sun
On your low-leaded window, Miss Joan Hunter Dunn.

The Hillman is waiting, the light's in the hall,
The pictures of Egypt are bright on the wall,
My sweet, I am standing beside the oak stair
And there on the landing's the light on your hair.

By roads "not adopted", by woodlanded ways,
She drove to the club in the late summer haze,
Into nine-o'clock Camberley, heavy with bells
And mushroomy, pine-woody, evergreen smells.

Miss Joan Hunter Dunn, Miss Joan Hunter Dunn,
I can hear from the car-park the dance has begun.
Oh! full Surrey twilight! importunate band!
Oh! strongly adorable tennis-girl's hand!

Around us are Rovers and Austins afar,
Above us, the intimate roof of the car,
And here on my right is the girl of my choice,
With the tilt of her nose and the chime of her voice,

And the scent of her wrap, and the words never said,
And the ominous, ominous dancing ahead.
We sat in the car-park till twenty to one
And now I'm engaged to Miss Joan Hunter Dunn.

YOUTH AND AGE ON BEAULIEU RIVER, HANTS

EARLY sun on Beaulieu water
    Lights the undersides of oaks,
Clumps of leaves it floods and blanches,
All transparent glow the branches
    Which the double sunlight soaks;
    To her craft on Beaulieu water
    Clemency the General's daughter
        Pulls across with even strokes.

Schoolboy-sure she is this morning;
    Soon her sharpie's rigg'd and free.
Cool beneath a garden awning
    Mrs. Fairclough, sipping tea

And raising large long-distance glasses
As the little sharpie passes,
     Sighs our sailor girl to see:

    Tulip figure, so appealing,
       Oval face, so serious-eyed,
Tree-roots pass'd and muddy beaches.
On to huge and lake-like reaches,
     Soft and sun-warm, see her glide—
    Slacks the slim young limbs revealing,
    Sun-brown arm the tiller feeling—
     With the wind and with the tide.

    Evening light will bring the water,
      Day-long sun will burst the bud,
    Clemency, the General's daughter,
     Will return upon the flood.
But the older woman only
Knows the ebb-tide leaves her lonely
     With the shining fields of mud.

ELIZABETH BISHOP, *born November 8, 1911, in Worcester, Massachusetts, lives in Brazil, where she spends summers in Rio de Janeiro and winters in the mountain resort town of Petropolis. As a child she lived for a number of years in Nova Scotia and later spent*

much of her time in Key West. She was educated at Vassar College and has published a number of short stories and a translation, Diary of Helena Morley. *The second of her two volumes of poetry,* A Cold Spring, *was awarded the Pulitzer Prize.*

In your next letter I wish you'd say
where you are going and what you are doing;
how are the plays, and after the plays
what other pleasures you're pursuing:

taking cabs in the middle of the night,
driving as if to save your soul
where the road goes round and round the park
and the meter glares like a moral owl,

and the trees look so queer and green
standing alone in big black caves
and suddenly you're in a different place
where everything seems to happen in waves,

and most of the jokes you just can't catch,
like dirty words rubbed off a slate,
and the songs are loud but somehow dim
and it gets so terribly late,

and coming out of the brownstone house
to the gray sidewalk, the watered street,
one side of the buildings rises with the sun
like a glistening field of wheat.

—Wheat, not oats, dear. I'm afraid
if it's wheat it's none of your sowing,
nevertheless I'd like to know
what you are doing and where you are going.

A COLD SPRING

For Jane Dewey. Maryland

Nothing is so beautiful as spring.—Hopkins

A COLD spring:
the violet was flawed on the lawn.
For two weeks or more the trees hesitated;
the little leaves waited,
carefully indicating their characteristics.
Finally a grave green dust
settled over your big and aimless hills.
One day, in a chill white blast of sunshine,
on the side of one a calf was born.
The mother stopped lowing
and took a long time eating the after-birth,
a wretched flag,
but the calf got up promptly
and seemed inclined to feel gay.

The next day
was much warmer.
Greenish-white dogwood infiltrated the wood,
each petal burned, apparently, by a cigarette-butt;
and the blurred redbud stood
beside it, motionless, but almost more
like movement than any placeable color.
Four deer practised leaping over your fences.
The infant oak-leaves swung through the sober oak.
Song-sparrows were wound up for the summer,
and in the maple the complementary cardinal
cracked a whip, and the sleeper awoke,
stretching miles of green limbs from the south.
In his cap the lilacs whitened,
then one day they fell like snow.

Now, in the evening,
a new moon comes.
The hills grow softer. Tufts of long grass show
where each cow-flop lies.
The bull-frogs are sounding,
slack strings plucked by heavy thumbs.
Beneath the light, against your white front door,
the smallest moths, like Chinese fans,
flatten themselves, silver and silver-gilt
over pale yellow, orange, or gray.
Now, from the thick grass, the fireflies
begin to rise:
up, then down, then up again:
lit on the ascending flight,
drifting simultaneously to the same height,
—exactly like the bubbles in champagne.
—Later on they rise much higher.
And your shadowy pastures will be able to offer
these particular glowing tributes
every evening now throughout the summer.

FLORIDA

THE state with the prettiest name,
the state that floats in brackish water,
held together by mangrove roots
that bear while living oysters in clusters,
and when dead strew white swamps with skeletons,
dotted as if bombarded, with green hummocks
like ancient cannon-balls sprouting grass.
The state full of long S-shaped birds, blue and white,
and unseen hysterical birds who rush up the scale
every time in a tantrum.

Tanagers embarrassed by their flashiness,
and pelicans whose delight it is to clown;
who coast for fun on the strong tidal currents
in and out among the mangrove islands
and stand on the sand-bars drying their damp gold wings
on sun-lit evenings.
Enormous turtles, helpless and mild,
die and leave their barnacled shells on the beaches,
and their large white skulls with round eye-sockets
twice the size of a man's.
The palm trees clatter in the stiff breeze
like the bills of the pelicans. The tropical rain comes down
to freshen the tide-looped strings of fading shells:
Job's Tear, the Chinese Alphabet, the scarce Junonia,
parti-colored pectins and Ladies' Ears,
arranged as on a gray rag of rotted calico,
the buried Indian Princess's skirt;
with these the monotonous, endless, sagging coast-line
is delicately ornamented.
Thirty or more buzzards are drifting down, down, down,
over something they have spotted in the swamp,
in circles like stirred up flakes of sediment
sinking through water.
Smoke from woods-fires filters fine blue solvents.
On stumps and dead trees the charring is like black velvet.
The mosquitoes
go hunting to the tune of their ferocious obbligatos.
After dark, the fire-flies map the heavens in the marsh
until the moon rises.
Cold white, not bright, the moonlight is coarse-meshed,
and the careless, corrupt state is all black specks
too far apart, and ugly whites; the poorest
post-card of itself.
After dark, the pools seem to have slipped away.

The alligator, who has five distinct calls:
friendliness, love, mating, war, and a warning,
whimpers and speaks in the throat
of the Indian Princess.

THE brown enormous odor he lived by
was too close, with its breathing and thick hair,
for him to judge. The floor was rotten; the sty
was plastered halfway up with glass-smooth dung.
Light-lashed, self-righteous, above moving snouts,
the pigs' eyes followed him, a cheerful stare—
even to the sow that always ate her young—
till, sickening, he leaned to scratch her head.
But sometimes mornings after drinking bouts
(he hid the pints behind a two-by-four),
the sunrise glazed the barnyard mud with red;
the burning puddles seemed to reassure.
And then he thought he almost might endure
his exile yet another year or more.

But evenings the first star came to warn.
The farmer whom he worked for came at dark
to shut the cows and horses in the barn
beneath their overhanging clouds of hay,
with pitchforks, faint forked lightnings, catching light,
safe and companionable as in the Ark.
The pigs stuck out their little feet and snored.
The lantern—like the sun, going away—
laid on the mud a pacing aureole.

Carrying a bucket along a slimy board,
he felt the bats' uncertain staggering flight,
his shuddering insights, beyond his control,
touching him. But it took him a long time
finally to make his mind up to go home.

LOUISE BOGAN, *born August 11, 1897, in Livermore Falls, Maine, lives in New York City. She attended Boston Girls' Latin School and Boston University and then was married and, within a few years, widowed with one daughter. Her second husband was the poet Raymond Holden, from whom she was divorced in 1937. For more than twenty years she has been poetry critic for* The New Yorker. *She was Consultant in Poetry at the Library of Congress in 1945 and 1946; in 1954 her* Collected Poems *was awarded the Bollingen Prize.*

Women have no wilderness in them,
They are provident instead,
Content in the tight hot cell of their hearts
To eat dusty bread.

They do not see cattle cropping red winter grass,
They do not hear
Snow water going down under culverts
Shallow and clear.

They wait, when they should turn to journeys,
They stiffen, when they should bend.
They use against themselves that benevolence
To which no man is friend.

They cannot think of so many crops to a field
Or of clean wood cleft by an axe.
Their love is an eager meaninglessness
Too tense, or too lax.

They hear in every whisper that speaks to them
A shout and a cry.
As like as not, when they take life over their door-sills
They should let it go by.

*This poem was originally published with the subtitle
"Imitated from Auden" and parodies the latter's
tendency, particularly in his early poems, to make
sociological observations in clinical terms and to
view the world as an enormous hospital in
which everyone is a patient.*

EVENING IN THE SANITARIUM

THE free evening fades, outside the windows fastened
    with decorative iron grilles.
The lamps are lighted; the shades drawn; the nurses
    are watching a little.
It is the hour of the complicated knitting on the safe
    bone needles; of the games of anagrams and bridge;
The deadly game of chess; the book held up like a mask.

The period of the wildest weeping, the fiercest delusion, is over.
The women rest their tired half-healed hearts; they are
    almost well.
Some of them will stay almost well always: the blunt-faced
    woman whose thinking dissolved
Under academic discipline; the manic-depressive girl
Now leveling off; one paranoiac afflicted with jealousy,
Another with persecution. Some alleviation has been
    possible.

O fortunate bride, who never again will become elated
    after childbirth!
O lucky older wife, who has been cured of feeling
    unwanted!
To the suburban railway station you will return, return,
To meet forever Jim home on the 5:35.
You will be again as normal and selfish and heartless as
    anybody else.

There is life left: the piano says it with its octave smile.
The soft carpets pad the thump and splinter of the suicide
       to be.
Everything will be splendid: the grandmother will not
       drink habitually.
The fruit salad will bloom on the plate like a bouquet
And the garden produce the blue-ribbon aquilegia.
The cats will be glad; the fathers feel justified; the
       mothers relieved.
The sons and husbands will no longer need to pay the bills.
Childhoods will be put away, the obscene nightmare abated.

At the ends of the corridors the baths are running.
Mrs. C. again feels the shadow of the obsessive idea.
Miss R. looks at the mantel-piece, which must mean something.

PHILIP BOOTH, *born 1925, in New Hampshire, lives with his wife and three daughters in Syracuse, New York, and in a summer home on the shore of Penobscot Bay, in Maine. He was educated at Dartmouth, where he won a varsity letter as a member of the skiing team, and in World War II served as a pilot in the Air Force. He has taught at Bowdoin, Dartmouth, Wellesley, and Syracuse.*

Wʜᴇɴ I was on Night Line,
flying my hands to park
a big-bird B-29,
I used to command the dark:
four engines were mine

to jazz; I was ground-crew,
an unfledged pfc,
but when I waved planes through
that flight line in Tennessee,
my yonder was wild blue.

Warming up, I was hot
on the throttle, logging an hour
of combat, I was the pilot
who rogered the tower.
I used to take off a lot.

With a flat-hat for furlough
and tin wings to sleep on,
I fueled my high-octane ego:
I buzzed, I landed my jeep on
the ramp, I flew low.

When a cross-country hop
let down, I was the big deal
who signaled big wheels to stop.
That's how I used to feel.
I used to get all revved up.

Lie back, daughter, let your head
be tipped back in the cup of my hand.
Gently, and I will hold you. Spread
your arms wide, lie out on the stream
and look high at the gulls. A deadman's float is face down. You will dive
and swim soon enough where this tidewater
ebbs to the sea. Daughter, believe
me, when you tire on the long thrash
to your island, lie up, and survive.
As you float now, where I held you
and let go, remember when fear
cramps your heart what I told you:
lie gently and wide to the light-year
stars, lie back, and the sea will hold you.

JOHN MALCOLM BRINNIN, *born September 13, 1916, in Halifax, Nova Scotia, lives in Cambridge, Massachusetts. He was educated at the University of Michigan and at Harvard, taught at Vassar College for five years, was director of the Poetry Center of the YM-YWHA in New York City from 1950 to 1956, and now teaches at the University of Connecticut. Besides poetry, his books include the memoir* Dylan Thomas in America *and the biography* The Third Rose: Gertrude Stein and Her World. *He makes annual visits to Europe and lectures widely there and in the United States on American literature in general and modern poetry in particular.*

ANOTHER hill town:
another dry Cinzano in the sun.
I couldn't sleep in that enormous echo—
silence and water music, sickly street lamps
neither on nor off—a night
of islands and forgotten languages.

Yet morning, marvellously frank, comes up
with bells, with loaves, with letters
distributed like gifts. I watch a fat priest
spouting grape seeds, a family weeping
in the fumes of a departing bus.

This place is nowhere
but on the map. Wheels spin the sun,
with a white clatter shutters are shut to,
umbrellas bloom in striped and sudden groves.
The day's away, impossibly the same,
and only minutes are at all important—
if women by a wall,
a lean dog, and a cheerful humpback
selling gum and ball-points
are important. My glass is empty.
It is Wednesday. It is not going to rain.

Observation
without speculation. How soon
the eye craves what it cannot see,
goes limpid, glazed, unanswerable,
lights on a pigeon walking in a circle,
hangs on a random shadow,
would rather sleep.

How old am I?
What's missing here? What do these people
feed on that won't feed on them? This town
needs scrolls, celestial delegations,
a swoon of virgins, apostles in apple green,
a landscape riding on a holy shoulder.

The morning stays.
As though I kept an old appointment,
I start by the cats' corridors (*Banco di Roma*,
wineshops, gorgeous butcheries)
toward some mild angel of annunciation—
upstairs, most likely, badly lit,
speaking in rivets on a band of gold.

Praise God, this town keeps one
unheard-of masterpiece to justify
a million ordinary mornings
and pardon this one.

NUNS AT EVE

O_N St. Martin's evening green
Imaginary diamond, between
The vestry buttress and the convent wall,
Solemn as sea-birds in a sanctuary,
Under the statue of the Virgin they play baseball.
They are all named Mary,
Sister Mary, Mary Anthony or Mary Rose,
And when the softball flies
In the shadow of the cross
The little chaplet of the Virgin's hands
Contains their soft excitements like a house.

A flying habit traces
The unprecedented rounding of the bases
By Sister Mary Agatha, who thanks God
For the easy triple and turns her eyes toward home;
As *Mary, Mother, Help Me* echoes in her head,
Mild cries from the proud team
Encourage her, and the obliging sun,
Dazzling the pitcher's box
With a last celestial light upon
The gold-spiked halo of the Virgin in her niche,
Leads Sister Mary John to a wild pitch.

Prayer wins the game.
As Sister Mary Agatha comes sailing home
Through infield dusk, like birds fan-wise
In the vague cloisters of slow-rising mist,
Winners and losers gather in to praise
The fleetness of a bride of Christ.
Flushed and humble, Agatha collects the bats
And balls, while at her belt
Catcher's and pitcher's mitts
—Brute fingers, toes and gross lopsided heads—
Fumble the ropes of her long swinging beads.

JOHN CIARDI, *born June 24, 1916, in Boston, lives with his wife and two children in Metuchen, New Jersey. He was educated at Bates College, Tufts College, and the University of Michigan and has taught at the University of Kansas City, Harvard, and Rutgers. During World War II he served in the Air Corps, flying many missions in the Pacific as an aerial gunner. He is an editor of the* Saturday Review *and a leading, sometimes controversial, spokesman for the dissemination and acceptance of the modern idiom in poetry.*

In this context, kaput *means* done for *and signalizes the end of the Nazi regime and the release of prisoners from its vast concentration camps, one of the most infamous of which was Dachau.*

THE GIFT

In 1945, when the keepers cried *kaput,*
Josef Stein, poet, came out of Dachau
like half a resurrection, his other
eighty pounds still in their invisible grave.

Slowly then the mouth opened and first
a broth, and then a medication, and then
a diet, and all in time and the knitting mercies,
the showing bones were buried back in flesh,

and the miracle was finished. Josef Stein,
man and poet, rose, walked, and could even
beget, and did, and died later of other causes
only partly traceable to his first death.

He noted—with some surprise at first—
that strangers could not tell he had died once.
He returned to his post in the library, drank his beer,
published three poems in a French magazine,

and was very kind to the son who at last was his.
In the spent of one night he wrote three propositions:
That Hell is the denial of the ordinary. That nothing lasts.
That clean white paper waiting under a pen

is the gift beyond history and hurt and heaven.

Here lie Ciardi's pearly bones
In their ripe organic mess.
Jungle blown, his chromosomes
Breed to a new address.

Was it bullets or a wind
Or a rip-cord fouled on Chance?
Artifacts the natives find
Decorate them when they dance.

Here lies the sgt.'s mortal wreck
Lily spiked and termite kissed,
Spiders pendant from his neck
And a beetle on his wrist.

Bring the tic and southern flies
Where the land crabs run unmourning
Through a night of jungle skies
To a climeless morning.

And bring the chalked eraser here
Fresh from rubbing out his name.
Burn the crew-board for a bier.
(Also Colonel what's-his-name.)

Let no dice be stored and still.
Let no poker deck be torn.
But pour the smuggled rye until
The barracks threshold is outworn.

File the papers, pack the clothes,
Send the coded word through air—
"We regret and no one knows
Where the sgt. goes from here."

"Missing as of inst. oblige,
Deepest sorrow and remain—"
Shall I grin at persiflage?
Could I have my skin again

Would I choose a business form
Stilted mute as a giraffe,
Or a pinstripe unicorn
On a cashier's epitaph?

Darling, darling, just in case
Rivets fail or engines burn,
I forget the time and place
But your flesh was sweet to learn.

Swift and single as a shark
I have seen you churn my sleep;
Now if beetles hunt my dark
What will beetles find to keep?

Fractured meat and open bone—
Nothing single or surprised.
Fragments of a written stone,
Undeciphered but surmised.

TRAM COMBS, *born September 25, 1924, in Riverview, Alabama, lives in St. Thomas, Virgin Islands, where he is an antiquarian bookseller specializing in literature and history of the Caribbean and Latin America. He studied physics at the University of California, meteorology at the University of Chicago, and did postgraduate work in electronic engineering at Harvard and MIT. Before moving permanently to St. Thomas in 1951, he lived in San Francisco, where he was associated with many of the writers who came into prominence with the "beat generation."*

The art of poetry as a means of worship is a familiar theme in literature. Here it is given a fresh restatement by the use of phrases from the lingo of the beat generation.

ARS POETICA ABOUT ULTIMATES

when   you   first   rub   up   against   God's   own   skin
He   turns   out   to   be   rougher   than   Christ's   men   most
    expect,
like   a   wood-rat,   -rasp   or   ravenous
connoisseur   with   tender   grapes   a   rough   trade!
yet   this   seduction   and   adoration
of   Him   we   must   get   done,   dangerous
though   it   go;   poetry's   ways're
strewn   with   the   early—de · railed,   · ridden,   · filed   who
heard   its   sirens;   and   rose   to   go
singing,   but   couldn't   make   it,   hammered
and   strove   but   with   beats   unsuccessful
to   get   on   to   come   on   with
the   real   jazz   and   sea   for   one's
self,   to   reach   follow · ,   fellow · ,   father ·
ship   with   Him!

AWARE   AWARE

that   corner   of   earth
where   I   beat   to   death
some   dozen   of   those   oozing   creatures
that   feed   on   the   garden's   rottings
haunts   me

they, too, sentient, Buddha—like, felt
and I hurt them

perhaps, though, it's the fresh un • life there
I sense that troubles me;
certainly my pangs to them were brief

cast here pyramidal we fleshes compete
for space, to feed each on others greens ——
our grace co-existence with mutual aid there-toward
          (in dry summers Thoreau would
          water the wood-land orchids.)
and he's most graceful in the butchery
who's most aware
all's done there.
          in these matters in space   of our meetings
          we 're to acts below the mind's potential
          visions.

animal cannibal creature born we strive to rise
by our mind's unsettling
lifts and ecstasies,
struggles
                    we re • vere to this
                    actuality we
find ourselves apart in, unable to understand,
but lift from our closes competing
                    wolf, ant, mouse;
                    and flesh—eaters will eat flesh ——
thus to this race
                    in these our circuits temporary

just after noon with fierce shears
I set to at the hibiscus trees,
hacking away their under branches,
for a tunnel to study the mornings in.

then at the banked—up flower—beds ——
withered iris out, down with vines dry for ten
    years ——
sparing with care the life—lines of the daisies ——
    African, orange ——
that plunge like comets from the spindling palm.

what a litter on the slates' dark—green!
rust cans, decay—gray'd paper, hunks of red brick,
    wilting leaves ——
I lean against the wall and all's silent.
and keeping the silence the lizards come —— one
    two three

I see now, six, a dozen they crawl
on the rotted wood chunks, run along walls;
one springs to a vine and flows down it, another
peers 'round a sphere of pink lace.

the bared and dying all-ways of their world
they stare at, walk over.
once in a life
such wonder.

I FLUNG UP MY ARM HALF FROM SLEEP

I flung up my arm half from sleep,
my fingers dangled past the bed

————— onto the dark house, minute
slivers of stars down spheres of air're
bounding and drifting gently to earth
into the elephant ears' darknesses
and waiting buds of hibiscus:
the house !swirling, laced in them —————
past the bed's edge fingers fell
and a soft rasp attached to them, a cat's tongue,
file of love.
I drew back,
and thought deliciously of the dark presences
amorphous tiny
two black kittens
back of the couch
in the next room
with enormous blue eyes
wondering
stillnesses

HILARY CORKE, *born July 12, 1921, in Malvern, England, lives with his wife, a granddaughter of Robert Bridges, and two young daughters at Abinger Hammer in a fifteenth-century house built on the site of a Roman market place. He was educated at Charterhouse and Christ Church, Oxford, and subsequently lectured in medieval English studies in Cairo and in Edinburgh. He is well known as a critic and reviewer and is a collector of rock crystal, ancient coins, Chinese artifacts, and sea shells.*

I HAVE known one bound to a bed by wrist and ankle
Scarred by the whips of a wasting ache
Who at the point of entering of the needle
Looked once around to take
The final view, then spoke:
The echo of that terribly witty joke
Pursued the surgeon to his home in Kew,
Deafened a nurse all night and leaden lay
On the heart of a thick-skinned anaesthetist
Long after they'd dispatched his ended clay.

That one lies in Oxford and is its earth.
Also a bright-eyed woman in Germany
In a sightless trap far below ground
Of which another held the key
Surveyed without visible alarm
Or twitch of pinioned arm
The instruments set out upon a table:
Then from her mouth there flowed a resolute
Stream of satire deliciously edged until
The tormentor tormented stopped it with a boot.

She fell as ash not bones in Herzen fields:
All brave men breathe her when the wind
Blows east from Danube. And Tom Caine
When the *Imperial* was mined
And water had flooded all but the wireless-room
Spoke without audible gloom
From fifty fathoms down for fifteen hours
To his mess-mates on land, told several stories,
Then to a doctor carefully described
Asphyxiation's onset and his doom.

He is grown water and surrounds the pole:
If ever you dip a cup in any sea
Tom Caine is in it somewhere. On the whole
Men die asleep or else disgracefully;
But not all men. Perhaps we are never
By any average mountain wood or river
More than a heart's-breadth from the dust
Of one who laughed with nothing left to lose.
Who saw the joke beneath the mammoth's foot?
And what shall I choose, if I am free to choose?

CALM WINTER SLEEP

SLEEP, calm winter sleep, the rides are woollen
Over the dreaming roots, thick snow in sunlight
Is sugar under the trees, wool or sugar,
Immaculate, crystalline, soft. All night this has fallen:

All night, like flaws in the night, under a singing
Steady moon, flutter of whirling frost-flakes
Settling in light packed cumulus has drifted
Into the copses, by the twig-sieves sifted.

We wake to this: from the bedroom window we see,
Leaning flank by flank in pyjamas and nightgown,
Its levelling laydown on the unregular earth;
We speak of this coldness with our joined warm breath—

As distance instructs us we think of the seamless snow
As a bride's dress hiding a rough brown secret body
In sleep, calm winter sleep, before the firegroom
Melts with one spring and lets her rivers go.

So distance says; but after oats and bacon,
The children mufflered, we venture and pass the wicket,

And how complicated the snow is, how alive a surface
As through all the flamboyant frettings of the thicket

The weak pale arrows of St. Lucy's sun
Yellow as an old apple strike in a brandished handful
Defining a paving crazed with mysterious blue;
With breezed shelving and with criss-crossed various

Other arrows of thrush-foot marking this mantle
Fitter for convict than bride; and with giddy drip-holes
Under the holly pointels, and deep in the bush
The nap worn through already in umber stipples!

Last night we spoke of the Bomb, of the perilous statesmen,
And those who shiver in tents, who are all our proper
Concern; this morning we laugh and look into the snow.
Have you forgotten your childhood that you grieve so?

Have you remembered your childhood that you grieve so?
It is not to explore too closely the heart's motions
Makes us quite wise: what dies is what's dissected.
Only I know that sometimes when least expected

What must be happiness is suddenly found,
Quite pointlessly, by following some small thing
Like the linked arrows of a bird, unguessed-at
In what from the window was one great trackless ground—

Though in the next night, under the silver eyeball
Of the bathed night-mistress, out of the castled west
The confetti's tourbillons again will bluster
And lay our happiness waste-wide with the rest.

E. E. CUMMINGS *was born October 14, 1894, in Cambridge, Massachusetts, and, until his death in September, 1962, lived with his wife, the photographer and former fashion model Marion Morehouse, in Greenwich Village, New York City, and in Silver Lake, New Hampshire. He was educated at Harvard and in World War I served with the Norton Harjes Ambulance Corps in France, where, through an error on the part of a military censor, he was imprisoned in a detention camp for three months, an experience recorded in his famous book* The Enormous Room. *Some of his works beside poetry include the play* Him; *the unorthodox journal of a trip through the Soviet Union,* Eimi; *and the published text of talks delivered when he was the Charles Eliot Norton lecturer at Harvard in 1952,* i: six nonlectures. *Eccentricity of language, punctuation, and typography is the hallmark of his poetry, and in his "nonlectures" he reasserted his lifelong position as an iconoclast, an individualist, an enemy of systems and restriction and regimentation.*

nobody loses all the time

i had an uncle named
Sol who was a born failure and
nearly everybody said he should have gone
into vaudeville perhaps because my Uncle Sol could
sing McCann He Was A Diver on Xmas Eve like Hell Itself which
may or may not account for the fact that my Uncle

Sol indulged in that possibly most inexcusable
of all to use a highfalootin phrase
luxuries that is or to
wit farming and be
it needlessly
added

my Uncle Sol's farm
failed because the chickens
ate the vegetables so
my Uncle Sol had a
chicken farm till the
skunks ate the chickens when

my Uncle Sol
had a skunk farm but
the skunks caught cold and
died and so
my Uncle Sol imitated the
skunks in a subtle manner

or by drowning himself in the watertank
but somebody who'd given my Uncle Sol a Victor
Victrola and records while he lived presented to
him upon the auspicious occasion of his decease a

scrumptious not to mention splendiferous funeral with
tall boys in black gloves and flowers and everything and

i remember we all cried like the Missouri
when my Uncle Sol's coffin lurched because
somebody pressed a button
(and down went
my Uncle
Sol

and started a worm farm)

*This poem, written in the sort of rhythm children
naturally fall into when they are playing games or
skipping rope, tells a very old and very simple story:
two little people, "anyone" and "noone," meet, fall
in love, marry, and die. These greatest of human
events take place against the wheeling movements
of the seasons and the stars, to which they are inti-
mately related in life but completely anonymous in time.*

anyone lived in a pretty how town

anyone lived in a pretty how town
(with up so floating many bells down)
spring summer autumn winter
he sang his didn't he danced his did.

Women and men(both little and small)
cared for anyone not at all
they sowed their isn't they reaped their same
sun moon stars rain

children guessed(but only a few
and down they forgot as up they grew

autumn winter spring summer)
that noone loved him more by more

when by now and tree by leaf
she laughed his joy she cried his grief
bird by snow and stir by still
anyone's any was all to her

someones married their everyones
laughed their cryings and did their dance
(sleep wake hope and then)they
said their nevers they slept their dream

stars rain sun moon
(and only the snow can begin to explain
how children are apt to forget to remember
with up so floating many bells down)

one day anyone died i guess
(and noone stooped to kiss his face)
busy folk buried them side by side
little by little and was by was

all by all and deep by deep
and more by more they dream their sleep
noone and anyone earth by april
wish by spirit and if by yes.

Women and men(both dong and ding)
summer autumn winter spring
reaped their sowing and went their came
sun moon stars rain

somewhere i have never travelled,gladly beyond

somewhere i have never travelled,gladly beyond
any experience,your eyes have their silence:
in your most frail gesture are things which enclose me,
or which i cannot touch because they are too near

your slightest look easily will unclose me
though i have closed myself as fingers,
you open always petal by petal myself as Spring opens
(touching skilfully,mysteriously)her first rose

or if your wish be to close me,i and
my life will shut very beautifully,suddenly,
as when the heart of this flower imagines
the snow carefully everywhere descending;

nothing which we are to perceive in this world equals
the power of your intense fragility:whose texture
compels me with the colour of its countries,
rendering death and forever with each breathing

(i do not know what it is about you that closes
and opens;only something in me understands
the voice of your eyes is deeper than all roses)
nobody,not even the rain,has such small hands

when serpents bargain for the right to squirm

when serpents bargain for the right to squirm
and the sun strikes to gain a living wage—
when thorns regard their roses with alarm
and rainbows are insured against old age

when every thrush may sing no new moon in
if all screech-owls have not okayed his voice
—and any wave signs on the dotted line
or else an ocean is compelled to close

when the oak begs permission of the birch
to make an acorn—valleys accuse their
mountains of having altitude—and march
denounces april as a saboteur

then we'll believe in that incredible
unanimal mankind(and not until)

ALAN DUGAN, *born February 12, 1923, in Brooklyn, New York, now lives in Manhattan with his wife, who is a daughter of the painter Ben Shahn. He is a graduate of Mexico City College and is employed as a model maker for a medical supply house. His first book, published in 1961, was the winner of the Yale Series of Younger Poets Award, the National Book Award, and the Pulitzer Prize, and brought him the chance to spend a year abroad as the winner of the* Prix de Rome.

I SEE that there it is on the beach. It is
ahead of me and I walk toward it: its
following vultures and contemptible dogs
are with it, and I walk toward it. If,
in the approach to it, I turn my back
to it, then I walk backwards: I
approach it as a limit. Even if I fall
to hands and knees, I crawl to it.
Backwards or forwards I approach it.

There is the land on one hand, rising, and
the ocean on the other, falling away;
what the sky does, I can not look to see,
but it's around, as ever, all around.
The courteous vultures move away in groups
like functionaries. The dogs circle and stare
like working police. One wants a heel
and gets it. I approach it, concentrating so
on not approaching it, going so far away
that when I get there I am sideways like
the crab, too limited by carapace to say:

"Oh here I am arrived, all; yours today."
No: kneeling and facing away, I will
fall over backwards in intensity of life
and lie convulsed, downed struggling,
sideways even, and should a vulture ask
an eye as its aperitif, I grant it,
glad for the moment wrestling by a horse
whose belly has been hollowed from the rear,
who's eyeless. The wild dog trapped in its ribs
grins as it eats its way to freedom. Not

conquered outwardly, and after rising once,
I fall away inside, and see the sky around
rush out away into the vulture's craw
and barely can not hear them calling, "Here's one."

THE MIRROR PERILOUS

I GUESS there is a garden named
"Garden of Love." If so, I'm in it:
I am the guesser in the garden.
There is a notice by the central pond
that reads: "Property of Narcissus.
Trespass at your own risk,"
so I went there. That is where,
having won but disdained a lady,
he fell for his own face and died,
rightly, "not having followed through,"
as the sentence read, read by the lady:
Oh you could hear her crying all about
the wilderness and wickedness of law.
I looked in that famous mirror perilous
and it wasn't much: my own face,
beautiful, and at the bottom,
bone, a rusty knife, two beads,
and something else I cannot name.
I drank my own lips on the dare
but could not drink the lips away.
The water was heavy, cool, and clear,
but did not quench. A lady laughed
behind my back; I learned the worst:
I could take it or leave it, go or stay,
and went back to the office drunk,
possessed of an echo but not a fate.

RICHARD EBERHART, *born
April 5, 1904, in Austin, Minnesota,
lives with his wife and two children
in Hanover, New Hampshire, where
he is professor of English at Dartmouth College. He studied at the
University of Minnesota for two
years, graduated from Dartmouth,
and then continued his education at
Cambridge, where he was a student
of I. A. Richards, and later at*

*Harvard. In 1930 he spent a year
as tutor to the son of King Prajadhi-
pok of Siam. He has taught at St.
Mark's School and, for short periods,
at a number of American universities, including Washington, Connecticut, and Princeton. During
World War II he served in the Navy
and was a lieutenant commander at
the time of his discharge. From
1959 to 1961 he was Consultant in
Poetry at the Library of Congress.*

NATURE had made them hide in crevices,
Two wasps so cold they looked like bark.
Why I do not know, but I took them
And I put them
In a metal pan, both day and dark.

Like God touching his finger to Adam
I felt, and thought of Michaelangelo,
For whenever I breathed on them,
The slightest breath,
They leaped, and preened as if to go.

My breath controlled them always quite.
More sensitive than electric sparks
They came into life
Or they withdrew to ice,
While I watched, suspending remarks.

Then one in a blind career got out,
And fell to the kitchen floor. I
Crushed him with my cold ski boot,
By accident. The other
Had not the wit to try or die.

And so the other is still my pet.
The moral of this is plain.
But I will shirk it.
You will not like it. And
God does not live to explain.

You would think the fury of aerial bombardment
Would rouse God to relent; the infinite spaces
Are still silent. He looks on shock-pried faces.
History, even, does not know what is meant.

You would feel that after so many centuries
God would give man to repent; yet he can kill
As Cain could, but with multitudinous will,
No farther advanced than in his ancient furies.

Was man made stupid to see his own stupidity?
Is God by definition indifferent, beyond us all?
Is the eternal truth man's fighting soul
Wherein the Beast ravens in his own avidity?

Of Van Wettering I speak, and Averill,
Names on a list, whose faces I do not recall
But they are gone to early death, who late in school
Distinguished the belt feed lever from the belt holding pawl.

T. S. ELIOT, *born September 26, 1888, in St.
Louis, Missouri, lives with his second wife in London, where for many years he has been a director
of the publishing house Faber and Faber, Ltd.
He was educated at Milton Academy, Harvard, the
Sorbonne, and Merton College, Oxford, and has
lived in England since World War I. He became a
British subject in 1927. His eminence as a poet is
internationally recognized, and as a critic he has
been a leading shaper of taste in literature. The
range of his work encompasses both epic poetry
—*The Waste Land—*and doggerel verse—*Old
Possum's Book of Practical Cats—*and he is the
only modern poet to have achieved wide public
success in the field of poetic drama, notably with*
The Cocktail Party *and* Murder in the Cathedral.
*He makes frequent trips to the United States, on
each of which he gives a limited number of public
readings. At a recent appearance at the University
of Minnesota he drew more people to hear him, it
was noted, than any poet since Sophocles. He
was awarded the Nobel Prize in 1948.*

I

THE winter evening settles down
With smell of steaks in passageways.
Six o'clock.
The burnt-out ends of smoky days.
And now a gusty shower wraps
The grimy scraps
Of withered leaves about your feet
And newspapers from vacant lots;
The showers beat
On broken blinds and chimney-pots,
And at the corner of the street
A lonely cab-horse steams and stamps.
And then the lighting of the lamps.

II

The morning comes to consciousness
Of faint stale smells of beer
From the sawdust-trampled street
With all its muddy feet that press
To early coffee-stands.
With the other masquerades
That time resumes,
One thinks of all the hands
That are raising dingy shades
In a thousand furnished rooms.

III

You tossed a blanket from the bed,
You lay upon your back, and waited;
You dozed, and watched the night revealing
The thousand sordid images
Of which your soul was constituted;

They flickered against the ceiling.
And when all the world came back
And the light crept up between the shutters
And you heard the sparrows in the gutters,
You had such a vision of the street
As the street hardly understands;
Sitting along the bed's edge, where
You curled the papers from your hair,
Or clasped the yellow soles of feet
In the palms of both soiled hands.

IV

His soul stretched tight across the skies
That fade behind a city block,
Or trampled by insistent feet
At four and five and six o'clock;
And short square fingers stuffing pipes,
And evening newspapers, and eyes
Assured of certain certainties,
The conscience of a blackened street
Impatient to assume the world.

I am moved by fancies that are curled
Around these images, and cling:
The notion of some infinitely gentle
Infinitely suffering thing.

Wipe your hand across your mouth, and laugh;
The worlds revolve like ancient women
Gathering fuel in vacant lots.

The epigraph to this poem may be translated thus: "If
I thought that my reply would be to one who would
ever return to the world, this flame would stay
without further movement; but since none has ever
returned alive from this depth, if what I hear is true,
I answer you without fear of infamy" (Dante, Inferno,
XXVII, 61–66). These are the words spoken to
Dante by Guido da Montelfeltro, who is shut up in
his flame as punishment for having been a false
counselor. He tells of his evil doings because
he thinks that Dante, like himself, is
doomed never to return to earth.
The speaker of this dramatic monologue is an acutely
sensitive and self-conscious man who feels out of
place in the only society he knows. He details the
triviality of his existence, sees himself in various dra-
matic attitudes, all of which he realizes are absurd,
and finally invokes a fantasy world of beauty
and simplicity—a world from which he is
kept by the intrusions of reality.

THE LOVE SONG OF J. ALFRED PRUFROCK

S'io credesse che mia risposta fosse
A persona che mai tornasse al mondo,
Questa fiamma staria senza piu scosse.
Ma perciocche giammai di questo fondo
Non torno vivo alcun, s'i'odo il vero,
Senza tema d'infamia ti rispondo.

LET us go then, you and I,
When the evening is spread out against the sky
Like a patient etherised upon a table;
Let us go, through certain half-deserted streets,
The muttering retreats
Of restless nights in one-night cheap hotels
And sawdust restaurants with oyster-shells:
Streets that follow like a tedious argument

Of insidious intent
To lead you to an overwhelming question . . .
Oh, do not ask, "What is it?"
Let us go and make our visit.

In the room the women come and go
Talking of Michelangelo.

The yellow fog that rubs its back upon the window-panes,
The yellow smoke that rubs its muzzle on the window-panes
Licked its tongue into the corners of the evening,
Lingered upon the pools that stand in drains,
Let fall upon its back the soot that falls from chimneys,
Slipped by the terrace, made a sudden leap,
And seeing that it was a soft October night,
Curled once about the house, and fell asleep.

And indeed there will be time
For the yellow smoke that slides along the street,
Rubbing its back upon the window-panes;
There will be time, there will be time
To prepare a face to meet the faces that you meet;
There will be time to murder and create,
And time for all the works and days of hands
That lift and drop a question on your plate;
Time for you and time for me,
And time yet for a hundred indecisions,
And for a hundred visions and revisions,
Before the taking of a toast and tea.

In the room the women come and go
Talking of Michelangelo.

And indeed there will be time
To wonder, "Do I dare?" and, "Do I dare?"
Time to turn back and descend the stair,
With a bald spot in the middle of my hair—

[They will say: "How his hair is growing thin!"]
My morning coat, my collar mounting firmly to the chin,
My necktie rich and modest, but asserted by a simple pin—
[They will say: "But how his arms and legs are thin!"]
Do I dare
Disturb the universe?
In a minute there is time
For decisions and revisions which a minute will reverse.

For I have known them all already, known them all:—
Have known the evenings, mornings, afternoons,
I have measured out my life with coffee spoons;
I know the voices dying with a dying fall
Beneath the music from a farther room.
So how should I presume?

And I have known the eyes already, known them all—
The eyes that fix you in a formulated phrase,
And when I am formulated, sprawling on a pin,
When I am pinned and wriggling on the wall,
Then how should I begin
To spit out all the butt-ends of my days and ways?
And how should I presume?

And I have known the arms already, know them all—
Arms that are braceleted and white and bare
[But in the lamplight, downed with light brown hair!]
Is it perfume from a dress
That makes me so digress?
Arms that lie along a table, or wrap about a shawl.
And should I then presume?
And how should I begin?

.   .   .   .   .

Shall I say, I have gone at dusk through narrow streets
And watched the smoke that rises from the pipes

Of lonely men in shirt-sleeves, leaning out of windows? . . .

    I should have been a pair of ragged claws
Scuttling across the floors of silent seas.

           . . . . .

And the afternoon, the evening, sleeps so peacefully!
Smoothed by long fingers,
Asleep . . . tired . . . or it malingers,
Stretched on the floor, here beside you and me.
Should I, after tea and cakes and ices,
Have the strength to force the moment to its crisis?
But though I have wept and fasted, wept and prayed,
Though I have seen my head [grown slightly bald] brought in upon
      a platter,
I am no prophet—and here's no great matter;
I have seen the moment of my greatness flicker,
And I have seen the eternal Footman hold my coat, and snicker,
And in short, I was afraid.

    And would it have been worth it, after all,
After the cups, the marmalade, the tea,
Among the porcelain, among some talk of you and me,
Would it have been worth while,
To have bitten off the matter with a smile,
To have squeezed the universe into a ball
To roll it toward some overwhelming question,
To say: "I am Lazarus, come from the dead,
Come back to tell you all, I shall tell you all"—
If one, settling a pillow by her head,
    Should say: "That is not what I meant at all.
    That is not it, at all."

    And would it have been worth it, after all,
Would it have been worth while,
After the sunsets and the dooryards and the sprinkled streets,

After the novels, after the teacups, after the skirts that trail along
     the floor—
And this, and so much more?—
It is impossible to say just what I mean!
But as if a magic lantern threw the nerves in patterns on a screen:
Would it have been worth while
If one, settling a pillow or throwing off a shawl,
And turning toward the window, should say:
    "That is not it at all,
    That is not what I meant, at all."

      . . . . .

No! I am not Prince Hamlet, nor was meant to be;
Am an attendant lord, one that will do
To swell a progress, start a scene or two,
Advise the prince; no doubt, an easy tool,
Deferential, glad to be of use,
Politic, cautious, and meticulous;
Full of high sentence, but a bit obtuse;
At times, indeed, almost ridiculous—
Almost, at times, the Fool.

    I grow old . . . I grow old . . .
I shall wear the bottoms of my trousers rolled.

    Shall I part my hair behind? Do I dare to eat a peach?
I shall wear white flannel trousers, and walk upon the beach.
I have heard the mermaids singing, each to each.

    I do not think that they will sing to me.

    I have seen them riding seaward on the waves
Combing the white hair of the waves blown back
When the wind blows the water white and black.

    We have lingered in the chambers of the sea
By sea-girls wreathed with seaweed red and brown
Till human voices wake us, and we drown.

As in the case of many likenesses made by painters,
this portrait tells more about the artist than
it does about the subject. The young man who is
involved in an ambiguous relationship with an older
woman at first feels superior to her and her obvious
romantic pretensions. However, as he continues to
see her through the course of a year, his attitude
toward her undergoes a change: she may be foolish
and hopelessly romantic, but his own character is not
sufficiently resolved to allow him to maintain the
smugness that marked their earlier encounters. As
the epigraph suggests, he would like to feel that this
episode is over and done with; but uncertainty plagues
him. He has done a kind of violence to a woman
and begins to suspect that his unresolved emotions
are as damaging to himself as they have been to her.

PORTRAIT OF A LADY

Thou hast committed—
Fornication: but that was in another country,
And besides, the wench is dead.
                                        THE JEW OF MALTA.

I

AMONG the smoke and fog of a December afternoon
You have the scene arrange itself—as it will seem to do—
With "I have saved this afternoon for you";
And four wax candles in the darkened room,
Four rings of light upon the ceiling overhead,
An atmosphere of Juliet's tomb
Prepared for all the things to be said, or left unsaid.
We have been, let us say, to hear the latest Pole
Transmit the Preludes, through his hair and fingertips.
"So intimate, this Chopin, that I think his soul
Should be resurrected only among friends

Some two or three, who will not touch the bloom
That is rubbed and questioned in the concert room."
—And so the conversation slips
Among velleities and carefully caught regrets
Through attenuated tones of violins
Mingled with remote cornets
And begins.
"You do not know how much they mean to me, my friends,
And how, how rare and strange it is, to find
In a life composed so much, so much of odds and ends,
[For indeed I do not love it . . . you knew? you are not blind!
How keen you are!]
To find a friend who has these qualities,
Who has, and gives
Those qualities upon which friendship lives.
How much it means that I say this to you—
Without these friendships—life, what *cauchemar*!"

    Among the windings of the violins
And the ariettes
Of cracked cornets
Inside my brain a dull tom-tom begins
Absurdly hammering a prelude of its own,
Capricious monotone
That is at least one definite "false note."
—Let us take the air, in a tobacco trance,
Admire the monuments,
Discuss the late events,
Correct our watches by the public clocks.
Then sit for half an hour and drink our bocks.

II

Now that lilacs are in bloom
She has a bowl of lilacs in her room
And twists one in her fingers while she talks.

"Ah, my friend, you do not know, you do not know
What life is, you who hold it in your hands";
(Slowly twisting the lilac stalks)
"You let it flow from you, you let it flow,
And youth is cruel, and has no remorse
And smiles at situations which it cannot see."
I smile, of course,
And go on drinking tea.
"Yet with these April sunsets, that somehow recall
My buried life, and Paris in the Spring,
I feel immeasurably at peace, and find the world
To be wonderful and youthful, after all."

The voice returns like the insistent out-of-tune
Of a broken violin on an August afternoon:
"I am always sure that you understand
My feelings, always sure that you feel,
Sure that across the gulf you reach your hand.

You are invulnerable, you have no Achilles' heel.
You will go on, and when you have prevailed
You can say: at this point many a one has failed.
But what have I, but what have I, my friend,
To give you, what can you receive from me?
Only the friendship and the sympathy
Of one about to reach her journey's end.

I shall sit here, serving tea to friends. . . ."

I take my hat: how can I make a cowardly amends
For what she has said to me?
You will see me any morning in the park
Reading the comics and the sporting page.
Particularly I remark
An English countess goes upon the stage.
A Greek was murdered at a Polish dance,

Another bank defaulter has confessed.
I keep my countenance,
I remain self-possessed
Except when a street piano, mechanical and tired
Reiterates some worn-out common song
With the smell of hyacinths across the garden
Recalling things that other people have desired.
Are these ideas right or wrong?

III

The October night comes down; returning as before
Except for a slight sensation of being ill at ease
I mount the stairs and turn the handle of the door
And feel as if I had mounted on my hands and knees.
"And so you are going abroad; and when do you return?
But that's a useless question.
You hardly know when you are coming back,
You will find so much to learn."
My smile falls heavily among the bric-à-brac.

　"Perhaps you can write to me."
My self-possession flares up for a second;
This is as I had reckoned.
"I have been wondering frequently of late
(But our beginnings never know our ends!)
Why we have not developed into friends."
I feel like one who smiles, and turning shall remark
Suddenly, his expression in a glass.
My self-possession gutters; we are really in the dark.

　"For everybody said so, all our friends,
They all were sure our feelings would relate
So closely! I myself can hardly understand.
We must leave it now to fate.
You will write, at any rate.

Perhaps it is not too late.
I shall sit here, serving tea to friends."

      And I must borrow every changing shape
To find expression . . . dance, dance
Like a dancing bear,
Cry like a parrot, chatter like an ape.
Let us take the air, in a tobacco trance—

      Well! and what if she should die some afternoon,
Afternoon grey and smoky, evening yellow and rose;
Should die and leave me sitting pen in hand
With the smoke coming down above the housetops;
Doubtful, for a while
Not knowing what to feel or if I understand
Or whether wise or foolish, tardy or too soon . . .
Would she not have the advantage, after all?
This music is successful with a "dying fall"
Now that we talk of dying—
And should I have the right to smile?

*Long after the event, one of the three wise men who
journeyed to the place of Christ's birth here
recalls his long trek from the East and meditates
upon the meaning of that experience.*

JOURNEY OF THE MAGI

'A COLD coming we had of it,
Just the worst time of the year
For a journey, and such a long journey:
The ways deep and the weather sharp,
The very dead of winter.'

And the camels galled, sore-footed, refractory,
Lying down in the melting snow.
There were times we regretted
The summer palaces on slopes, the terraces,
And the silken girls bringing sherbet.
Then the camel men cursing and grumbling
And running away, and wanting their liquor and women,
And the night-fires going out, and the lack of shelters.
And the cities hostile and the towns unfriendly
And the villages dirty and charging high prices:
A hard time we had of it.
At the end we preferred to travel all night,
Sleeping in snatches,
With the voices singing in our ears, saying
That this was all folly.

Then at dawn we came down to a temperate valley,
Wet, below the snow line, smelling of vegetation;
With a running stream and a water-mill beating the darkness,
And three trees on the low sky,
And an old white horse galloped away in the meadow.
Then we came to a tavern with vine-leaves over the lintel,
Six hands at an open door dicing for pieces of silver,
And feet kicking the empty wine-skins.
But there was no information, and so we continued
And arrived at evening, not a moment too soon
Finding the place; it was (you may say) satisfactory.

All this was a long time ago, I remember,
And I would do it again, but set down
This set down
This: were we led all that way for
Birth or Death? There was a Birth, certainly,
We had evidence and no doubt. I had seen birth and death,
But had thought they were different; this Birth was

Hard and bitter agony for us, like Death, our death.
We returned to our places, these Kingdoms,
But no longer at ease here, in the old dispensation,
With an alien people clutching their gods.
I should be glad of another death.

D. J. ENRIGHT, *born March 11, 1920, in Leamington, Warwickshire, lives with his wife and daughter in Singapore, where he teaches at the University of Malaya. He was educated at Leamington College and Downing College, Cambridge, and then took teaching assignments in England, Egypt, Japan, Germany, and Thailand before assuming his present post.*

For him, it seems, everything was molten. Court-ladies flow in gentle
    streams,
Or, gathering lotus, strain sideways from their curving boat,
A donkey prances, or a kite dances in the sky, or soars like sacrificial
    smoke.
All is flux: waters fall and leap, and bridges leap and fall.
Even his Tortoise undulates, and his Spring Hat is lively as a pool
    of fish.
All he ever saw was sea: a sea of marble splinters—
Long bright fingers claw across his pages, fjords and islands and
    shattered trees—

And the Laughing Hyena, cavalier of evil, as volcanic as the rest:
Elegant in a flowered gown, a face like a bomb-burst,
Featured with fangs and built about a rigid laugh,
Ever moving, like a pond's surface where a corpse has sunk.

Between the raised talons of the right hand rests an object—
At rest, like a pale island in a savage sea—a child's head,
Immobile, authentic, torn and bloody—
The point of repose in the picture, the point of movement in us.

Terrible enough, this demon. Yet it is present and perfect,
Firm as its horns, curling among its thick and handsome hair.
I find it an honest visitant, even consoling, after all
Those sententious phantoms, choked with rage and uncertainty,
Who grimace from contemporary pages. It, at least,
Knows exactly why it laughs.

Players are British cigarettes; Akhenaton was a king
of ancient Egypt who believed that the sun was
god and god alone and attempted to found
a new religion based on his belief.

UNIVERSITY EXAMINATIONS IN EGYPT

THE air is thick with nerves and smoke: pens tremble in sweating
    hands:
Domestic police flit in and out, with smelling salts and aspirin:
And servants, grave-faced but dirty, pace the aisles,
With coffee, Players and Coca-Cola.

Was it like this in my day, at my place? Memory boggles
Between the aggressive fly and curious ant—but did I really
Pause in my painful flight to light a cigarette or swallow drugs?

The nervous eye, patrolling these hot unhappy victims,
Flinches at the symptoms of a year's hard teaching—
'Falstaff indulged in drinking and sexcess', and then,
'Doolittle was a dusty man' and 'Dr. Jonson edited the Yellow Book.'

Culture and aspirin: the urgent diploma, the straining brain—all in
    the evening fall
To tric-trac in the café, to Hollywood in the picture-house:
Behind, like tourist posters, the glamour of laws and committees,
Wars for freedom, cheap textbooks, national aspirations—

And, farther still and very faint, the foreign ghost of happy Shakespeare,
Keats who really loved things, Akhenaton who adored the Sun,
And Goethe who never thought of Thought.

IRVING FELDMAN, *born September 22,*
1928, in Coney Island, New York, lives with
his wife and young son in Gambier, Ohio,
where he teaches in the English department
of Kenyon College. He was educated at the
City College of New York and at Columbia
University. Subsequently he taught at the
University of Puerto Rico, in Rio Piedras
and in Mayaguez, where he met his wife, and
spent two years in France on a Fulbright
fellowship.

*Vitellozzo Vitelli, a nobleman who was murdered by
Cesare Borgia in 1502, is here presented in circum-
stances that reflect the whimsical, or predetermined,
course of the fate of any man.*

THE DEATH OF VITELLOZZO VITELLI

VITELLI rides west toward Fano, the morning sun
Has spread his shadow before him, his head is cast
Upon the road beyond the horse, and now in vain

He works his spurs and whip. For all his speed, his past
Like a heavy wind has thrown his death far before
Him, and not till midday shall he fill the waste

Of light he has made with the goldness of his spur
And the greenness of his cape. Then shall he stand
At last by the bridge at Fano and know no more

His way than the farmer at noon who looks from his land
To his heart and knows not where next to turn his plow;
Or lovers who have stayed abed and reach a hand

And yet have turned away, even as they do so,
To move their legs and sigh, wearied of their embrace
—Yet nothing else seems worth their while. His road shall go

Before him, having broken itself in two ways:
One goes to Borgia in Fano, and one toward Rome.
But his shadow hurries from his feet to his face.

FLOOD

THE first day it rained we were glad.
How could we know? The heavy air
Had lain about us like a scarf, though work

Got done. Everything seemed easier.
In the streets a little mud.

With the first faint drops, a tiny breeze
Trembled the cornsilk, and the frailest leaves
Turned on their stems this way and that.
Coming from the fields for lunch
I thought it my sweat.

On the second day streamlets ran
In the furrows; the plow stuck,
The oxen balked. On the third day
The rain ran from the roof like a sea.
I thought I would visit town.

Farmers from their farms, merchants from stores,
Laborers, we filled the town. I
Stayed with a cousin. We were told
The granary was full, we could live
A thousand days should the river rise impetuously.

The fifth day the clouds seemed hung
From the tops of the tallest trees. The sun
We did not see at all. And the rain
Beat down as if to crush the roof.
I did not shave or write my wife.

On the sixth day, we moved the women
And children to the town church, built
On the highest ground hard by the granary.
We finished work on the levee.
The river was thick with silt.

A dark drizzle started in my head.
Next day it trickled on the walls of my skull
Like black earth drifting down a grave.
We resolved to stay in the church come what will.
That day I did not leave my bed.

From where the rain? and why on us?
Not even the wisest knows or dares guess.
Did we not plan, care, save, toil,
Did we lay idle or lust, did we waste or spoil?
Therefore, why on us?

The husbandman from his flock,
Husband from wife, the miser from his heap,
The wise man from his wit, from her urn
The widow—are tumbled all, as a man might knock
The ashes from his pipe.

And the days descended in a stream,
So fast they could not be told apart.
In the church all went black.
Once I lay with Lenah as in a dream.
Another time I found myself at Adah's back.

If no one gets up at dawn to wind
The clock, shall not the state run down?
If no one gets up to go to the fields
To feed the cows, to sow the wheat,
To reap, how shall the state grow fat?

One comes telling us Noah has built a boat
That through the flood he may ride about,
And filled it all with animals.
Just like the drunken fool, that slut-
Chaser, to think of no one else.

I feed my friends and kin; twenty-nine thrived
In my home. But mad Noah harangues the air
Or goes muttering in his cuff
As though a god were up his sleeve.
Who is Noah to get saved?

I am a farmer, I love my wife,
My sons are many and strong, my land is green.

This is my cousin, he lives in town,
An honest man, he rises at dawn.
We were children together.

Shall not the world run down?
Why on us? Did we not plan?
Does not black blood flow before my eyes
And blackness brim inside my skull?
Did we lie idle? Did we spoil?

Out of its harness the mind wild as a horse
Roams the rooms and streets. There are some that say
Noah sits amid the rude beasts in his ark
And they feed one upon the other in the dark
And in the dark they mate. And some say worse:

That a griffin was born, and centaur
And sphinx hammer at the door.
Groans and moans are heard, by some the roar
Of giant Hippogriff. Still others cry
That all about the earth is dry!

Dry as if no rain had fallen,
As if we were not awaiting the swollen
River, as if the clouds did not sit
On our chimneys, or the waters
Tumble past our windows in spate.

And some here say a dove has come,
Sure, they think, the sign of a god.
And others say that Noah walks the street
Puffed with news. But bid him wait!
We are busy with our flood.

Ho! Persephone brings flowers, to them
New styles in spring. In seven glittering
Greys, under round grey hats of straw
—Lo! to the fifing sun's tune
The old men come on, stride, march,
Drill, straight as the ties of lovers!
(And their bones have drawn together
In gentle communities of joints,
Like weary soldiers dreaming head to head.)

Hup, they go, ho! in grey jackets,
Grey shoes, sleek as boys, smiling,
Striding on, the gay granite legions,
Persephone's grooms, all together, raise
Chins, link arms, step out, hiking, marching,
Down down into the earth!

ROBERT FITZGERALD, *born October 12,
1910, in Geneva, New York, lives with his wife and
six children in Italy. He was educated at Choate,
Harvard, and Trinity College, Cambridge, where
he studied philosophy and classical languages. He
once worked as a reporter on the* New York Herald
Tribune *and for a number of years was a leading
writer in several departments of* Time. *During
World War II he was on the staff of the Commander in Chief, Pacific Ocean Areas, first at Pearl
Harbor and later at Guam. His reputation is based
not only on his own original work but on his
widely praised and frequently performed translations, in collaboration with Dudley Fitts, of the
Greek playwrights. He returned in 1961 to the
United States for a visit when his translation of
Homer's* Odyssey *was published.*

I

The newsvendor with his hut and crutch
And black palm polished by pennies
Chinked me swiftly my worn-out silver;
Then I went underground.

                  Many went down there,
Down blowing passages and dimness where
Rocketing cars were sucked out of sound in the tunnel.

A train came and expired, opening slots to us
All alacritous moving in voiceless numbers,
Haunch to haunch, elbow to hard elbow.

One would sleep, gaping and sagged in a corner,
One might wish for a seat by the girl yonder;
Each a-sway with his useless heavy headpiece.

II

Tenements: "islands" in the ancient city.
Neither under the old law nor the new
Could any insulation make them gentle.

Here I retired, here I did lay me down—

Beyond the washing lines reeled in at evening,
Beyond the roofpots and the lightless skylights,
The elevated grated round a curve
To pick up pitch diminishing toward silence—
And took my ease amid that hardihood:
The virago at her sill obscenely screeching
Or the lutanist plucking away at "My Lady Greensleeves."

III

The down beat, off beat, beat.
A hopped up drummer's perfect
Tocking periodicity and abandon.

Cush a cush cush a cush. Whang.
Diddle di daddle di yup yup
Whisper to me daddy. On the
Down, the down beat, beat.

The spot's on blondie, see her croon,
See that remarkable subtle pelvic
Universal joint softly rolling.
Honey take it sweet and slow,
Honey, take your time.
Roll those eyes and send, baby, send.

And swing it. O cats
Express your joys and savoir faire
You hot lick connoisseurs: shake
A laig like New Orleans. Or

Rumba. O you Arthur Murray, O you Murray boys
With your snappy steward jackets keeping young,
Steer and sway, you accomplished dancers.
Won't you come over to my table.
Meet Rosemary. This is Rosemary.

IV

The manhole disks were prone shields of morning
Where the sun greeted the avenue.
O lumbering conveyances! O yellow
Gliding of cabs, thousand-footed dimpling stir!
The fresh net placed on the fair hair!

The steel shutters removed at Tiffany's
And the doorman pulling his beige gloves on;

The elevator boy holding down his yawn
And the cool engineer with his briefcase;

The sun striking over the void city room
And the first hasteners through the concourse;

The riveter walking out on the flaking plank
And the welder donning his goggles;

The steel drawer sliding from the office file
And the receptionist fixing her lipline;

The towsled showgirl a-drool on the pillow
And the schoolyard filling with cries;

The roominghouse suicide at peace by the gasjet
And the nun smiling across the ward—

Against the shine of windows, visual
Madness of intersecting multitudes,
Their speech torn to bits in the torrent.

> *The baseball immortal, Ty Cobb, died in 1961. In a*
> *kind of poetic shorthand, the poem attempts to*
> *catch the speech and rhythm of the national pastime*
> *without any sort of imposed comment.*

COBB WOULD HAVE CAUGHT IT

IN sunburnt parks where Sundays lie,
Or the wide wastes beyond the cities,
Teams in grey deploy through sunlight.

Talk it up, boys, a little practice.

Coming in stubby and fast, the baseman
Gathers a grounder in fat green grass,
Picks it stinging and clipped as wit
Into the leather: a swinging step
Wings it deadeye down to first.
Smack. Oh, attaboy, attyoldboy.

Catcher reverses his cap, pulls down
Sweaty casque, and squats in the dust:
Pitcher rubs new ball on his pants,
Chewing, puts a jet behind him;
Nods past batter, taking his time.
Batter settles, tugs at his cap:
A spinning ball: step and swing to it,
Caught like a cheek before it ducks
By shivery hickory: socko, baby:
Cleats dig into dust. Outfielder,
On his way, looking over shoulder,
Makes it a triple. A long peg home.

Innings and afternoons. Fly lost in sunset.
Throwing arm gone bad. There's your old ball game.
Cool reek of the field. Reek of companions.

SOULS LAKE

THE evergreen shadow and the pale magnolia
Stripping slowly to the air of May
Stood still in the night of the honey trees.
At rest above a star pool with my friends,
Beside that grove most fit for elegies,
I made my phrase to out-enchant the night.

The epithalamion, the hush were due,
For I had fasted and gone blind to see
What night might be beyond our passages;
Those stars so chevalier in fearful heaven
Could not but lay their steel aside and come
With a grave glitter into my low room.

Vague though the population of the earth
Lay stretched and dry below the cypresses,
It was not round-about but in my night,
Bone of my bone, as an old man would say;
And all its stone weighed my mortality;
The pool would be my body and my eyes,

The air my garment and material
Whereof that wateriness and mirror lived—
The colorable, meek and limpid world.
Though I had sworn my element alien
To the pure mind of night, the cold princes,
Behold them there, and both worlds were the same.

The heart's planet seemed not so lonely then,
Seeing what kin it found in that reclining.
And ah, though sweet the catch of your chorales,
I heard no singing there among my friends;
But still were the great waves, the lions shining,
And infinite still the discourse of the night.

ROBERT FROST, *born March 26, 1874, in San Francisco, lives in Cambridge, Massachusetts, during the winter and on his farm in Ripton, Vermont, during the summer. He attended Dartmouth and Harvard but took degrees from neither. After an early and unsuccessful career of farming and intermittent school teaching, he went with his wife and young family to England in 1912, and there his first book,* A Boy's Will, *was published. He returned in 1915, his reputation as a poet already established. Honored by more awards and greater public favor than that granted to any other American poet, he has for many years lectured and read his poems throughout the United States. On March 24, 1950, the United States Senate unanimously adopted a resolution honoring him. His poems, according to the citation, ". . . have helped to guide American thought with humor, and wisdom, setting forth to our minds a reliable representation of ourselves and of all men. . . ." In 1958 he went to England to receive honorary degrees from both Oxford and Cambridge. In 1961 he read his poem "The Gift Outright" as part of the ceremonies attending the inauguration of President John F. Kennedy.*

I HAVE been one acquainted with the night.
I have walked out in rain—and back in rain.
I have outwalked the furthest city light.

I have looked down the saddest city lane.
I have passed by the watchman on his beat
And dropped my eyes, unwilling to explain.

I have stood still and stopped the sound of feet
When far away an interrupted cry
Came over houses from another street,

But not to call me back or say good-bye;
And further still at an unearthly height,
One luminary clock against the sky

Proclaimed the time was neither wrong nor right.
I have been one acquainted with the night.

WHOSE woods these are I think I know.
His house is in the village though;
He will not see me stopping here
To watch his woods fill up with snow.

My little horse must think it queer
To stop without a farmhouse near
Between the woods and frozen lake
The darkest evening of the year.

He gives his harness bells a shake
To ask if there is some mistake.

The only other sound's the sweep
Of easy wind and downy flake.

The woods are lovely, dark and deep.
But I have promises to keep,
And miles to go before I sleep,
And miles to go before I sleep.

THE ROAD NOT TAKEN

Two roads diverged in a yellow wood,
And sorry I could not travel both
And be one traveler, long I stood
And looked down one as far as I could
To where it bent in the undergrowth;

Then took the other, as just as fair,
And having perhaps the better claim,
Because it was grassy and wanted wear;
Though as for that the passing there
Had worn them really about the same,

And both that morning equally lay
In leaves no step had trodden black.
Oh, I kept the first for another day!
Yet knowing how way leads on to way,
I doubted if I should ever come back.

I shall be telling this with a sigh
Somewhere ages and ages hence:
Two roads diverged in a wood, and I—
I took the one less traveled by,
And that has made all the difference.

Once when the snow of the year was beginning to fall,
We stopped by a mountain pasture to say, 'Whose colt?'
A little Morgan had one forefoot on the wall,
The other curled at his breast. He dipped his head
And snorted at us. And then he had to bolt.
We heard the miniature thunder where he fled,
And we saw him, or thought we saw him, dim and grey,
Like a shadow against the curtain of falling flakes.
'I think the little fellow's afraid of the snow.
He isn't winter-broken. It isn't play
With the little fellow at all. He's running away.
I doubt if even his mother could tell him, "Sakes,
It's only weather." He'd think she didn't know!
Where is his mother? He can't be out alone.'
And now he comes again with clatter of stone,
And mounts the wall again with whited eyes
And all his tail that isn't hair up straight.
He shudders his coat as if to throw off flies.
'Whoever it is that leaves him out so late,
When other creatures have gone to stall and bin,
Ought to be told to come and take him in.'

PROVIDE PROVIDE

The witch that came (the withered hag)
To wash the steps with pail and rag,
Was once the beauty Abishag,

The picture pride of Hollywood.
Too many fall from great and good
For you to doubt the likelihood.

Die early and avoid the fate.
Or if predestined to die late,
Make up your mind to die in state.

Make the whole stock exchange your own!
If need be occupy a throne,
Where nobody can call *you* crone.

Some have relied on what they knew;
Others on being simply true.
What worked for them might work for you.

No memory of having starred
Atones for later disregard,
Or keeps the end from being hard.

Better to go down dignified
With boughten friendship at your side
Than none at all. Provide, provide!

A tribute to the poet's wife, this poem, a sonnet,
is remarkable, not only for the fact that the spiritual
qualities of a woman are metaphorically seen in
relation to the physical properties of a pitched tent
on a summer's day, but for the technical mas-
tery by which a fourteen-line poem is
presented as one sentence.

THE SILKEN TENT

SHE is as in a field a silken tent
At midday when a sunny summer breeze
Has dried the dew and all its ropes relent,
So that in guys it gently sways at ease,

And its supporting central cedar pole,
That is its pinnacle to heavenward
And signifies the sureness of the soul,
Seems to owe naught to any single cord,
But strictly held by none, is loosely bound
By countless silken ties of love and thought
To everything on earth the compass round,
And only by one's going slightly taut
In the capriciousness of summer air
Is of the slightest bondage made aware.

JEAN GARRIGUE, *born December 8, 1914, in Evansville, Indiana, lives in Greenwich Village, New York City. She graduated from the University of Chicago and during World War II edited a publication sheet for the USO. She then went to the University of Iowa to begin a teaching career that eventually included brief residences at Queens College, Bard College, and the University of Connecticut. After receiving a Guggenheim fellowship and an award from the National Academy of Arts and Letters in 1961, she went to Europe to continue work on her fifth volume of poetry.*

WHEN the mouse died at night
He was all overgrown with delight,
His whiskers thick as a wood
From exploring the Polar cupboard
And his eyes still agape
From risky accomplishment.
No honor or drum was his bait.
The more glorious, he
Who with no shame for time
Then boldly died,
Three weeks a rich spell
Of sound and pure smell
And all his long leisure
For meat of short measure
(An ant could carry it.)
Praise him who sweetens
On a small hate.

Now upon this piteous year
I sit in Denmark beside the quai
And nothing that the fishers say
Or the children carrying boats
Can recall me from that place
Where sense and wish departed me
Whose very shores take on
The whiteness of anon.
For I beheld a stranger there
Who moved ahead of me

So tensile and so dancer made
That like a thief I followed her
Though my heart was so alive
I thought myself the equal beauty.
But when at last a turning came
Like the branching of a river
And I saw if she walked on
She would be gone forever,
Fear, then, so wounded me
As fell upon my ear
The voice a blind man dreams
And broke on me the smile
I dreamed as deaf men hear,
I stood there like a spy,
My tongue and eyelids taken
In such necessity.
Now upon this piteous year
The rains of Autumn fall.
Where may she be?
I suffered her to disappear
Who hunger in the prison of my fear.
That lean and brown, that stride,
That cold and melting pride,
For whom the river like a clear,
Melodic line and the distant carrousel
Where lovers on their beasts of play
Rose and fell, that wayfare where the swan adorned
With every wave and eddy
The honor of his sexual beauty,
Create her out of sorrow
That, never perishing,
Is a stately thing.

We are large with pity, slow and awkward,
In the false country of the zoo.
For the beasts our hearts turn over and sigh.
With the gazelle we long to look eye to eye.
Laughter at the stumbling, southern giraffes
Urges our anger, righteous despair.
As the hartebeest plunges, giddy, eccentric,
From out of the courtyard into his stall,
We long to seize his forehead's steep horns
Which are like the staves of a lyre.
Fleeter than greyhounds the hartebeest
Long-muzzled, small-footed and shy.
Another runner, the emu, is even better
At kicking. Oh, the coarse chicken feet
Of this bird reputed a fossil!
His body, deep as a table,
Droops gracelessly downwise,
His small head shakes like an old woman's eye.
The emu, ostrich, the cassowary,
Continue to go on living their lives
In conditions unnatural to them
And in relations most strange,
Remain the same.
As for the secretary bird,
Snake-killer, he suggests
A mischievous bird-maker.
Like a long-legged boy in short pants
He runs teetering, legs far apart,
On his toes, part gasping girl.
What thought him up, this creature
Eminently equipped by his nervous habits
To kill venomous snakes with his strong,

Horny feet, first jumping on them,
And then leaping away?
At the reptile and monkey houses
Crowds gather, to enjoy the ugly,
But mock the kangaroo who walks like a cripple.

In the false country of the zoo
Where Africa is well represented
By Australia,
The emu, the ostrich and the cassowary
Survive like kings, poor antiquated strays,
Deceased in all but vestiges
Who did not have to change, preserved
In their peculiarities by rifts,
From emigration barred.
Now melancholy, like old continents
Unmodified and discontinued, they
Survive by some discreet permission
Like older souls too painfully handicapped.
Running birds who cannot fly,
Whose virtue is their liability,
Whose stubborn, very resistance, is their sorrow.
See, as they run, how we laugh
At the primitive, relic procedure.

In the false country of the zoo
Grief is well represented there
From those continents of the odd
And outmoded, Africa and Australia.
Sensation is foremost at a zoo—
The sensation of gaping at the particular:
The striped and camouflaged,
The bear, wallowing in his anger,
The humid tiger wading in a pool.
As for those imports

From Java and India,
The pale, virginal peafowl,
The stork, cracking his bill against a wall,
The peacock, plumes up, though he walks as if weighted,
—All that unconscionable tapestry—
Till a wind blows the source of his pride
And it becomes his embarrassment—
The eye, plunged in sensation, closes.
Thought seizes the image. This shrieking
Jungle of spot, stripe, orange,
Blurs. The oil from the deer's eye
That streaks like a tear his cheek
Seems like a tear, is, is,
As our love and our pity are, are.

DAVID GASCOYNE, *born October, 1916,*
in Harrow, Middlesex, England, lives in
London. He was educated at Salisbury
Cathedral Choir School and Regent Street
Polytechnic. He lived for a number of years
in France, where he wrote a book about
surrealism, a movement which deeply influ-
enced an important phase of his poetic
career. In 1952 he spent several months in
the United States.

Friend, whose unnatural early death
In this year's cold, chaotic Spring
Is like a clumsy wound that will not heal:
What can I say to you, now that your ears
Are stoppered-up with distant soil?
Perhaps to speak at all is false; more true
Simply to sit at times alone and dumb
And with most pure intensity of thought
And concentrated inmost feeling, reach
Towards your shadow on the years' crumbling wall.

I'll say not any word in praise or blame
Of what you ended with the mere turn of a tap;
Nor to explain, deplore nor yet exploit
The latent pathos of your living years—
Hurried, confused and unfulfilled—
That were the shiftless years of both our youths
Spent in the monstrous mountain-shadow of
Catastrophe that chilled you to the bone:
The certain imminence of which always pursued
You from your heritage of fields and sun . . .

I see your face in hostile sunlight, eyes
Wrinkled against its glare, behind the glass
Of a car's windscreen, while you seek to lose
Your self in swift devouring of white roads
Unwinding across Europe or America;
Taciturn at the wheel, wrapped in a blaze
Of restlessness that no fresh scene can quench;
In cities of brief sojourn that you pass
Through in your quest for respite, heavy drink
Alone enabling you to bear each hotel night.

Sex, Art and Politics: those poor
Expedients! You tried them each in turn,
With the wry inward smile of one resigned
To join in every complicated game
Adults affect to play. Yet girls you found
So prone to sentiment's corruptions; and the joy
Of sensual satisfaction seemed so brief, and left
Only new need. It proved hard to remain
Convinced of the Word's efficacity; or even quite
Certain of World-Salvation through "the Party Line" . . .

Cased in the careful armour that you wore
Of wit and nonchalance, through which
Few quizzed the concealed countenance of fear,
You waited daily for the sky to fall;
At moments wholly panic-stricken by
A sense of stifling in your brittle shell;
Seeing the world's damnation week by week
Grow more and more inevitable; till
The conflagration broke out with a roar,
And from those flames you fled through whirling smoke,

To end at last in bankrupt exile in
That sordid city, scene of *Ulysses*; and there,
While War sowed all the lands with violent graves,
You finally succumbed to a black, wild
Incomprehensibility of fate that none could share . . .
Yet even in your obscure death I see
The secret candour of that lonely child
Who, lost in the storm-shaken castle-park,
Astride his crippled mastiff's back was borne
Slowly away into the utmost dark.

W. S. GRAHAM, *born 1921, in Liverpool, of Scottish parentage, had little formal schooling. He spent his early years in the north of England and then went to London, where his work was recognized by publication and reading appearances on the BBC. In 1953 he came to America for a lecture tour.*

Listen. Put on morning.
Waken into falling light.
A man's imagining
Suddenly may inherit
The handclapping centuries
Of his one minute on earth.
And hear the virgin juries
Talk with his own breath
To the corner boys of his street
And hear the Black Maria
Searching the town at night.
And hear the playropes caa
The sister Mary in.
And hear Willie and Davie
Among bracken of Narnain
Sing in a mist heavy
With myrtle and listeners.
And hear the higher town
Weep a petition of fears
At the poorhouse close upon
The public heartbeat.
And hear the children tig
And run with my own feet
Into the netting drag
Of a suiciding principle.

Listen. Put on lightbreak.
Waken into miracle.
The audience lies awake
Under the tenements
Under the sugar docks
Under the printed moments.

The centuries turn their locks
And open under the hill
Their inherited books and doors
All gathered to distill
Like happy berry pickers
One voice to talk to us.
Yes listen. It carries away
The second and the years
Till the heart's in a jacket of snow
And the head's in a helmet of white
And the song sleeps to be wakened
By the morning ear bright.
Listen. Put on morning.
Waken into falling light.

ROBERT GRAVES, *born July 24, 1895, in London, lives in Spain on the island of Majorca. His early career was identified with that of the "trench poets" of World War I, during which, as a member of the Royal Welch Fusiliers, he saw much action and was wounded. He later studied at Oxford and taught for a year at the University of Cairo.*

He is one of the most prolific of contemporary authors, famous for his historical novels as well as for his critical essays, translations, and mythological studies, notably The White Goddess. *In recent years he has made several visits to the United States to read his poems; in 1961 he was elected professor of poetry at Oxford, a position in which he succeeded W. H. Auden.*

THE butterfly, a cabbage-white,
(His honest idiocy of flight)
Will never now, it is too late,
Master the art of flying straight,
Yet has—who knows so well as I?—
A just sense of how not to fly:
He lurches here and here by guess
And God and hope and hopelessness.
Even the aerobatic swift
Has not his flying-crooked gift.

Robert Graves's seventh child, Juan, was born on De-
cember 21, 1945. The fact that the winter solstice falls
on this date and that it is also the traditional
birthday of many figures of divinity such as the
Greek Apollo, Dionysus, Zeus, Hermes, the Syrian
Tammuz, the Egyptian Horus, the Welsh Merlin and
Llew Llaw, etc., leads the poet to address his son
as one in a great succession of heroes. His fate, like
theirs, he suggests, will be a retelling of "one story
and one story only": the Moon Goddess will appear
to him in her different characters at different seasons
of the year, i.e., at different years of his life span,
as mother, lover, and widow. The Boreal Crown is
Corona Borealis, which was the purgatory where many
such heroes went after death. The "log" in the fifth
stanza is the yule log, traditionally burned at the end
of the year. The "great boar" is the beast that kills
heroes at the fall of the year. Understand your fate,
the poet says to his infant son, accept it, and live it.

TO JUAN AT THE WINTER SOLSTICE

THERE is one story and one story only
That will prove worth your telling,
Whether as learned bard or gifted child;
To it all lines or lesser gauds belong
That startle with their shining
Such common stories as they stray into.

Is it of trees you tell, their months and virtues,
Or strange beasts that beset you,
Of birds that croak at you the Triple will?
Or of the Zodiac and how slow it turns
Below the Boreal Crown,
Prison of all true kings that ever reigned?

Water to water, ark again to ark,
From woman back to woman:

So each new victim treads unfalteringly
The never altered circuit of his fate,
Bringing twelve peers as witness
Both to his starry rise and starry fall.

Or is it of the Virgin's silver beauty,
All fish below the thighs?
She in her left hand bears a leafy quince;
When, with her right she crooks a finger smiling,
How may the King hold back?
Royally then he barters life for love.

Or of the undying snake from chaos hatched,
Whose coils contain the ocean,
Into whose chops with naked sword he springs,
Then in black water, tangled by the reeds,
Battles three days and nights,
To be spewed up beside her scalloped shore?

Much snow is falling, winds roar hollowly,
The owl hoots from the elder,
Fear in your heart cries to the loving-cup:
Sorrow to sorrow as the sparks fly upward.
The log groans and confesses
There is one story and one story only.

Dwell on her graciousness, dwell on her smiling,
Do not forget what flowers
The great boar trampled down in ivy time.
Her brow was creamy as the crested wave,
Her sea-blue eyes were wild
But nothing promised that is not performed.

OFTEN, half-way to sleep,
Not yet sunken deep—
The sudden moment on me comes
From a mountain shagged and steep,
With terrible roll of dream drums,
Reverberations, cymbals, horns replying.
When with standards flying,
Horsemen in clouds behind,
The coloured pomps unwind,
The Carnival wagons
With their saints and their dragons
On the scroll of my teeming mind:
The Creation and Flood
With our Saviour's Blood
And fat Silenus' flagons,
And every rare beast
From the South and East,
Both greatest and least,
On and on,
In endless, different procession.
I stand at the top rungs
Of a ladder reared in the air,
And I rail in strange tongues,
So the crowds murmur and stare;
Then volleys again the blare
Of horns, and summer flowers
Fly scattering in showers,
And the sun leaps in the sky,
While the drums thumping by
Proclaim me . . . .
    Oh, then, when I wake,
Could I courage take

To renew my speech,
Could I stretch and reach
The flowers and the ripe fruit
Laid out at the ladder's foot,
Could I rip a silken shred
From the banner tossed ahead,
Could I call a double-flam
From the drums, could the goat
Horned with gold, could the ram
With a flank like a barn-door,
The dwarf, the blackamoor,
Could Jonah and the Whale
And the Holy Grail,
The Ape with his platter
Going clitter-clatter,
The Nymphs and the Satyr,
And every marvellous matter
Come before me here,
Standing near and clear—
Could I make it so that you
Might wonder at them too!
—Glories of land and sea,
Of Heaven glittering free,
Castles hugely built in Spain,
Glories of Cockaigne,
Of that spicy kingdom, Cand,
Of the Delectable Land,
Of the Land of Crooked Stiles.
Of the Fortunate Isles,
Of the more than three-score miles
That to Babylon lead
(A pretty city indeed
Built on a four-square plan),
Of the Land of the Gold Man

Whose eager horses whinny
In their cribs of gold,
Of the Land of Whipperginny,
Of the land where none grows old . . . .
But cowardly I tell,
Rather, of the Town of Hell—
A huddle of dirty woes
And houses in fading rows
Straggled through space:
Hell has no market-place,
Nor point where four ways meet,
Nor principal street,
Nor barracks, nor Town Hall,
Nor shops at all,
Nor rest for weary feet,
Nor theatre, square, or park,
Nor lights after dark,
Nor churches, nor inns,
Nor convenience for sins—
Neither ends nor begins,
Rambling, limitless, hated well,
This Town of Hell
Where between sleep and sleep I dwell.

THOM GUNN, *born 1929, in Gravesend, England, lives in Berkeley, where he is a member of the English department of the University of California. He was educated at Cambridge, after which he moved permanently to the United States, first as a student of Yvor Winters at Stanford and later as a teacher.*

'Man, you gotta Go.'

THE blue jay scuffling in the bushes follows
Some hidden purpose, and the gust of birds
That spurts across the field, the wheeling swallows,
Have nested in the trees and undergrowth.
Seeking their instinct, or their poise, or both,
One moves with an uncertain violence
Under the dust thrown by a baffled sense
Or the dull thunder of approximate words.

On motorcycles, up the road, they come:
Small, black, as flies hanging in heat, the Boys,
Until the distance throws them forth, their hum
Bulges to thunder held by calf and thigh.
In goggles, donned impersonality,
In gleaming jackets trophied with the dust,
They strap in doubt—by hiding it, robust—
And almost hear a meaning in their noise.

Exact conclusion of their hardiness
Has no shape yet, but from known whereabouts
They ride, direction where the tires press.
They scare a flight of birds across the field:
Much that is natural, to the will must yield.
Men manufacture both machine and soul,
And use what they imperfectly control
To dare a future from the taken routes.

It is a part solution, after all.
One is not necessarily discord
On earth; or damned because, half animal,
One lacks direct instinct, because one wakes
Afloat on movement that divides and breaks.

One joins the movement in a valueless world,
Choosing it, till, both hurler and the hurled,
One moves as well, always toward, toward.

A minute holds them, who have come to go:
The self-defined, astride the created will
They burst away; the towns they travel through
Are home for neither bird nor holiness,
For birds and saints complete their purposes.
At worst, one is in motion; and at best,
Reaching no absolute, in which to rest,
One is always nearer by not keeping still.

BLACK JACKETS

In the silence that prolongs the span
Rawly of music when the record ends,
    The red-haired boy who drove a van
In weekday overalls but, like his friends,

    Wore cycle boots and jacket here
To suit the Sunday hangout he was in,
    Heard, as he stretched back from his beer,
Leather creak softly round his neck and chin.

    Before him, on a coal-black sleeve
Remote exertion had lined, scratched, and burned
    Insignia that could not revive
The heroic fall or climb where they were earned.

    On the other drinkers bent together,
Concocting selves for their impervious kit,
    He saw it as no more than leather
Which, taut across the shoulders grown to it,

Sent through the dimness of a bar
As sudden and anonymous hints of light
    As those that shipping give, that are
Now flickers in the Bay, now lost in night.

    He stretched out like a cat, and rolled
The bitterish taste of beer upon his tongue,
    And listened to a joke being told:
The present was the things he stayed among.

    If it was only loss he wore,
He wore it to assert, with fierce devotion,
    Complicity and nothing more.
He recollected his initiation,

    And one especially of the rites.
For on his shoulders they had put tattoos:
    The group's name on the left, The Knights,
And on the right the slogan Born To Lose.

CONSIDERING THE SNAIL

THE snail pushes through a green
night, for the grass is heavy
with water and meets over
the bright path he makes, where rain
has darkened the earth's dark. He
moves in a wood of desire,

pale antlers barely stirring
as he hunts. I cannot tell
what power is at work, drenched there
with purpose, knowing nothing.
What is a snail's fury? All
I think is that if later

I parted the blades above
the tunnel and saw the thin
trail of broken white across
litter, I would never have
imagined the slow passion
to that deliberate progress.

NOTHING in this bright region melts or shifts.
The local names are concepts: the Ravine,
Pemmican Ridge, North Col, Death Camp, they mean
The streetless rise, the dazzling abstract drifts,
To which particular names adhere by chance,
From custom lightly, not from character.
We stand on a white terrace and confer;
This is the last camp of experience.

What is that sudden yelp upon the air?
And whose are these cold droppings? whose malformed
Purposeless tracks about the slope? We know.
The abominable endures, existing where
Nothing else can: it is—unfed, unwarmed—
Born of rejection, of the boundless snow.

DONALD HALL, *born 1928, in New Haven, Connecticut, lives with his wife and son in Ann Arbor, where he teaches in the English department of the University of Michigan. He was educated at Harvard and Oxford, where his poem "Exile" was awarded the Newdigate Prize. With Robert Pack and Louis Simpson, he was editor of the anthology* The New Poets of England and America *(1957).*

THE SLEEPING GIANT

(A Hill, So Named, in Hamden, Connecticut)

THE whole day long, under the walking sun
That poised an eye on me from its high floor,
Holding my toy beside the clapboard house
I looked for him, the summer I was four.

I was afraid the waking arm would break
From the loose earth and rub against his eyes
A fist of trees, and the whole country tremble
In the exultant labor of his rise;

Then he with giant steps in the small streets
Would stagger, cutting off the sky, to seize
The roofs from house and home because we had
Covered his shape with dirt and planted trees;

And then kneel down and rip with fingernails
A trench to pour the enemy Atlantic
Into our basin, and the water rush,
With the streets full and all the voices frantic.

That was the summer I expected him.
Later the high and watchful sun instead
Walked low behind the house, and school began,
And winter pulled a sheet over his head.

THE BODY POLITIC

I SHOT my friend to save my country's life,
And when the happy bullet struck him dead,
I was saluted by the drum and fife
Corps of a high school, while the traitor bled.

I never thought until I pulled the trigger
But that I did the difficult and good.
I thought republics stood for something bigger,
For the mind of man, as Plato said they stood.

So when I heard the duty they assigned,
Shooting my friend seemed only sanity;
To keep disorder from the state of mind
Was mental rectitude, it seemed to me.

The audience dispersed. I felt depressed.
I went to where my orders issued from,
But the right number on the street was just
A rickety old house, vacant and dumb.

I tried to find the true address, but where?
Nobody told me what I really wanted;
Just secretaries sent me here and there
To other secretaries. I was daunted.

Poor Fred. His presence will be greatly missed
By children and by cronies by the score.
The State (I learn too late) does not exist;
Man lives by love, and not by metaphor.

MICHAEL HAMBURGER, *born March
22, 1924, in Berlin, Germany, lives with his
wife and three children in Reading, Berkshire, where he teaches at the University of
Reading. He was educated at Christ Church,
Oxford, and spent four years in the armed
services. He has published many critical
essays, some of which are included in his
volume* Reason and Energy (1957), *and
is well known as a translator of German
literature.*

To my twin who lives in a cruel country
    I wrote a letter at last;
For my bones creaked out in our long silence
    That seven years had passed,

Seven whole years since he and I
    By word or token exchanged
The message I dare not do without:
    That still we are not estranged,

Though I watch figures in a city office
    And he the waves of the sea,
Keeping no count since he hardly cares
    What happens to him or to me;

Since to names and numbers he closed his head
    When, children still, we were parted,
Chose birth and death for his calendar,
    But leaves the dates uncharted,

Being one who forgets what I remember,
    Who knows what I do not,
Who has learnt the ways of otter and raven
    While I've grown polyglot.

Lately I found a cactus in flower
    And feared for his apple-trees,
Dozed in the club and saw his cattle
    Drag with a foul disease,

And my bones grown stiff with leaning and lying
    Cried out that I'll labour in vain
Till I help my twin to rebuild his hovel
    That's open to wind and rain.

So I sent him a note, expecting no answer,
    And a cheque he'd never cash.
For I knew he was one who'd smile if he heard
    His own roof come down with a crash,

But above the porpoise-leaping bay
    Where ploughshare fin and tail
Cut furrows the foam-flecked sea fills up
    He'd stand in the swishing gale,

Calm as the jackdaws that nest in crannies
    And no more prone to doubt,
With gull and cormorant perched on the rocks
    Would wait the weather out.

Yet he wrote by return: "Have no fear for your dwelling
    Though dry-rot gnaws at the floors;
Only lighten their load of marble and metal,
    Keep clear the corridors,

Move out the clocks that clutter your study,
    And the years will leave you alone:
Every frame I know of lasts long enough,
    Though but cardboard, wood or bone.

And spare me your nightmares, brother, I beg you,
    They make my daemons laugh,
They scare the spirits that rarely will visit
    A man with no wand or staff,

With no symbol, no book and no formula,
    No lore to aid him at all,
Who wherever he walks must find the image
    That holds his mentors in thrall.

But your waking cares put down on paper
    For me to give to the wind,

That the seed may fall and the dry leaf crumble,
    Not a wisp be left behind

Of the tangle that hides the dual site
    Where even you and I
Still may meet again and together build
    One house before we die."

JOHN HEATH-STUBBS *was born July 9, 1918, in London, where he now lives. He was educated at schools in Sussex and the Isle of Wight until he was sixteen, when failing eyesight caused him to be put under private tutors. After an operation when he was eighteen, he was sent for a year to the Worcester College for the Blind and then entered Oxford, where he took a "first class" in English language and literature. In 1952 he was appointed poet-in-residence at the University of Leeds and later taught at the University of Cairo. He has written one volume of criticism,* The Darkling Plain.

Venerable Mother Tooth-ache
Climb down from the white battlements,
Stop twisting in your yellow fingers
The fourfold rope of nerves;
And tomorrow I will give you a tot of whiskey
To hold in your cupped hands,
A garland of anise-flowers,
And three cloves like nails.

And tell the attendant gnomes
It is time to knock off now,
To shoulder their little pick-axes,
Their cold-chisels and drills.
And you may mount by a silver ladder
Into the sky, to grind
In the cracked polished mortar
Of the hollow moon.

By the lapse of warm waters,
And the poppies nodding like red coals,
The paths on the granite mountains,
And the plantation of my dreams.

THE LADY'S COMPLAINT

I speak of that lady I heard last night,
    Maudlin over her gin and water,
In a sloppy bar with a fulvous light
    And an air that was smeared with smoke and laughter:
    How youth decamps and cold age comes after,

In fifty years she had found it true—
    She sighed for the damage that time had brought her:
'Oh, after death there's a judgement due.

'What once was as sleek as a seal's pelt,
    My shapeless body has fallen from grace;
My soul and my shoes are worn down to the welt,
    And no cosmetic can mask my face,
    As under talcum and oxide you trace
How the bones stick out, and the ghost peeps through—
    A wanderer, I, in Wraith-bone Place,
And after death there's a judgement due.

'My roundabout horses have cantered away,
    The gilded and garrulous seasons are flown;
What echo is left of the rag-time bray
    Of the tenor sax and the susaphone?
    But I was frightened to sleep alone
(As now I must do, as now I must do)
    And a chittering bat-voice pipes "Atone,
For after death there's a judgement due."

'Green apples I bit when I was green,
    My teeth are on edge at the maggotty core;
Life is inclement, obscure, obscene;
    Nothing's amusing—not any more;
    But love's abrasions have left me sore—
To hairy Harry and half-mast Hugh
    I gave the love I was starving for,
And after death there's a judgement due.

'Potentate, swirling in stark cold air
    The corn from the husks—I offer to you
My terror-struck and incredulous prayer,
    For after death there's a judgement due.'

ANTHONY HECHT, *born January 16, 1923, in New York, now lives in his native city. He was educated at Bard College and Columbia University and, for a number of years, was on the English faculty of Smith College. Married and divorced, he has two sons, Jason and Adam.*

Samuel Sewall (1652–1750) was a leading jurist in Puritan times in Massachusetts. Having once been a minister, he gave up the cloth for a public career and became one of the judges responsible for the conviction of nineteen persons in the famous Salem witchcraft trials. In this poem, Anthony Hecht is concerned, not with Sewall as a public man, but solely with the humanly engaging aspects of the courtship of a man of exemplary, and sometimes frightening, rectitude.

SAMUEL SEWALL

SAMUEL Sewall, in a world of wigs,
Flouted opinion in his personal hair;
For foppery he gave not any figs,
But in his right and honor took the air.

Thus in his naked style, though well attired,
He went forth in the city, or paid court
To Madam Winthrop, whom he much admired,
Most godly, but yet liberal with the port.

And all the town admired for two full years
His excellent address, his gifts of fruit,
Her gracious ways and delicate white ears,
And held the course of nature absolute.

But yet she bade him suffer a peruke,
"That One be not distinguished from the All";
Delivered of herself this stern rebuke
Framed in the resonant language of St. Paul.

"Madam," he answered her, "I have a Friend
Furnishes me with hair out of His strength,
And He requires only I attend
Unto His charity and to its length."

And all the town was witness to his trust:
On Monday he walked out with the Widow Gibbs,
A pious lady of charm and notable bust,
Whose heart beat tolerably beneath her ribs.

On Saturday he wrote proposing marriage,
And closed, imploring that she be not cruel,
"Your favorable answer will oblige,
Madam, your humble servant, Samuel Sewall."

A botanical garden in Brooklyn becomes the model for a jungle Eden and leads the poet into a meditation upon "the botanical condition" of all living things, importantly including man. Ischia is an island off Italy, a resort as fashionable today as it was in Roman times. Madame Curie was the Polish-born chemist who with her French husband, Pierre, discovered radium in 1898. Lilith was the first wife of Adam, according to popular medieval belief. "Lullay myn lykyng, myn owyn dere derlyng" *is the refrain of an old lullaby. The* Gare du Nord *is a railway station in Paris. Polyphemus was a mythical Greek Cyclops who imprisoned Odysseus and his men in a cave and devoured two of the group every day until Odysseus got him drunk and blinded him.* Mort' saison *is taken from the* Little Testament *of François Villon, the second stanza of which begins*: "En ce temps que j'ai dit devant,/ Sur le Noel, morte saison,/ Que les loups se vivent de vent/ Et qu'on se tient en sa maison, . . ." *Pyrites is the technical term for fool's gold, the name given to any of a number of metallic-looking sulfides that resemble gold. Making a pun of the similarity between pyrites and Stylites, the name of an ascetic of Antioch who lived on the top of a pillar, the poet creates "Simeon Pyrites," patron saint of a fool's paradise.*

LA CONDITION BOTANIQUE

Romans, rheumatic, gouty, came
   To bathe in Ischian springs where water steamed,
Puffed and enlarged their bold imperial thoughts, and which
Later Madame Curie declared to be so rich
   In radioactive content as she deemed
     Should win them everlasting fame.

   Scattered throughout their ice and snow
   The Finns have built airtight cabins of log
Where they may lie, limp and entranced by the sedative purr

Of steam pipes, or torment themselves with flails of fir
    To stimulate the blood, and swill down grog,
        Setting the particles aglow.

        Similarly the Turks, but know
    Nothing of the more delicate thin sweat
Of plants, breathing their scented oxygen upon
Brooklyn's botanical gardens, roofed with glass and run
    So to the pleasure of each leafy pet,
        Manured, addressed in Latin, so

        To its thermostatic happiness—
Spreading its green and innocence to the ground
Where pipes, like Satan masquerading as the snake,
Coil and uncoil their frightful liquid length, and make
    Gurglings of love mixed with a rumbling sound
        Of sharp intestinal distress—

        So to its pleasure, as I said,
    That each particular vegetable may thrive,
Early and late, as in the lot first given Man,
Sans interruption, as when Universal Pan
    Led on the Eternal Spring. The spears of chive,
        The sensitive plant, showing its dread,

        The Mexican flytrap, that can knit
    Its quilled jaws pitilessly, and would hurt
A fly with pleasure, leading Riley's life in bed
Of peat moss and of chemicals, and is thoughtfully fed
    Flies for the entrée, flies for the dessert,
        Fruit flies for fruit, and all of it

        Administered as by a wife—
    Lilith our lady, patroness of plants,
Who sings, *Lullay myn lykyng, myn owyn dere derlyng,*

Madrigals nightly to the spiny stalk in sterling
  Whole notes of admiration and romance—
    This, then, is what is called The Life.

    And we, like disinherited heirs,
  Old Adams, can inspect the void estate
At visiting hours: the unconditional garden spot,
The effortless innocence preserved, for God knows what,
  And think, as we depart by the toll gate:
    No one has lived here these five thousand years.

    Our world is turned on points, is whirled
  On wheels, Tibetan prayer wheels, French verb wheels,
The toothy wheels of progress, the terrible torque
Insisting, and in the sky, even above New York
  Rotate the marvelous four-fangled seals
    Ezekiel saw. The mother-of-pearled

    Home of the bachelor oyster lies
  Fondled in fluent shifts of bile and lime
As sunlight strikes the water, and it is of our world,
And will appear to us sometime where the finger is curled
  Between the frets upon a mandolin,
    Fancy cigar boxes, and eyes

    Of ceremonial masks; and all
  The places where Kilroy inscribed his name,
For instance, the ladies' rest room in the Gare du Nord,
The iron rump of Buddha, whose hallowed, hollowed core
  Admitted tourists once but all the same
    Housed a machine gun, and let fall

    A killing fire from its eyes
  During the war; and Polyphemus hurled
Tremendous rocks that stand today off Sicily's coast

Signed with the famous scrawl of our most traveled ghost;
    And all these various things are of our world.
        But what's become of Paradise?

        Ah, it is lodged in glass, survives
    In Brooklyn, like a throwback, out of style,
Like an incomprehensible veteran of the Grand
Army of the Republic in the reviewing stand
    Who sees young men in a mud-colored file
        March to the summit of their lives,

        For glory, for their country, with the flag
    Joining divergent stars of North and South
In one blue field of heaven, till they fall in blood
And are returned at last unto their native mud—
    The eyes weighed down with stones, the sometimes mouth
        Helpless to masticate or gag

        Its old inheritance of earth.
    In the sweat of thy face shalt thou manage, said the Lord.
And we, old Adams, stare through the glass panes and wince,
Fearing to see the ancestral apple, pear, or quince,
    The delicacy of knowledge, the fleshed Word,
        The globe of wisdom that was worth

        Our lives, or so our parents thought,
    And turn away to strengthen our poor breath
And body, keep the flesh rosy with hopeful dreams,
Peach-colored, practical, to decorate the bones, with schemes
    Of life insurance, Ice-Cream-After-Death,
        Hormone injections, against the *mort'*

        Saison, largely to babble praise
    Of Simeon Pyrites, patron saint
Of our Fools' Paradise, whose glittering effigy

Shines in God's normal sunlight till the blind men see
    Visions as permanent as artists paint:
        The body's firm, nothing decays

        Upon the heirloom set of bones
    In their gavotte. Yet we look through the glass
Where green lies ageless under snow-stacked roofs in steam-
Fitted apartments, and reflect how bud and stem
    Are wholly flesh, and the immaculate grass
        Does without buttressing of bones.

    In open field or public bed
    With ultraviolet help, man hopes to learn
The leafy secret, pay his most outstanding debt
To God in the salt and honesty of his sweat,
    And in his streaming face manly to earn
        His daily and all-nourishing bread.

DANIEL HOFFMAN, *born 1923, in New York City, lives with his wife and two children in Swarthmore, Pennsylvania, where he is associate professor of English literature at Swarthmore College. He was educated at Columbia University, served in the Army Air Force in World War II, and subsequently taught at Columbia and at the University of Dijon, in France. Beyond poetry, his works include several scholarly studies of phases of American literature.*

THE SEALS IN PENOBSCOT BAY

hadn't heard of the atom bomb,
so I shouted a warning to them.

Our destroyer (on trial run) slid by
the rocks where they gamboled and played;

they must have misunderstood,
or perhaps not one of them heard

me over the engines and tides.
As I watched them over our wake

I saw their sleek skins in the sun
ripple, light-flecked, on the rock,

plunge, bubbling, into the brine,
and couple & laugh in the troughs

between the waves' whitecaps and froth.
Then the males clambered clumsily up

and lustily crowed like seacocks,
sure that their prowess held thrall

DANIEL HOFFMAN   *159*

all the sharks, other seals, and seagulls.
And daintily flipped the females,

seawenches with musical tails;
each looked at the Atlantic as

though it were her looking-glass.
If my warning had ever been heard

it was sound none would now ever heed.
And I, while I watched those far seals,

tasted honey that buzzed in my ears
and saw, out to windward, the sails

of an obsolete ship with banked oars
that swept like two combs through the spray.

And I wished for a vacuum of wax
to ward away all those strange sounds,

yet I envied the sweet agony
of him who was tied to the mast,

when the boom, when the boom, when the boom
of guns punched dark holes in the sky.

JOHN HOLLANDER, *born 1929, lives with his wife and young daughter in New Haven, Connecticut, where he is on the faculty of Yale University. He was educated at Columbia, Indiana, and Harvard, where he was a member of the Society of Fellows. He is poetry editor of the* Partisan Review *and the author of* The Untuning of the Sky: Ideas of Music in English Poetry 1500–1706. *Before going to Yale, he taught at Connecticut College for Women, in New London.*

WHEN Adam found his rib was gone
He cursed and sighed and cried and swore,
And looked with cold resentment on
The creature God had used it for.
All love's delights were quickly spent
And soon his sorrows multiplied;
He learned to blame his discontent
On something stolen from his side.

And so in every age we find
Each Jack, destroying every Joan,
Divides and conquers womankind
In vengeance for the missing bone;
By day he spins out quaint conceits
With gossip, flattery and song
And then at night, between the sheets
He wrongs the girl to right the wrong.

Though shoulder, bosom, lip and knee
Are praised in every kind of art,
Here is Love's true anatomy:
His rib is gone; he'll have her heart.
So women bear the debt alone
And live eternally distressed,
For though we throw the dog his bone
He wants it back with interest.

THE GREAT BEAR

EVEN on clear nights, lead the most supple children
Out onto hilltops, and by no means will

They make it out. Neither the gruff round image
From a remembered page nor the uncertain
Finger tracing that image out can manage
To mark the lines of what ought to be there,
Passing through certain bounding stars, until
The whole massive expanse of bear appear
Swinging, across the ecliptic; and, although
The littlest ones say nothing, others respond,
Making us thankful in varying degrees
For what we would have shown them: "There it is!"
"I see it now!" Even "Very like a bear!"
Would make us grateful. Because there is no bear

We blame our memory of the picture: trudging
Up the dark, starlit path, stooping to clutch
An anxious hand, perhaps the outline faded
Then; perhaps could we have retained the thing
In mind ourselves, with it we might have staged
Something convincing. We easily forget
The huge, clear, homely dipper that is such
An event to reckon with, an object set
Across the space the bear should occupy;
But even so, the trouble lies in pointing
At any stars. For one's own finger aims
Always elsewhere: the man beside one seems
Never to get the point. "No! The bright star
Just above my fingertip." The star,

If any, that he sees beyond one's finger
Will never be the intended one. To bring
Another's eye to bear in such a fashion
On any single star seems to require
Something very like a constellation
That both habitually see at night;
Not in the stars themselves, but in among

Their scatter, perhaps, some old familiar sight
Is always there to take a bearing from.
And if the smallest child of all should cry
Out on the wet, black grass because he sees
Nothing but stars, though claiming that there is
Some bear not there that frightens him, we need
Only reflect that we ourselves have need

Of what is fearful (being really nothing)
With which to find our way about the path
That leads back down the hill again, and with
Which to enable the older children standing
By us to follow what we mean by "This
Star," "That one," or "The other one beyond it."
But what of the tiny, scared ones?—Such a bear,
Who needs it? We can still make do with both
The dipper that we always knew was there
And the bright, simple shapes that suddenly
Emerge on certain nights. To understand
The signs that stars compose, we need depend
Only on stars that are entirely there
And the apparent space between them. There

Never need be lines between them, puzzling
Our sense of what is what. What a star does
Is never to surprise us as it covers
The center of its patch of darkness, sparkling
Always, a point in one of many figures.
One solitary star would be quite useless,
A frigid conjecture, true but trifling;
And any single sign is meaningless
If unnecessary. Crab, bull, and ram,
Or frosty, irregular polygons of our own
Devising, or finally the Great Dark Bear
That we can never quite believe is there—

Having the others, any one of them
Can be dispensed with. The bear, of all of them,

Is somehow most like any one, taken
At random, in that we always tend to say
That just because it might be there; because
Some Ancients really traced it out, a broken
And complicated line, webbing bright stars
And fainter ones together; because a bear
Habitually appeared—then even by day
It is for us a thing that should be there.
We should not want to train ourselves to see it.
The world is everything that happens to
Be true. The stars at night seem to suggest
The shapes of what might be. If it were best,
Even, to have it there (such a great bear!
All hung with stars!), there still would be no bear.

BARBARA HOWES, *born 1914, in Boston, lives with her husband, the poet William Jay Smith, and their two sons in North Pownal, Vermont. After graduating from Bennington, she lived in New York City, where she was founder and editor of the distinguished literary magazine* Chimera. *Since her marriage she has lived with her family for long periods in Italy and in France.*

A chimera is a creature out of mythology that breathes fire and has a lion's head, a goat's body, and a serpent's tail. It is usually considered a horrible and unreal figment of the imagination, but in this poem it is judged differently. Hippocampi are sea horses with two forefeet and bodies that end in tails like those of dolphins or of fish.

CHIMERA

AFTER a fearful maze where doubt
Crept at my side down the terrible lightless channel,
I came in my dream to a sandspit parting
Wind-tossed fields of ocean. There,
Lightstepping, appeared
A trio of moose or mules,
Ugly as peat,
Their trotters slim as a queen's.
"Hippocampi!" cried a voice as they sped
Over black water, their salty course,
And away. From the heaving sea
Then sprang a fabulous beast
For its evening gallop.
Head of a lion, goat's head rearing
Back, derisive, wild—the dragon
Body scaling the waves; each reckless
Nature in balance, flying apart
In one. How it sported
Across the water, how it ramped and ran!
My heart took heart. Awaking, I thought:
What was disclosed in this vision
Was good; phantom or real,
I have looked on a noble animal.

WITH seven matching calfskin cases for his new suits—
Wife and three children following up the plank—
The Colonel shepherds his brood on board.

As the band pumps out "Arrivederci
Roma," the airman's apple
Face bobs over the first-class rail;
Across the watery gap, Sicilian
Crowds like lemmings rush at the narrowing pier.

Poised on the balls of his feet, the athlete
Goes below. Headwaiters
Screen him with menus; sommeliers
Approach on the double; corks pop to the creaking
Of timbers, while he dreams
Of winning every ship's pool.

Florid, the airman bunts
Favors around the dance floor: sky-blue-pink
Balloons doze on the air. It is the Captain's
Dinner; haloed in streamers, he romps
With a Duchess and wins
At Musical Chairs.

Later, on the boat-deck, laced
Tight as a hammock by Irish
Whiskey, the athlete nuzzles the nurse. Collapsed
Like a tent around her, he rolls
With the ship.

After breakfast, the children on deck, New York
Near, balling his fists, the hero
Turns on his wife:
He hits out as if to do her honor.

With seven matching calfskin cases for his new suits—
Wife and children following down the plank—
The Colonel shepherds his brood ashore.

In forest-green sportcoat and desert brogans, he passes
Through Customs like quicksilver. His wife
Is heavily veiled; her three
Children follow like figures in effigy.

TED HUGHES, *born August 17, 1930, in Mytholmroyd, Yorkshire, lives with his wife, the American poet Sylvia Plath, in Devonshire. During World War II he served with the Royal Air Force as a ground wireless mechanic and then studied at Cambridge, where he met his wife, who was attending Newnham College on a Fulbright fellowship. During a long visit to the United States, during which he lived in Northampton and Boston, Massachusetts, his first book,* The Hawk in the Rain, *was the winner of the First Publication Award of the Poetry Center of the YM–YWHA in New York City.*

I sit in the top of the wood, my eyes closed.
Inaction, no falsifying dream
Between my hooked head and hooked feet:
Or in sleep rehearse perfect kills and eat.

The convenience of the high trees!
The air's buoyancy and the sun's ray
Are of advantage to me;
And the earth's face upward for my inspection.

My feet are locked upon the rough bark.
It took the whole of Creation
To produce my foot, my each feather:
Now I hold Creation in my foot

Or fly up, and revolve it all slowly—
I kill where I please because it is all mine.
There is no sophistry in my body:
My manners are tearing off heads—

The allotment of death.
For the one path of my flight is direct
Through the bones of the living.
No arguments assert my right:

The sun is behind me.
Nothing has changed since I began.
My eye has permitted no change.
I am going to keep things like this.

The pig lay on a barrow dead.
It weighed, they said, as much as three men.
Its eyes closed, pink white eyelashes.
Its trotters stuck straight out.

Such weight and thick pink bulk
Set in death seemed not just dead.
It was less than lifeless, further off.
It was like a sack of wheat.

I thumped it without feeling remorse.
One feels guilty insulting the dead,
Walking on graves. But this pig
Did not seem able to accuse.

It was too dead. Just so much
A poundage of lard and pork.
Its last dignity had entirely gone.
It was not a figure of fun.

Too dead now to pity.
To remember its life, din, stronghold
Of earthly pleasure as it had been,
Seemed a false effort, and off the point.

Too deadly factual. Its weight
Oppressed me—how could it be moved?
And the trouble of cutting it up!
The gash in its throat was shocking, but not pathetic.

Once I ran at a fair in the noise
To catch a greased piglet
That was faster and nimbler than a cat,
Its squeal was the rending of metal.

Pigs must have hot blood, they feel like ovens.
Their bite is worse than a horse's—
They chop a half-moon clean out.
They eat cinders, dead cats.

Distinctions and admirations such
As this one was long finished with.
I stared at it a long time. They were going to scald it,
Scald it and scour it like a doorstep.

RANDALL JARRELL, *born May 6, 1914, in Nashville,*
Tennessee, lives with his wife and two daughters in
Greensboro, North Carolina, where he is professor of
English at the Women's College of the University of
North Carolina. He was educated at Vanderbilt University
and has taught at the University of Texas, Sarah Lawrence,
Kenyon, and in Europe at the Salzburg Seminar in
American Civilization. He has been Consultant in Poetry
at the Library of Congress and a literary editor of
The Nation, *and during World War II he served for three*
and a half years in the Army Air Force. His writings
include a novel, Pictures from an Institution, *and two*
volumes of essays, Poetry and the Age *and* A Sad Heart
at the Supermarket.

Nestus Gurley is only the boy who delivers the papers, but in this poem he looms as large as a character out of mythology. Dorian mode refers to the music of the Dorians, which the more sophisticated Athenians regarded as harsh and rough. Moravian Star is a decoration manufactured in Moravia, central Czechoslovakia. Rauwolfia is the original name for the medical extract known as snakeroot, sometimes used for treatment of mental patients.

NESTUS GURLEY

SOMETIMES waking, sometimes sleeping,
Late in the afternoon, or early
In the morning, I hear on the lawn,
On the walk, on the lawn, the soft quick step,
The sound half song, half breath: a note or two
That with a note or two would be a tune.
It is Nestus Gurley.

It is an old
Catch or snatch or tune
In the Dorian mode: the mode of the horses
That stand all night in the fields asleep
Or awake, the mode of the cold
Hunter, Orion, wheeling upside-down,
All space and stars, in cater-cornered Heaven.
When, somewhere under the east,
The great march begins, with birds and silence;
When, in the day's first triumph, dawn
Rides over the houses, Nestus Gurley
Delivers to me my lot.

As the sun sets, I hear my daughter say:
"He has four routes and makes a hundred dollars."

RANDALL JARRELL *175*

Sometimes he comes with dogs, sometimes with children,
Sometimes with dogs and children.
He collects, today.
I hear my daughter say:
"Today Nestus has got on his derby."
And he says, after a little: "It's two-eighty."
"How could it be two-eighty?"
"Because this month there're five Sundays: it's two-eighty."

He collects, delivers. Before the first, least star
Is lost in the paling east; at evening
While the soft, side-lit, gold-leafed day
Lingers to see the stars, the boy Nestus
Delivers to me the Morning Star, the Evening Star
—Ah no, only the Morning *News*, the Evening *Record*
Of what I have done and what I have not done
Set down and held against me in the Book
Of Death, on paper yellowing
Already, with one morning's sun, one evening's sun.

Sometimes I only dream him. He brings then
News of a different morning, a judgment not of men.
The bombers have turned back over the Pole,
Having met a star. . . . I look at that new year
And, waking, think of our Moravian Star
Not lit yet, and the pure beeswax candle
With its red flame-proofed paper pompom
Not lit yet, and the sweetened
Bun we brought home from the love-feast, still not eaten,
And the song the children sang: *O Morning Star*—

And at this hour, to the dew-hushed drums
Of the morning, Nestus Gurley
Marches to me over the lawn; and the cat Elfie,
Furred like a musk-ox, coon-tailed, gold-leaf-eyed,

Looks at the paper boy without alarm
But yawns, and stretches, and walks placidly
Across the lawn to his ladder, climbs it, and begins to purr.

I let him in,
Go out and pick up from the grass the paper hat
Nestus has folded: this tricorne fit for a Napoleon
Of our days and institutions, weaving
Baskets, being bathed, receiving
Electric shocks, Rauwolfia. . . . I put it on
—Ah no, only unfold it.
There is dawn inside; and I say to no one
About—
        it is a note or two
That with a note or two would—
                  say to no one
About nothing: "He delivers dawn."

When I lie coldly
—Lie, that is, neither with coldness nor with warmth—
In the darkness that is not lit by anything,
In the grave that is not lit by anything
Except our hope: the hope
That is not proofed against anything, but pure
And shining as the first, least star
That is lost in the east on the morning of Judgment—
May I say, recognizing the step
Or tune or breath. . . .
             recognizing the breath,
May I say, "It is Nestus Gurley."

The saris go by me from the embassies.

Cloth from the moon. Cloth from another planet.
They look back at the leopard like the leopard.

And I. . . .
          this print of mine, that has kept its color
Alive through so many cleanings; this dull null
Navy I wear to work, and wear from work, and so
To my bed, so to my grave, with no
Complaints, no comment: neither from my chief,
The Deputy Chief Assistant, nor his chief—
Only I complain. . . . this serviceable
Body that no sunlight dyes, no hand suffuses
But, dome-shadowed, withering among columns,
Wavy beneath fountains—small, far-off, shining
In the eyes of animals, these beings trapped
As I am trapped but not, themselves, the trap,
Aging, but without knowledge of their age,
Kept safe here, knowing not of death, for death—
Oh, bars of my own body, open, open!

The world goes by my cage and never sees me.
And there come not to me, as come to these,
The wild beasts, sparrows pecking the llamas' grain,
Pigeons settling on the bears' bread, buzzards
Tearing the meat the flies have clouded. . . .
                      Vulture,
When you come for the white rat that the foxes left,
Take off the red helmet of your head, the black
Wings that have shadowed me, and step to me as man:
The wild brother at whose feet the white wolves fawn,
To whose hand of power the great lioness

Stalks, purring. . . .

                You know what I was,
You see what I am: change me, change me!

HIS pads furring the scarp's rime,
Weightless in greys and ecru, gliding
Invisibly, incuriously
As the crystals of the cirri wandering
A mile below his absent eyes,
The leopard gazes at the caravan.
The yaks groaning with tea, the burlaps
Lapping and lapping each stunned universe
That gasps like a kettle for its thinning life
Are pools in the interminable abyss
That ranges up through ice, through air, to night.
Raiders of the unminding element,
The last cold capillaries of their kind,
They move so slowly they are motionless
To any eye less stubborn than a man's. . . .
From the implacable jumble of the blocks
The grains dance icily, a scouring plume,
Into the breath, sustaining, unsustainable,
They trade to that last stillness for their death.
They sense with misunderstanding horror, with desire,
Behind the world their blood sets up in mist
The brute and geometrical necessity:
The leopard waving with a grating purr
His six-foot tail; the leopard, who looks sleepily—
Cold, fugitive, secure—at all he knows,
At all that he is: the heart of heartlessness.

ELIZABETH JENNINGS, *born July 26, 1926,
in Boston, England, lives in Oxford, where she
pursues a career as free-lance writer. Educated
in private schools and at Oxford University, she
has been a fellow of the Royal Society of Literature and, in 1956, was winner of the Somerset
Maugham Award. She spends as much time as
she can in Rome.*

Nobody stays here long;
    Deliberate visitors know
There is nothing here the guide-books show,
    No ruin or statue to sustain
Some great emotion in their stone.
    So visitors soon go.

Some travellers stay a little
    To collect wine or corn
And here breathe in the over-subtle
    Smell of places worn
Not by a marvellous death or battle
    But by their insignificance brought down.

Yet good, a place like this,
    For one grown tired of histories
To shape a human myth,
    A story but for his
Delight, where he might make the place
    His own success
Building what no one else had bothered with—
    A simple life or death.

IN THE NIGHT

Out of my window late at night I gape
And see the stars but do not watch them really,
And hear the trains but do not listen clearly;
Inside my mind I turn about to keep
Myself awake, yet am not there entirely.
Something of me is out in the dark landscape.

How much am I then what I think, how much what I feel?
How much the eye that seems to keep stars straight?
Do I control what I can contemplate
Or is it my vision that's amenable?
I turn in my mind, my mind is a room whose wall
I can see the top of but never completely scale.

All that I love is, like the night, outside,
Good to be gazed at, looking as if it could
With a simple gesture be brought inside my head
Or in my heart. But my thoughts about it divide
Me from my object. Now deep in my bed
I turn and the world turns on the other side.

GALWAY KINNELL, *born February 1, 1927, in Pawtucket, Rhode Island, lives in New York City. He was educated at Princeton and the University of Rochester and has taught at Alfred University, the University of Chicago, the University of Grenoble, New York University, and in Iran at the University of Teheran. Married and divorced, he devotes his time to translating and free-lance literary work.*

THEN it was dusk in Illinois, the small boy
After an afternoon of carting dung
Hung on the rail fence, a sapped thing
Weary to crying. Dark was growing tall
And he began to hear the pond frogs all
Calling upon his ear with what seemed their joy.

Soon their sound was pleasant for a boy
Listening in the smoky dusk and the nightfall
Of Illinois, and then from the field two small
Boys came bearing cornstalk violins
And rubbed three cornstalk bows with resins,
And they set fiddling with them as with joy.

It was now fine music the frogs and the boys
Did in the towering Illinois twilight make
And into dark in spite of a right arm's ache
A boy's hunched body loved out of a stalk
The first song of his happiness, and the song woke
His heart to the darkness and into the sadness of joy.

DUCK-CHASING

I SPIED a very small brown duck
Riding the swells of the sea
Like a rocking-chair. "Little duck!"
I cried. It paddled away,
I paddled after it. When it dived,
Down I dived: too smoky was the sea,
We were lost. It surfaced
In the west, I torpedoed west

And when it dived I dived,
And we were lost and lost and lost
In the slant smoke of the sea.
When I came floating up on it
From the side, like a deadman,
And yelled suddenly, it took off,
It skimmed the swells as it ascended,
Brown wings burning and flashing
In the sun as the sea it rose over
Burned and flashed underneath it.
I did not see the little duck again.
Duck-chasing is a game like any game.
When it is over it is all over.

TO CHRIST OUR LORD

The legs of the elk punctured the snow's crust
And wolves floated lightfooted on the land
Hunting Christmas elk living and frozen;
Inside snow melted in a basin, and a woman basted
A bird spread over coals by its wings and head.

Snow had sealed the windows; candles lit
The Christmas meal. The Christmas grace chilled
The cooked bird, being long-winded and the room cold.
During the words a boy thought, is it fitting
To eat this creature killed on the wing?

He had killed it himself, climbing out
Alone on snowshoes in the Christmas dawn,
The fallen snow swirling and the snowfall gone,
Heard its throat scream as the rifle shouted,
Watched it drop, and fished from the snow the dead.

He had not wanted to shoot. The sound
Of wings beating into the hushed air
Had stirred his love, and his fingers
Froze in his gloves, and he wondered,
Famishing, could he fire? Then he fired.

Now the grace praised his wicked act. At its end
The bird on the plate
Stared at his stricken appetite.
There had been nothing to do but surrender,
To kill and to eat; he ate as he had killed, with wonder.

At night on snowshoes on the drifting field
He wondered again, for whom had love stirred?
The stars glittered on the snow and nothing answered.
Then the Swan spread her wings, cross of the cold north,
The pattern and mirror of the acts of earth.

STANLEY KUNITZ, *born July 29, 1905, in Worcester,*
Massachusetts, lives in New York City with his third wife,
the painter Elise Asher. He was educated at Harvard and
then worked for many years as an editor of biographical
reference books. In World War II he was a noncom-
missioned officer in charge of information and education
in the Air Transport Command. Subsequently he taught
at Bennington, at Brandeis, and, as a visiting professor,
at other American colleges. Although he had been pub-
lishing for twenty years, his wide recognition came suddenly
when, in 1958, the publication of his Selected Poems
brought him the Pulitzer Prize and a favorable revaluation
of his career by many critics and reviewers.

Isolation, even at the pitch of love, is a recurrent
theme of poets. The following lines may best be
read as the meditation of a lover keenly aware of the
proximity of his love and just as keenly aware of
the terrible singleness of any human soul. The cir-
cumstance of the poem is focused in the line "My
touch is on you, who are light-years gone."

THE SCIENCE OF THE NIGHT

I TOUCH you in the night, whose gift was you,
My careless sprawler,
And I touch you cold, unstirring, star-bemused,
That are become the land of your self-strangeness.
What long seduction of the bone has led you
Down the imploring roads I cannot take
Into the arms of ghosts I never knew,
Leaving my manhood on a rumpled field
To guard you where you lie so deep
In absent-mindedness,
Caught in the calcium snows of sleep?

And even should I track you to your birth
Through all the cities of your mortal trial,
As in my jealous thought I try to do,
You would escape me—from the brink of earth
Take off to where the lawless auroras run,
You with your wild and metaphysic heart.
My touch is on you, who are light-years gone.
We are not souls but systems, and we move
In clouds of our unknowing
                              like great nebulae.
Our very motives swirl and have their start
With father lion and with mother crab.

Dreamer, my own lost rib,
Whose planetary dust is blowing
Past archipelagoes of myth and light,
What far Magellans are you mistress of
To whom you speed the pleasure of your art?
As through a glass that magnifies my loss
I see the lines of your spectrum shifting red,
The universe expanding, thinning out,
Our worlds flying, oh flying, fast apart.

From hooded powers and from abstract flight
I summon you, your person and your pride.
Fall to me now from outer space,
Still fastened desperately to my side;
Through gulfs of streaming air
Bring me the mornings of the milky ways
Down to my threshold in your drowsy eyes;
And by the virtue of your honeyed word
Restore the liquid language of the moon,
That in gold mines of secrecy you delve.
Awake!

      My whirling hands stay at the noon,
Each cell within my body holds a heart
And all my hearts in unison strike twelve.

Dreams as a source of understanding have always
figured importantly in poetry. The dream recorded
here, which, actual or imagined, comes to the same
thing, recapitulates a man's personal history and his
arrival, just before waking, at wisdom that neverthe-
less involves the deepest sense of loss. Gemara is that
part of the Talmud, the Jewish civil and canonical law,
that serves as commentary on the Mishnah, or text.

FATHER AND SON

Now in the suburbs and the falling light
I followed him, and now down sandy road
Whiter than bone-dust, through the sweet
Curdle of fields, where the plums
Dropped with their load of ripeness, one by one.
Mile after mile I followed, with skimming feet,
After the secret master of my blood,
Him, steeped in the odor of ponds, whose indomitable love
Kept me in chains. Strode years; stretched into bird;
Raced through the sleeping country where I was young,
The silence unrolling before me as I came,
The night nailed like an orange to my brow.

How should I tell him my fable and the fears,
How bridge the chasm in a casual tone,
Saying, "The house, the stucco one you built,
We lost. Sister married and went from home,
And nothing comes back, it's strange, from where she goes.
I lived on a hill that had too many rooms:
Light we could make, but not enough of warmth,
And when the light failed, I climbed under the hill.
The papers are delivered every day;
I am alone and never shed a tear."

At the water's edge, where the smothering ferns lifted
Their arms, "Father!" I cried, "Return! You know
The way. I'll wipe the mudstains from your clothes;
No trace, I promise, will remain. Instruct
Your son, whirling between two wars,
In the Gemara of your gentleness,
For I would be a child to those who mourn
And brother to the foundlings of the field
And friend of innocence and all bright eyes.
O teach me how to work and keep me kind."

Among the turtles and the lilies he turned to me
The white ignorant hollow of his face.

JOSEPH LANGLAND, *born
1917, in Spring Grove, Minnesota, lives with his wife and
children in Amherst, Massachusetts, where he is a member
of the English department of
the University of Massachusetts.
Of second-generation Norwegian-
American parentage, he was
brought up on a Midwestern
farm, attended the State University of Iowa, and served for
four years in the United States
Army. He has taught at the
University of Wyoming and, for
the greater part of a year, lived
with his family in Positano, Italy.*

THE hooded reptile, in his guile,
Knows how to dance and how to smile.

Some say he merely writhes and grins
Through solemn subtleties of sins,

But look, his jeweled body turns
To rings and bracelets in the ferns.

He grazes on the velvet grasses
With coral feet, then dewlike passes

Flickering on the darkling ground
In neural sandals of no sound.

Glimpsed at the lily pool, he glides
Serene among its undertides

And wakes soft ripples into bells
Of water sepulchered in shells;

So kissed, he resurrects his head
Above the broad-leafed lily bed

And blasts the ivory blooms among
Pale whispered powders of his tongue.

Standing in water like a spring
Long-coiled for Satan's underling,

Spinning through subterranean loves,
Feeding upon pure lily groves,

He makes an ikon with his thin
Needle of spiraled medicine.

Seductive, convoluted, poised,
He equals elements, unvoiced

Except for one hushed song of death,
A sudden exodus of breath.

And now he floats and slides and soars,
Glistening, upon the further shores

And waves toward Calvary, his gloss
All intersected in a cross;

There, hung in haloes, all amazed,
So slyly caught, so subtly praised,

Fleeing among his purple stings
Love dances, smiles. Oh, how he sings!

WHEN my young brother was killed
By a mute and dusty shell in the thorny brush
Crowning the boulders of the Villa Verde Trail
On the island of Luzon,

I laid my whole dry body down,
Dropping my face like a stone in a green park
On the east banks of the Rhine;

On an airstrip skirting the Seine
His sergeant brother sat like a stick in his barracks
While cracks of fading sunlight
Caged the dusty air;

In the rocky rolling hills west of the Mississippi
His father and mother sat in a simple Norwegian parlor
With a photograph smiling between them on the table
And their hands fallen into their laps
Like sticks and dust;

And still other brothers and sisters,
Linking their arms together,
Walked down the dusty road where once he ran
And into the deep green valley
To sit on the stony banks of the stream he loved
And let the murmuring waters
Wash over their blood-hot feet with a springing crown of tears.

PHILIP LARKIN, *born August
9, 1922, in Coventry, England, lives
in Hull, where he is librarian of*

*the university. He was educated at
St. John's College, Oxford, and
has published a novel,* A Girl in
Winter.

SOMETIMES you hear, fifth-hand,
As epitaph:
He chucked up everything
And just cleared off,
And always the voice will sound
Certain you approve
This audacious, purifying,
Elemental move.

And they are right, I think.
We all hate home
And having to be there:
I detest my room,
Its specially-chosen junk,
The good books, the good bed,
And my life, in perfect order:
So to hear it said

He walked out on the whole crowd
Leaves me flushed and stirred,
Like *Then she undid her dress*
Or *Take that you bastard;*
Surely I can, if he did?
And that helps me stay
Sober and industrious.
But I'd go today,

Yes, swagger the nut-strewn roads,
Crouch in the fo'c'sle
Stubbly with goodness, if
It weren't so artificial,
Such a deliberate step backwards

To create an object:
Books; china; a life
Reprehensibly perfect.

ONCE I am sure there's nothing going on
I step inside, letting the door thud shut.
Another church: matting, seats, and stone,
And little books; sprawlings of flowers, cut
For Sunday, brownish now; some brass and stuff
Up at the holy end; the small neat organ;
And a tense, musty unignorable silence,
Brewed God knows how long. Hatless, I take off
My cycle-clips in awkward reverence,

Move forward, run my hand around the font.
From where I stand, the roof looks almost new—
Cleaned, or restored? Someone would know: I don't.
Mounting the lectern, I peruse a few
Hectoring large-scale verses, and pronounce
'Here endeth' much more loudly than I'd meant.
The echoes snigger briefly. Back at the door
I sign the book, donate an Irish sixpence,
Reflect the place was not worth stopping for.

Yet stop I did: in fact I often do,
And always end much at a loss like this,
Wondering what to look for; wondering, too,
When churches fall completely out of use
What we shall turn them into; if we shall keep
A few cathedrals chronically on show,

Their parchment, plate and pyx in locked cases,
And let the rest rent-free to rain and sheep.
Shall we avoid them as unlucky places?

Or, after dark, will dubious women come
To make their children touch a particular stone;
Pick simples for a cancer; or on some
Advised night see walking a dead one?
Power of some sort or other will go on
In games, in riddles, seemingly at random;
But superstition, like belief, must die,
And what remains when disbelief has gone?
Grass, weedy pavement, brambles, buttress, sky,

A shape less recognisable each week,
A purpose more obscure. I wonder who
Will be the last, the very last, to seek
This place for what it was; one of the crew
That tap and jot and know what rood-lofts were?
Some ruin-bibber, randy for antique,
Or Christmas-addict, counting on a whiff
Of gown-and-bands and organ-pipes and myrrh?
Or will he be my representative,

Bored, uninformed, knowing the ghostly silt
Dispersed, yet tending to this cross of ground
Through suburb scrub because it held unspilt
So long and equably what since is found
Only in separation—marriage, and birth,
And death, and thoughts of these—for whom was built
This special shell? For, though I've no idea
What this accoutred frowsty barn is worth,
It pleases me to stand in silence here;

A serious house on serious earth it is,
In whose blent air all our compulsions meet,

Are recognised, and robed as destinies.
And that much never can be obsolete,
Since someone will forever be surprising
A hunger in himself to be more serious,
And gravitating with it to this ground,
Which, he once heard, was proper to grow wise in,
If only that so many dead lie round.

JOHN LEHMANN, *born 1907, at Bourne End,*
in the Thames valley, of an English father and
an American mother, lives in London, where he
is editor of The London Magazine. *He was edu-*
cated at Eton and Trinity College, Cambridge,
and then began a long and distinguished editorial
career in which, among many other related activi-
ties, he founded the Penguin New Writing *and*
served as managing director of The Hogarth Press
in association with its owners, Leonard and
Virginia Woolf. He has two famous sisters:
Rosamond, the novelist, and Beatrix, the actress.
His autobiography was published in two volumes
under the titles The Listening Gallery *and*
I Am My Brother.

He sent us letters, which we read
Drinking our coffee by the lake,
And when we heard the promised day
And which express he planned to take,

A quickened silence fell on all:
Could we believe that it was true?
Under the ridge the water seemed
To gleam a deeper peacock blue.

Great were our plans to greet this friend
So long a legend to our love,
And while we filled his room with flowers
And sent for cakes and wine, we strove

Each to recapture from the past
A glance, a gesture that would bring
His clear-eyed presence out of night:
But it was hard remembering.

Then on the morning of the feast
A cable came: we were afraid:
There was no other news, except
Once more his journey was delayed.

So far away it sinks, the dream
That flushed our days, and made us one;
The long weeks melted, and the guests
Packed as each end came and were gone.

The young explorer was the first:
O that was sharp: he seemed to make
A furrow on our hearts that hour
He rowed away across the lake;

And there were tears that had to flow
Breaking on laughter in farewell,
As down the vine-linked valley road
Those comrades from the citadel

One afternoon of dust and songs
Turned, and were swallowed in the glare;
Yet still good-bye, though few remained
Grew like a weed of rank despair,

Till I was left alone to meet
(As I had always known must be)
In the damp house, at summer's end,
The dark Lieutenant from the sea.

CECIL DAY LEWIS, *born
April 27, 1904, in Beallintogher,
Ireland, lives with his second wife
in London, where he is a director
of the publishing house, Chatto
and Windus. Educated at Oxford,
he taught at schools in England and
Scotland until 1935. During World
War II he was an editor of books
and pamphlets for the Ministry of
Information and later returned to
academic life first as a lecturer at
Trinity College and then as professor of poetry at Oxford. He is
widely known as the author of
many expert detective stories, which
he publishes under the pseudonym
Nicholas Blake.*

*In the third and fourth stanzas of this poem there is
an extended allusion to the Biblical story of the de-
livery of the Israelites, under Moses, from
imprisonment and bondage in Egypt to "a desert
of freedom" and the Promised Land.*

DEPARTURE IN THE DARK

Nothing so sharply reminds a man he is mortal
As leaving a place
In a winter morning's dark, the air on his face
Unkind as the touch of sweating metal:
Simple goodbyes to children or friends become
A felon's numb
Farewell, and love that was a warm, a meeting place—
Love is the suicide's grave under the nettles.

Gloomed and clemmed as if by an imminent ice-age
Lies the dear world
Of your street-strolling, field-faring. The senses, curled
At the dead end of a shrinking passage,
Care not if close the inveterate hunters creep,
And memories sleep
Like mammoths in lost caves. Drear, extinct is the world,
And has no voice for consolation or presage.

There is always something at such times of the passover,
When the dazed heart
Beats for it knows not what, whether you part
From home or prison, acquaintance or lover—
Something wrong with the time-table, something unreal
In the scrambled meal
And the bag ready packed by the door, as though the heart
Has gone ahead, or is staying here forever.

No doubt for the Israelites that early morning
It was hard to be sure
If home were prison or prison home: the desire
Going forth meets the desire returning.
This land, that had cut their pride down to the bone
Was now their own
By ancient deeds of sorrow. Beyond, there was nothing sure
But a desert of freedom to quench their fugitive yearnings.

At this blind hour the heart is informed of nature's
Ruling that man
Should be nowhere a more tenacious settler than
Among wry thorns and ruins, yet nurture
A seed of discontent in his ripest ease.
There's a kind of release
And a kind of torment in every goodbye for every man—
And will be, even to the last of his dark departures.

RECONCILIATION

ALL day beside the shattered tank he'd lain
Like a limp creature hacked out of its shell,
Now shrivelling on the desert's grid,
Now floating above a sharp-set ridge of pain.

There came a roar, like water, in his ear.
The mortal dust was laid. He seemed to be lying
In a cool coffin of stone walls,
While memory slid towards a plunging weir.

The time that was, the time that might have been
Find in this shell of stone a chance to kiss
Before they part eternally:
He feels a world without, a world within

Wrestle like old antagonists, until each is
Balancing each. Then, in a heavenly calm,
The lock gates open, and beyond
Appear the argent, swan-assemblied reaches.

*The dead here are ordinary people who lived ordinary
lives, unaware of the life of the intellect as represented by such world-shaking figures as Karl Marx
and Sigmund Freud, and died in anonymous multitudes
in the bombing of London. Speaking as one who is
aware of philosophies and scientific discoveries that
shape history, the poet pays homage to those who keep
the world going simply by enduring the hazards of
existence and the darkness of their own ignorance.*

THE DEAD

THEY lie in the sunday street
Like effigies thrown down after a fête
Among the bare-faced houses frankly yawning revulsion,
Fag-ends of fires, litter of rubble, stale
Confetti-sprinkle of blood. Was it defeat
With them, or triumph? Purification
Or All Fools' Day? On this they remain silent.
Their eyes are closed to honour and hate.

We cannot blame the great
Alone—the mad, the calculating or effete
Rulers. Whatever grotesque scuffle and piercing
Indignant orgasm of pain took them,
All that enforced activity of death
Did answer and compensate
Some voluntary inaction, soft option, dream retreat.

Each man died for the sins of a whole world:
For the ant's self-abdication, the fat-stock's patience
Are sweet goodbye to human nations.

Still, they have made us eat
Our knowing words, who rose and paid
The bill for the whole party with their uncounted courage.
And if they chose the dearer consolations
Of living—the bar, the dog race, the discreet
Establishment—and let Karl Marx and Freud go hang,
Now they are dead, who can dispute their choice?
Not I, nor even Fate.

IN THE HEART OF CONTEMPLATION

IN the heart of contemplation—
Admiring, say, the frost-flowers of the white lilac,
Or lark's song busily sifting like sand-crystals
Through the pleased hourglass an afternoon of summer,
Or your beauty, dearer to me than these—
Discreetly a whisper in the ear,
The glance of one passing my window recall me
From lark, lilac, you, grown suddenly strangers.

In the plump and pastoral valley
Of a leisure time, among the trees like seabirds
Asleep on a glass calm, one shadow moves—
The sly reminder of the forgotten appointment.
All the shining pleasures, born to be innocent,
Grow dark with a truant's guilt:
The day's high heart falls flat, the oaks tremble,
And the shadow sliding over your face divides us.

In the act of decision only,
In the hearts cleared for action like lovers naked
For love, this shadow vanishes: there alone
There is nothing between our lives for it to thrive on.
You and I with lilac, lark and oak-leafed
Valley are bound together
As in the astounded clarity before death.
Nothing is innocent now but to act for life's sake.

ROBERT LOWELL, *born March 1, 1917,
in Boston, lives in New York with his wife,
the writer Elizabeth Hardwick, and their
young daughter. He went to Harvard for
two years and then transferred to Kenyon
College, where he was a student of John
Crowe Ransom. During World War II he
refused to register for the draft and was
imprisoned as a conscientious objector.
After his release, he lived with his first wife,
the novelist Jean Stafford, in New York City
and in Maine. In recent years he has taught
in the English departments of Kenyon College and Boston University, and he is currently visiting professor at Harvard.*

*Ford Madox Ford was an Anglo-German writer who,
in the fanatical anti-German climate of World War I,
changed his name from Hueffer to Ford. He wrote
one outstanding novel,* The Good Soldier, *which turned
to advantage innovations made by Flaubert and other
French naturalists, but most of his other novels
were mere potboilers. He befriended and encouraged
many writers at the beginnings of their careers,
even when he himself had outlived his reputation and
fallen into poverty and neglect. In his last years he
was often in New York, a wheezing gourmand and
failing* bon vivant *who was habitually seen at the
Brevoort Hotel, the last resort of Edwardian
grandeur in the city, in the neighborhood of
both Washington Square and Stuyvesant Square.*

FORD MADOX FORD

1873–1939

The lobbed ball plops, then dribbles to the cup . . . .
(a birdie Fordie!) But it nearly killed
the ministers. Lloyd George was holding up
the flag. He gabbled, 'Hop-toad, hop-toad, hop-toad!
Hueffer has used a niblick on the green;
it's filthy art, Sir, filthy art!'
You answered, 'What is art to me and thee?
Will a blacksmith teach a midwife how to bear?'
That cut the puffing statesman down to size,
Ford. You said, 'Otherwise,
I would have been general of a division.' Ah Ford!
Was it war, the sport of kings, that your *Good Soldier,*
the best French novel in the language, taught
those Georgian Whig magnificoes at Oxford,
at Oxford decimated on the Somme?

Ford, five times black-balled for promotion,
then mustard gassed voiceless some seven miles
behind the lines at Nancy or Belleau Wood:
you emerged in your 'worn uniform,
gilt dragons on the revers of the tunic,'
a Jonah—O divorced, divorced
from the whale-fat of post-war London! Boomed,
cut, plucked and booted! In Provence, New York . . .
marrying, blowing . . . nearly dying
at Boulder, when the altitude
pressed the world on your heart,
and your audience, almost football-size,
shrank to a dozen, while you stood
mumbling, with fish-blue eyes,
and mouth pushed out
fish-fashion, as if you gagged for air . . . .
Sandman! Your face, a childish O. The sun
is pernod-yellow and it gilds the heirs
of all the ages there on Washington
and Stuyvesant, your Lilliputian squares,
where writing turned your pockets inside out.
But master, mammoth mumbler, tell me why
the bales of your left-over novels buy
less than a bandage for your gouty foot.
Wheel-horse, O unforgetting elephant,
I hear you huffing at your old Brevoort,
Timon and Falstaff, while you heap the board
for publishers. Fiction! I'm selling short
your lies that made the great your equals. Ford,
you were a kind man and you died in want.

In the long view of this elegy, specific landmarks of the city of Boston are seen against a mythological background. Phillips House is a hospital. In Latin, the word cancer *means* crab, *the fourth sign of the Zodiac. Charon is the mythical figure who ferried dead souls across the Styx, the chief river of the underworld. Acheron is the "river of woe" in Hades. This poem is one of four under the general title "In Memory of Arthur Winslow."*

DEATH FROM CANCER

THIS Easter, Arthur Winslow, less than dead,
Your people set you up in Phillips' House
To settle off your wrestling with the crab—
The claws drop flesh upon your yachting blouse
Until longshoreman Charon come and stab
Through your adjusted bed
And crush the crab. On Boston Basin, shells
Hit water by the Union Boat Club wharf:
You ponder why the coxes' squeakings dwarf
The *resurrexit dominus* of all the bells.

Grandfather Winslow, look, the swanboats coast
That island in the Public Gardens, where
The bread-stuffed ducks are brooding, where with tub
And strainer the mid-Sunday Irish scare
The sun-struck shallows for the dusky chub
This Easter, and the ghost
Of risen Jesus walks the waves to run
Arthur upon a trumpeting black swan
Beyond Charles River to the Acheron
Where the wide waters and their voyager are one.

Relinquunt omnia servare rem publicam.

THE old South Boston Aquarium stands
in a Sahara of snow now. Its broken windows are boarded.
The bronze weathervane cod has lost half its scales.
The airy tanks are dry.

Once my nose crawled like a snail on the glass;
my hand tingled
to burst the bubbles,
drifting from the noses of the cowed, compliant fish.

My hand draws back. I often sigh still
for the dark downward and vegetating kingdom
of the fish and reptile. One morning last March,
I pressed against the new barbed and galvanized

fence on the Boston Common. Behind their cage,
yellow dinosaur steam shovels were grunting
as they cropped up tons of mush and grass
to gouge their underworld garage.

Parking lots luxuriate like civic
sand piles in the heart of Boston.
A girdle of orange, Puritan-pumpkin-colored girders
braces the tingling Statehouse, shaking

over the excavations, as it faces Colonel Shaw
and his bell-cheeked Negro infantry
on St. Gaudens' shaking Civil War relief,
propped by a plank splint against the garage's earthquake.

Two months after marching through Boston,
half the regiment was dead;
at the dedication,
William James could almost hear the bronze Negroes breathe.

The monument sticks like a fishbone
in the city's throat.
Its colonel is as lean
as a compass needle.

He has an angry wrenlike vigilance,
a greyhound's gentle tautness;
he seems to wince at pleasure
and suffocate for privacy.

He is out of bounds. He rejoices in man's lovely,
peculiar power to choose life and die—
when he leads his black soldiers to death,
he cannot bend his back.

On a thousand small-town New England greens,
the old white churches hold their air
of sparse, sincere rebellion; frayed flags
quilt the graveyards of the Grand Army of the Republic.

The stone statues of the abstract Union Soldier
grow slimmer and younger each year—
wasp-waisted, they doze over muskets,
and muse through their sideburns.

Shaw's father wanted no monument
except the ditch,
where his son's body was thrown
and lost with his "niggers."

The ditch is nearer.
There are no statues for the last war here;
on Boylston Street, a commercial photograph
showed Hiroshima boiling

over a Mosler Safe, "the Rock of Ages,"
that survived the blast. Space is nearer.
When I crouch to my television set,
the drained faces of Negro school children rise like balloons.

Colonel Shaw
is riding on his bubble,
he waits
for the blessed break.

The Aquarium is gone. Everywhere,
giant finned cars nose forward like fish;
a savage servility
slides by on grease.

*Mr. Edwards, the speaker in this poem, is Jonathan
Edwards, the great Calvinist theologian and preacher
whose zeal was largely responsible for the religious
revival in New England known as the Great Awaken-
ing. He was born in what is now Windsor, Connecticut,
and as a child demonstrated his great aptitude as a
naturalist by writing a series of scientific observations
on the spider. In this poem, reminiscent of one of
his famous sermons,* Sinners in the Hands of an Angry
God, *he particularly addresses Josiah Hawley, a
Revolutionary patriot who was one of the leaders of the
opposition to Edwards' fiery revivalist preachings.*

MR. EDWARDS AND THE SPIDER

I saw the spiders marching through the air,
Swimming from tree to tree that mildewed day
    In latter August when the hay
    Came creaking to the barn. But where
        The wind is westerly,
Where gnarled November makes the spiders fly
Into the apparitions of the sky,
    They purpose nothing but their ease and die
Urgently beating east to sunrise and the sea;

What are we in the hands of the great God?
It was in vain you set up thorn and briar
    In battle array against the fire
    And treason crackling in your blood;
        For the wild thorns grow tame
And will do nothing to oppose the flame;
Your lacerations tell the losing game
You play against a sickness past your cure.
How will the hands be strong? How will the heart endure?

A very little thing, a little worm,
Or hourglass-blazoned spider, it is said,
    Can kill a tiger. Will the dead
    Hold up his mirror and affirm
        To the four winds the smell
And flash of his authority? It's well
If God who holds you to the pit of hell,
Much as one holds a spider, will destroy,
Baffle and dissipate your soul. As a small boy

On Windsor Marsh, I saw the spider die
When thrown into the bowels of fierce fire:
    There's no long struggle, no desire
    To get up on its feet and fly—
        It stretches out its feet
And dies. This is the sinner's last retreat;
Yes, and no strength exerted on the heat
Then sinews the abolished will, when sick
And full of burning, it will whistle on a brick.

But who can plumb the sinking of that soul?
Josiah Hawley, picture yourself cast
    Into a brick-kiln where the blast
    Fans your quick vitals to a coal—
        If measured by a glass,

How long would it seem burning! Let there pass
A minute, ten, ten trillion; but the blaze
Is infinite, eternal: this is death,
To die and know it. This is the Black Widow, death.

ARCHIBALD MACLEISH,
born May 7, 1892, in Glencoe,
Illinois, lives with his wife in
Cambridge, Massachusetts,
where until recently he was
Boylston Professor of Rhetoric
and Oratory at Harvard, and for
part of each year in Antigua,
British West Indies. He was
educated at Yale and the Har-
vard Law School, served in the
Field Artillery in France during
World War I, practiced law in
Boston, and later became an
editor of Fortune. *During the*
administration of Franklin D.
Roosevelt he was, successively,
Librarian of Congress and
Undersecretary of State. Among
his writings are a number of
radio and television plays, the
poetic dramas Panic *and* J.B.,
and works of a documentary
nature.

The "cue" or point of departure for this poem is
Andrew Marvell's famous love poem "To His Coy
Mistress." Time and eternity, represented by the
movement of the sun, is a theme common to these
poems, both of which are otherwise concerned with
human awareness. Geographically, the point from
which the westward passage of night is observed
is the southwestern shore of Lake Michigan.

YOU, ANDREW MARVELL

AND here face down beneath the sun
And here upon earth's noonward height
To feel the always coming on
The always rising of the night:

To feel creep up the curving east
The earthy chill of dusk and slow
Upon those under lands the vast
And ever climbing shadow grow

And strange at Ecbatan the trees
Take leaf by leaf the evening strange
The flooding dark about their knees
The mountains over Persia change

And now at Kermanshah the gate
Dark empty and the withered grass
And through the twilight now the late
Few travelers in the westward pass

And Baghdad darken and the bridge
Across the silent river gone
And through Arabia the edge
Of evening widen and steal on

And deepen on Palmyra's street
The wheel rut in the ruined stone
And Lebanon fade out and Crete
High through the clouds and overblown

And over Sicily the air
Still flashing with the landward gulls
And loom and slowly disappear
The sails above the shadowy hulls

And Spain go under and the shore
Of Africa the gilded sand
And evening vanish and no more
The low pale light across that land

Nor now the long light on the sea:

And here face downward in the sun
To feel how swift how secretly
The shadow of the night comes on . . .

"NOT MARBLE NOR THE GILDED MONUMENTS"

For Adele

THE praisers of women in their proud and beautiful poems,
Naming the grave mouth and the hair and the eyes,
Boasted those they loved should be forever remembered:
These were lies.

The words sound but the face in the Istrian sun is forgotten.
The poet speaks but to her dead ears no more.
The sleek throat is gone—and the breast that was troubled to listen:
Shadow from door.

Therefore I will not praise your knees nor your fine walking
Telling you men shall remember your name as long
As lips move or breath is spent or the iron of English
Rings from a tongue.

I shall say you were young, and your arms straight, and your mouth
    scarlet:
I shall say you will die and none will remember you:
Your arms change, and none remember the swish of your garments,
Nor the click of your shoe.

Not with my hand's strength, not with difficult labor
Springing the obstinate words to the bones of your breast
And the stubborn line to your young stride and the breath to your
    breathing
And the beat to your haste
Shall I prevail on the hearts of unborn men to remember.

(What is a dead girl but a shadowy ghost
Or a dead man's voice but a distant and vain affirmation
Like dream words most)

Therefore I will not speak of the undying glory of women.
I will say you were young and straight and your skin fair
And you stood in the door and the sun was a shadow of leaves on your
    shoulders
And a leaf on your hair—

I will not speak of the famous beauty of dead women:
I will say the shape of a leaf lay once on your hair.
Till the world ends and the eyes are out and the mouths broken
Look! It is there!

LOUIS MACNEICE, *born September 12, 1907, in Belfast, Ireland, lives in London, where he is program director for the BBC. He was educated at Merton College, Oxford, and later had a brief teaching career as a lecturer in Greek in London. His early poetry is identified with that of his friends*

in the "English Group"—Spender, Lewis, and Auden—and with the last he is coauthor of the travel book Letters from Iceland. *He has lived for extended periods in Greece; in 1954 he made a reading and concert tour in the United States with his second wife, the singer Hedli Anderson.*

THE SUNLIGHT ON THE GARDEN

THE sunlight on the garden
Hardens and grows cold,
We cannot cage the minute
Within its nets of gold;
When all is told
We cannot beg for pardon.

Our freedom as free lances
Advances towards its end;
The earth compels, upon it
Sonnets and birds descend;
And soon, my friend,
We shall have no time for dances.

The sky was good for flying
Defying the church bells
And every evil iron
Siren and what it tells:
The earth compels,
We are dying, Egypt, dying

And not expecting pardon,
Hardened in heart anew,

But glad to have sat under
Thunder and rain with you,
And grateful too
For sunlight on the garden.

SHUTTLES of trains going north, going south, drawing threads of blue,
The shining of the lines of trams like swords,
Thousands of posters asserting a monopoly of the good, the beautiful,
    the true,
Crowds of people all in the vocative, you and you,
The haze of the morning shot with words.

Yellow sun comes white off the wet streets but bright
Chromium yellows in the gay sun's light,
Filleted sun streaks the purple mist,
Everything is kissed and reticulated with sun
Scooped-up and cupped in the open fronts of shops
And bouncing on the traffic that never stops.

And the street fountain blown across the square
Rainbow-trellises the air and sunlight blazons
The red butcher's and scrolls of fish on marble slabs,
Whistled bars of music crossing silver sprays
And horns of cars, touché, touché, rapiers' retort, a moving cage,
A turning page of shine and sound, the day's maze.

But when the sun goes out, the streets go cold, the hanging meat
And tiers of fish are colourless and merely dead,
And the hoots of cars neurotically repeat and the tiptoed feet
Of women hurry and falter whose faces are dead;
And I see in the air but not belonging there

The blown grey powder of the fountain grey as the ash
That forming on a cigarette covers the red.

Even poisons praise thee.—George Herbert

I AM not yet born; O hear me.
Let not the bloodsucking bat or the rat or the stoat or the
      club-footed ghoul come near me.

I am not yet born, console me.
I fear that the human race may with tall walls wall me,
      with strong drugs dope me, with wise lies lure me,
         on black racks rack me, in blood-baths roll me.

I am not yet born; provide me
With water to dandle me, grass to grow for me, trees to talk
      to me, sky to sing to me, birds and a white light
         in the back of my mind to guide me.

I am not yet born; forgive me
For the sins that in me the world shall commit, my words
      when they speak me, my thoughts when they think me,
         my treason engendered by traitors beyond me,
            my life when they murder by means of my
               hands, my death when they live me.

I am not yet born; rehearse me
In the parts I must play and the cues I must take when
      old men lecture me, bureaucrats hector me, mountains
         frown at me, lovers laugh at me, the white
            waves call me to folly and the desert calls
               me to doom and the beggar refuses
                  my gift and my children curse me.

I am not yet born; O hear me,
Let not the man who is beast or who thinks he is God
      come near me.

I am not yet born; O fill me
With strength against those who would freeze my
      humanity, would dragoon me into a lethal automaton,
          would make me a cog in a machine, a thing with
             one face, a thing, and against all those
                who would dissipate my entirety, would
                  blow me like thistledown hither and
                    thither or hither and thither
                      like water held in the
                        hands would spill me.
Let them not make me a stone and let them not spill me.
Otherwise kill me.

JAMES MERRILL, *born
March 3, 1926, in New York
City, lives in the old seaport
village of Stonington, Connecticut. He is a graduate of
Amherst College, where, for one
year, he was a member of the
English department. He has
published a novel,* The Seraglio,
and his play The Immortal
Husband *was produced off
Broadway. A world traveler, he
has spent long periods of residence abroad, particularly in
Greece and in Italy.*

"ONE is reminded of a certain person,"
Continued the parson, settling back in his chair
With a glass of port, "who sought to emulate
The sport of birds (it was something of a chore)
By climbing up on a kite. They found his coat
Two counties away; the man himself was missing."

His daughters tittered: it was meant to be a lesson
To them—they had been caught kissing, or some such nonsense,
The night before, under the crescent moon.
So, finishing his pheasant, their father began
This thirty-minute discourse, ending with
A story improbable from the start. He paused for breath,

Having shown but a few of the dangers. However, the wind
Blew out the candles and the moon wrought changes
Which the daughters felt along their stockings. Then,
Thus persuaded, they fled to their young men
Waiting in the sweet night by the raspberry bed,
And kissed and kissed, as though to escape on a kite.

LABORATORY POEM

CHARLES used to watch Naomi, taking heart
    And a steel saw, open up turtles, live.
    While she swore they felt nothing, he would gag
    At blood, at the blind twitching, even after
    The murky dawn of entrails cleared, revealing
    Contours he knew, egg-yellows like lamps paling.

    Well then. She carried off the beating heart
    To the kymograph and rigged it there, a rag

In fitful wind, now made to strain, now stopped
By her solutions tonic or malign
Alternately in which it would be steeped.
What the heart bore, she noted on a chart,

For work did not stop only with the heart.
He thought of certain human hearts, their climb
Through violence into exquisite disciplines
Of which, as it now appeared, they all expired.
Soon she would fetch another and start over,
Easy in the presence of her lover.

VOICES FROM THE OTHER WORLD

PRESENTLY at our touch the teacup stirred,
    Then circled lazily about
    From A to Z. The first voice heard
    (If they are voices, these mute spellers-out)
Was that of an engineer

Originally from Cologne.
    Dead in his 22nd year
    Of cholera in Cairo, he had 'known
    No happiness.' He once met Goethe, though.
Goethe had told him: *Persevere.*

Our blind hound whined. With that, a horde
    Of voices gathered above the Ouija board,
    Some childish and, you might say, blurred
    By sleep; one little boy
Named Will, reluctant possibly in a ruff

Like a large-lidded page out of El Greco, pulled
    Back the arras for that next voice,
    Cold and portentous: 'All is lost.

Flee this house. Otto von Thurn und Taxis.
Obey. You have no choice.'

Frightened, we stopped; but tossed
Till sunrise striped the rumpled sheets with gold.
Each night since then, the moon waxes,
Small insects flit round a cold torch
We light, that sends them pattering to the porch . . .

But no real Sign. New voices come,
Dictate addresses, begging us to write;
Some warn of lives misspent, and all of doom
In ways that so exhilarate
We are sleeping sound of late.

Last night the teacup shattered in a rage.
Indeed, we have grown nonchalant
Towards the other world. In the gloom here,
Our elbows on the cleared
Table, we talk and smoke, pleased to be stirred

Rather by buzzings in the jasmine, by the drone
Of our own voices and poor blind Rover's wheeze,
Than by those clamoring overhead,
Obsessed or piteous, for a commitment
We still have wit to postpone

Because, once looked at lit
By the cold reflections of the dead
Risen extinct but irresistible,
Our lives have never seemed more full, more real,
Nor the full moon more quick to chill.

W. S. MERWIN, *born September 30, 1927, in Pennsylvania, lives with his British wife in New York City and on a farm in the Lot, France. The son of a Presbyterian minister, he went to Princeton, where he majored in Romance languages. After his graduation he spent several years in France, Portugal, and Spain as a tutor and eventually went to England, where his early reputation as a poet was made. His translation of* The Cid *was published in 1961.*

Walking out in the late March midnight
With the old blind bitch on her bedtime errand
Of ease stumbling beside me, I saw

At the hill's edge, by the blue flooding
Of the arc-lamps, and the moon's suffused presence
The first leaves budding pale on the thorn trees,

Uncurling with that crass light coming through them,
Like the translucent wings of insects
Dilating in the dampness of birth;

And their green seemed already more ghostly
Than the hour drowned beneath bells, and the city sleeping,
Or even than the month with its round moon sinking.

As a white lamb the month's entrance had been:
The day warm, and at night unexpectedly
An hour of soft snow falling silently,

Soon ceasing, leaving transfigured all traceries,
These shrubs and trees, in white and white shadows; silk screens
Where were fences. And all restored again in an hour.

And as a lamb, I could see now, it would go,
Breathless, into its own ghostliness,
Taking with it more than its tepid moon.

And here there would be no lion at all that is
The beast of gold, and sought as an answer,
Whose pure sign in no solution is,

But between its two lambs the month would have run
As its varying moon, all silver,
That is the colour of questions.

Oh there as it went was such a silence
Before the water of April should be heard singing
Strangely as ever under the knowing ground

As fostered in me the motion of asking
In hope of no answer that fated leaves,
Sleep, or the sinking moon might proffer,

And in no words, but as it seemed in love only
For all breath, whose departing nature is
The spirit of question, whatever least I knew,

Whatever most I wondered. In which devotion
I stayed until the bell struck and the silver
Ebbed before April, and might have stood unseizing

Among answers less ghostly than the first leaves
On the thorn trees, since to seize had been
Neither to love nor to possess;

While the old bitch nosed and winded, conjuring
A congenial spot, and the constellations
Sank nearer already, listing toward summer.

THE DRUNK IN THE FURNACE

For a good decade
The furnace stood in the naked gulley, fireless
And vacant as any hat. Then when it was
No more to them than a hulking black fossil
To erode unnoticed with the rest of the junk-hill
By the poisonous creek, and rapidly to be added
        To their ignorance,

        They were afterwards astonished
To confirm, one morning, a twist of smoke like a pale

Resurrection, staggering out of its chewed hole,
And to remark then other tokens that someone,
Cosily bolted behind the eye-holed iron
Door of the drafty burner, had there established
     His bad castle.

     Where he gets his spirits
It's a mystery. But the stuff keeps him musical:
Hammer-and-anvilling with poker and bottle
To his jugged bellowings, till the last groaning clang
As he collapses onto the rioting
Springs of a litter of car-seats ranged on the grates,
     To sleep like an iron pig.

     In their tar-paper church
On a text about stoke-holes that are sated never
Their Reverend lingers. They nod and hate trespassers.
When the furnace wakes, though, all afternoon
Their witless offspring flock like piped rats to its siren
Crescendo, and agape on the crumbling ridge
     Stand in a row and learn.

MARIANNE MOORE, *born November 15, 1887, in St. Louis, Missouri, lives in Brooklyn, New York. She is a graduate of Bryn Mawr and for a brief time after college taught commercial subjects at the United States Indian school in Carlisle, Pennsylvania. For a number of years she was employed in the New York Public Library system and, from 1925 to 1929, was editor of* The Dial, *the most distinguished literary magazine of its time. She is the most honored of women poets in America and in recent years has made many reading appearances at colleges and universities. About her own work she has said: "To be trusted is an ennobling experience; and poetry is a peerless proficiency of the imagination. I prize it, but am myself an observer; I can see no reason for calling my work poetry except that there is no other category in which to put it."*

*A Swedish country cart in Brooklyn, New York, "this
city of freckled integrity," provides the anomaly on
which this lively meditation is based. Gustavus
Adolphus is the name of several kings of Sweden,
one of whom was a contemporary of George Washington. Kracken, usually spelled* kraken, *is a fabulous
Scandinavian sea monster. Dalgrén was a Swedish inven-
tor who contributed to the improvement of lighthouses.*

A CARRIAGE FROM SWEDEN

THEY say there is a sweeter air
      where it was made, than we have here;
      a Hamlet's castle atmosphere.
At all events there is in Brooklyn
something that makes me feel at home.

Noone may see this put-away
      museum-piece, this country cart
      that inner happiness made art;
and yet, in this city of freckled
integrity it is a vein

of resined straightness from north-wind
      hardened Sweden's once-opposed-to-
      compromise archipelago
of rocks. Washington and Gustavus
Adolphus, forgive our decay.

Seats, dashboard and sides of smooth gourd-
      rind texture, a flowered step, swan-
      dart brake, and swirling crustacean-
tailed equine amphibious creatures
that garnish the axle-tree! What

a fine thing! What unannoying
     romance! And how beautiful, she
     with the natural stoop of the
snowy egret, gray-eyed and straight-haired,
for whom it should come to the door,—

of whom it reminds me. The split
     pine fair hair, steady gannet-clear
     eyes and the pine-needled-path deer-
swift step; that is Sweden, land of the
free and the soil for a spruce-tree—

vertical though a seedling—all
     needles: from a green trunk, green shelf
     on shelf fanning out by itself.
The deft white-stockinged dance in thick-soled
shoes! Denmark's sanctuaried Jews!

The puzzle-jugs and hand-spun rugs,
     the root-legged kracken shaped like dogs,
     the hanging buttons and the frogs
that edge the Sunday jackets! Sweden,
you have a runner called the Deer, who

When he's won a race, likes to run
     more; you have the sun-right gable-
     ends due east and west, the table
spread as for a banquet; and the put-
in twin vest-pleats with a fish-fin

effect when you need none. Sweden,
     what makes the people dress that way
     and those who see you wish to stay?
The runner, not too tired to run more
at the end of the race? And that

cart, dolphin-graceful? A Dalgrén
    lighthouse, self-lit? responsive and
    responsible, I understand;
it's not pine-needle-paths that give spring
when they're run on, it's a Sweden

of moated white castles,—the bed
    of densely grown flowers in an S
    meaning Sweden and stalwartness,
skill, and a surface that says
Made in Sweden: carts are my trade.

*In the following annotations, Marianne Moore
suggests how phrases from her reading and observation are fitted, in the manner of mosaics,
into the text of her poem:*

"In America." Les Idéals de l'Éducation Française;
lecture, December 3, 1931, by M. Auguste Desclos,
Director-adjoint, Office National des Universités
et Écoles Françaises de Paris.

The singing tree. Each leaf was a mouth, and every
leaf joined in concert. *Arabian Nights.*

Lux et veritas (Yale) ; *Christo et ecclesiae*
(Harvard) ; sapiet felici,—

"Science is never finished." Professor Einstein
to an American student; *New York Times.*

Jack Bookworm in Goldsmith's
The Double Transformation.

A variety of hero: Emerson in *The American Scholar;*
"there can be no scholar without the heroic
mind;" "let him hold by himself; . . .
patient of neglect, patient of reproach."

The wolf. Edmund Burke, November, 1781, in
reply to Fox: "there is excellent wool on the

back of a wolf and therefore he must be
sheared. . . . But will he comply?"

"Gives his opinion." Henry McBride in the *New York
Sun*, December 12, 1931: "Dr. Valentiner . . . has
the typical reserve of the student. He does not enjoy
the active battle of opinion that invariably rages
when a decision is announced that can be
weighed in great sums of money. He gives
his opinion firmly and rests upon that."

THE STUDENT

"In America," began
the lecturer, "everyone must have a
degree. The French do not think that
all can have it, they don't say everyone
            must go to college." We
do incline to feel
        that although it may be unnecessary

to know fifteen languages,
one degree is not too much. With us, a
school—like the singing tree of which
the leaves were mouths singing in concert—is
        both a tree of knowledge
and of liberty,—
        seen in the unanimity of college

mottoes, *lux et veritas*,
Christo et ecclesiae, sapiet
felici. It may be that we
have not knowledge, just opinions, that we
        are undergraduates,
not students; we know
        we have been told with smiles, by expatriates

of whom we had asked "When will
your experiment be finished?" "Science
is never finished." Secluded
from domestic strife, Jack Bookworm led a
         college life, says Goldsmith;
and here also as
         in France or Oxford, study is beset with

dangers,—with bookworms, mildews,
and complaisancies. But someone in New
England has known enough to say
the student is patience personified,
         is a variety
of hero, "patient
         of neglect and of reproach,"—who can "hold by

himself." You can't beat hens to
make them lay. Wolf's wool is the best of wool,
but it cannot be sheared because
the wolf will not comply. With knowledge as
         with the wolf's surliness,
the student studies
         voluntarily, refusing to be less

than individual. He
"gives his opinion and then rests on it;"
he renders service when there is
no reward, and is too reclusive for
         some things to seem to touch
him, not because he
         has no feeling but because he has so much.

Bell T. leaflet, 1939, *"The World's Most Accurate Clocks"*: In the Bell Telephone Laboratories in New York, in a 'time vault' whose temperature is maintained within 1/100 of a degree, at 41° centigrade, are the most accurate clocks in the world—the four quartz crystal clocks. . . . When properly cut and inserted in a suitable circuit, they will control the rate of electric vibration to an accuracy of one part in a million. . . . When you call MEridian 7-1212 for correct time you get it every 15 seconds."

Jean Giraudoux: "Appeler à l'aide d'un camouflage ces instruments fait pour la vérité qui sont la radio, le cinéma, la presse?" "J'ai traversé voilà un an des pays arabes où l'on ignorait encore que Napoléon était mort." *Une allocation radiodiffusée de M. Giraudoux aux Françaises à propos de Sainte Catherine;* the *Figaro*, November, 1939.

The cannibal Chronos. Rhea, mother of Zeus, hid him from Chronos who "devoured all his children except Jupiter (air), Neptune (water), and Pluto (the grave). These Time cannot consume." Brewer's *Dictionary of Phrase and Fable*.

FOUR QUARTZ CRYSTAL CLOCKS

THERE are four vibrators, the world's exactest clocks;
    and these quartz time-pieces that tell
time intervals to other clocks,
    these worksless clocks work well;
and all four, independently the
    same, are there in the cool Bell
        Laboratory time

vault. Checked by a comparator with Arlington,
    they punctualize the "radio,

cinéma," and "presse,"—a group the
        Giraudoux truth-bureau
of hoped-for accuracy has termed
        "instruments of truth." We know—
                as Jean Giraudoux says

certain Arabs have not heard—that Napoleon
        is dead; that a quartz prism when
the temperature changes, feels
        the change and that the then
electrified alternate edges
        oppositely charged, threaten
                careful timing; so that

this water-clear crystal as the Greeks used to say,
        this "clear ice" must be kept at the
same coolness. Repetition, with
        the scientist, should be
synonymous with accuracy.
The lemur-student can see
        that an aye-aye is not

an angwan-tíbo, potto, or loris. The sea-
        side burden should not embarrass
the bell-buoy with the buoy-ball
        endeavoring to pass
hotel patronesses; nor could a
        practiced ear confuse the glass
                eyes for taxidermists

with eye-glasses from the optometrist. And as
        MEridian-7 1, 2
1, 2 gives, each fifteenth second
        in the same voice, the new
data—"The time will be" so and so—
        you realize that "when you
                hear the signal," you'll be

hearing Jupiter or jour pater, the day god—
    the salvaged son of Father Time—
telling the cannibal Chronos
    (eater of his proxime
newborn progeny) that punctual-
    ity is not a crime.

HOWARD MOSS, *born January 22, 1921,*
in New York, has been a lifelong resident of
his native city and, for many years, an editor
of The New Yorker. *He was educated at the*
University of Michigan and the University
of Wisconsin and then, for two years, taught
at Vassar College. His play The Folding
Green *was produced by The Poets' Theatre*
in Cambridge, Massachusetts, in 1958, and
his critical appreciation The Magic Lantern
of Marcel Proust *was published in 1962.*

This poem is a tribute written on the death of Albert Einstein, the great modern physicist whose theories, especially in their relevance to the development of the atomic bomb and its more lethal variations, have influenced the life of everyone on earth. His own life was one of endearing simplicity, and yet it was shadowed by the irony that he who hated the misuses of science should have been largely responsible for making atomic warfare possible.

THE GIFT TO BE SIMPLE

Breathing something German at the end,
Which no one understood, he died, a friend,
  Or so he meant to be, to all of us.
  Only the stars defined his radius;
His life, restricted to a wooden house,
Was in his head. He saw a fledgling fall.
  Two times he tried to nest it, but it fell
  Once more, and died; he wandered home again—
  We save so plain a story for great men.
      An angel in ill-fitting sweaters,
      Writing children naive letters,
  A violin player lacking vanities,
  A giant wit among the homilies—
We have no parallel to that immense
      Intelligence.

But if he were remembered for the Bomb,
As some may well remember him, such a tomb,
  For one who hated violence and ceremony
  Equally, would be a wasted irony.
He flew to formal heavens from his perch,
A scientist become his own research,
  And even if the flames were never gold

That lapped his body to an ash gone cold,
Even if his death no trumpets tolled,
    There is enough of myth inside the truth
    To make a monument to fit him with;
And since the universe is in a jar,
There is no weeping where his heavens are,
And I would remember, now the world is less,
    His gentleness.

> *Underwood is the brand name of a famous typewriter,*
> *and in this poem the word is used punningly to sug-*
> *gest that, beyond the office world of "blotters,*
> *folders,/ Memos, carbons, pencils, papers" is the*
> *world of the imagination and jungle freedom. All*
> *of this has been evoked by the sun through Venetian*
> *blinds, the sudden creation of a "harp of light" that*
> *transforms the pedestrian activity of an office and*
> *makes it lively with hazards and surprises.*

UNDERWOOD

FROM the thin slats of the Venetian blinds
The sun has plucked a sudden metaphor:
A harp of light, reflected on the floor,
Disorients the chair and desk and door.
Those much too delicate hands still tapping
The Underwood seem now Hindu dancers
Or five or ten young Balinese children
Hopping up and down in a clearing where
The striped light scrapes through bamboo seedlings
And moves from skinny shade to thin veneer
And changes as the harp of light is changing
Its twanging image on the office floor,

Being so remarkably the blinding heir
Of something that is not, and yet is, there.

Once I watched at the water cooler
A face bent over the jet-thin water:
The iris of the bent eye changed its color
As if the water jet had stained it green;
I saw the animal head's slight shudder,
Lifted from the surface of that running stream.
Tall branches then grew green in the hallway,
Arching above a green-ferned pathway;
A screen of green leaves hung in the doorway.
Was that a mirror where I saw the beaked birds,
The sluggish coffin of the alligator,
The monkeys climbing up the sunlit tree trunks?
Or did imagination, in that corridor,
Create, like the harp, its sudden metaphor?

Inside that drawer, among the blotters, folders,
Memos, carbons, pencils, papers,
Is the youngest animal of all awaking
In that coarse nest where he's been sleeping?
If I should reach into that dangerous drawer,
What singular teeth might pierce my skin?
Of if he should leap, should I then kill him,
And watch, where the harp had set its lightness,
The marvelous animal blood go thin?

WATER ISLAND

(To the memory of a friend, drowned off Water Island, April, 1960)

FINALLY, from your house there is no view;
The bay's blind mirror shattered over you

And Patchogue took your body like a log
The wind rolled up to shore. The senseless drowned
Have faces nobody would care to see,
But water loves those gradual erasures
Of flesh and shoreline, greenery and glass,
And you belonged to water, it to you,
Having built, on a hillock, above the bay,
Your house, the bay giving you reason to,
Where now, if seasons still are running straight,
The horseshoe crabs clank armor night and day,
Their couplings far more ancient than the eyes
That watched them from your porch. I saw one once
Whose back was a history of how we live;
Grown onto every inch of plate, except
Where the hinges let it move, were living things,
Barnacles, mussels, water weeds—and one
Blue bit of polished glass, glued there by time:
The origins of art. It carried them
With pride, it seemed, as if endurance only
Matters in the end. Or so I thought.

Skimming traffic lights, starboard and port,
Steer through planted poles that mark the way,
And other lights, across the bay, faint stars
Lining the border of Long Island's shore,
Come on at night, they still come on at night,
Though who can see them now I do not know.
Wild roses, at your back porch, break their blood,
And bud to test surprises of sea air,
And the birds fly over, gliding down to feed
At the two feeding stations you set out with seed,
Or splash themselves in a big bowl of rain
You used to fill with water. Going across
That night, too fast, too dark, no one will know,
Maybe you heard, the last you'll ever hear,

The cry of the savage and endemic gull
Which shakes the blood and always brings to mind
The thought that death, the scavenger, is blind,
Blunders and is stupid, and the end
Comes with ironies so fine the seed
Falters in the marsh and the heron stops
Hunting in the weeds below your landing stairs,
Standing in a stillness that now is yours.

HOWARD NEMEROV, *born March 1, 1920,*
in New York City, lives with his wife and children
in Bennington, Vermont, where he is on the
faculty of Bennington College. He is a graduate
of Harvard and, during World War II, served
with the Royal Canadian Air Force and the
United States Army Air Force in Canada and
in England. He has published three novels: The
Melodramatists; Federigo, or the Power of Love;
and The Homecoming Game, *which was adapted*
as a Broadway play, Tall Story, *and later as a*
motion picture.

My son invites me to witness with him
a children's program, a series of cartoons,
on television. Addressing myself to share
his harmless pleasures, I am horrified
by the unbridled violence and hostility
of the imagined world he takes in stride,
where human beings dressed in the skins of mice
are eaten by portcullises and cowcatchers,
digested through the winding corridors
of organs, overshoes, boa constrictors
and locomotive boilers, to be excreted
in waters where shark and squid and abalone
wait to employ their tentacles and jaws.
It seems there is no object in this world
unable to become a gullet with great lonely teeth;
sometimes a set of teeth all by itself
comes clacking over an endless plain
after the moving mouse; and though the mouse
wins in the end, the tail of one cartoon
is spliced into the mouth of the next, where his
rapid and trivial agony repeats itself
in another form. My son has seen these things
a number of times, and knows what to expect;
he does not seem disturbed or anything more
than mildly amused. Maybe these old cartoons
refer to my childhood and not to his
(The ogres in them wear Mussolini's face),
so that when mice are swallowed by skeletons
or empty suits of armor, when a tribe
of savage Negro mice is put through a wringer
and stacked flat in the cellar, he can take
the objective and critical view, while I

am shaken to see the giant picassoid
parents eating and voiding their little mice
time and again. And when the cheery announcer
cries, "Well, kids, that's the end," my son gets up
obediently and runs outside to play.
I hope he will ride over this world as well,
and that his crudest and most terrifying dreams
will not return with such wide publicity.

BOOM!

SEES BOOM IN RELIGION, TOO

Atlantic City, June 23, 1957 (AP).—President Eisenhower's pastor said tonight
that Americans are living in a period of "unprecedented religious activity"
caused partially by paid vacations, the eight-hour day and modern conveniences.

"These fruits of material progress," said the Rev. Edward L. R. Elson of the
National Presbyterian Church, Washington, "have provided the leisure, the
energy, and the means for a level of human and spiritual values never before
reached."

HERE at the Vespasian-Carlton, it's just one
religious activity after another; the sky
is constantly being crossed by cruciform
airplanes, in which nobody disbelieves
for a second, and the tide, the tide
of spiritual progress and prosperity
miraculously keeps rising, to a level
never before attained. The churches are full,
the beaches are full, and the filling-stations
are full, God's great ocean is full
of paid vacationers praying an eight-hour day
to the human and spiritual values, the fruits,
the leisure, the energy, and the means, Lord,

the means for the level, the unprecedented level,
and the modern conveniences, which also are full.
Never before, O Lord, have the prayers and praises
from belfry and phonebooth, from ballpark and barbecue
the sacrifices, so endlessly ascended.

It was not thus when Job in Palestine
sat in the dust and cried, cried bitterly;
when Damien kissed the lepers on their wounds
it was not thus; it was not thus
when Francis worked a fourteen-hour day
strictly for the birds; when Dante took
a week's vacation without pay and it rained
part of the time, O Lord, it was not thus.

But now the gears mesh and the tires burn
and the ice chatters in the shaker and the priest
in the pulpit, and Thy Name, O Lord,
is kept before the public, while the fruits
ripen and religion booms and the level rises
and every modern convenience runneth over,
that it may never be with us as it hath been
with Athens and Karnak and Nagasaki,
nor Thy sun for one instant refrain from shining
on the rainbow Buick by the breezeway
or the Chris Craft with the uplift life raft;
that we may continue to be the just folks we are,
plain people with ordinary superliners and
disposable diaperliners, people of the stop'n'shop
'n'pray as you go, of hotel, motel, boatel,
the humble pilgrims of no deposit no return
and please adjust thy clothing, who will give to Thee,
if Thee will keep us going, our annual
Miss Universe, for Thy Name's Sake, Amen.

SYLVIA PLATH, *born October 27, 1932, in Boston, Massachusetts, lives in the village of North Tawton, Devonshire, with her husband, the English poet Ted Hughes, and their two children. She was educated at Smith College and at Newnham College, Cambridge, where she met her husband while she was spending a year abroad on a Fulbright fellowship.*

On the stiff twig up there
Hunches a wet black rook
Arranging and rearranging its feathers in the rain.
I do not expect miracle
Or an accident

To set the sight on fire
In my eye, nor seek
Any more in the desultory weather some design,
But let spotted leaves fall as they fall,
Without ceremony, or portent.

Although, I admit, I desire,
Occasionally, some backtalk
From the mute sky, I can't honestly complain:
A certain minor light may still
Leap incandescent

Out of kitchen table or chair
As if a celestial burning took
Possession of the most obtuse objects now and then—
Thus hallowing an interval
Otherwise inconsequent

By bestowing largesse, honour,
One might say love. At any rate, I now walk
Wary (for it could happen
Even in this dull, ruinous landscape); sceptical,
Yet politic; ignorant

Of whatever angel may choose to flare
Suddenly at my elbow. I only know that a rook
Ordering its black feathers can so shine
As to seize my senses, haul
My eyelids up, and grant

A brief respite from fear
Of total neutrality. With luck,
Trekking stubborn through this season
Of fatigue, I shall
Patch together a content

Of sorts. Miracles occur,
If you care to call those spasmodic
Tricks of radiance miracles. The wait's begun again,
The long wait for the angel,
For that rare, random descent.

THE COLOSSUS

I SHALL never get you put together entirely,
Pieced, glued, and properly jointed.
Mule-bray, pig-grunt and bawdy cackles
Proceed from your great lips.
It's worse than a barnyard.

Perhaps you consider yourself an oracle,
Mouthpiece of the dead, or of some god or other.
Thirty years now I have laboured
To dredge the silt from your throat.
I am none the wiser.

Scaling little ladders with gluepots and pails of lysol
I crawl like an ant in mourning
Over the weedy acres of your brow
To mend the immense skull-plates and clear
The bald, white tumuli of your eyes.

A blue sky out of the Oresteia
Arches above us. O father, all by yourself
You are pithy and historical as the Roman Forum.

I open my lunch on a hill of black cypress.
Your fluted bones and acanthine hair are littered

In their old anarchy to the horizon-line.
It would take more than a lightning-stroke
To create such a ruin.
Nights, I squat in the cornucopia
Of your left ear, out of the wind,

Counting the red stars and those of plum-colour.
The sun rises under the pillar of your tongue.
My hours are married to shadow.
No longer do I listen for the scrape of a keel
On the blank stones of the landing.

WILLIAM PLOMER, *born December 10, 1903, in the Northern Transvaal, Africa, of English parents, lives in Rustington, Sussex. He was educated at Rugby and then returned to South Africa for a number of years, working as a farmer and a trader. Subsequently he spent two years in Japan and long periods in Greece before settling permanently in England. He is well known as a novelist and short-story writer, and as a writer of comic poetry he has established his own particular genre. He wrote the libretto for Benjamin Britten's opera* Gloriana, *performed during the coronation celebration for Queen Elizabeth II.*

This poem is based upon an incident recorded in the
memoirs of an Edwardian hostess, Mrs. Hwfa Williams,
whose husband's given name is pronounced Hoofer.

1

IN the light beneath the leafage
In the afternoon in May
In the Park and near the Row
Gracefully from Hwfa
Mrs. Hwfa Williams turned away,
Saying 'Hwfa, I must go,
I expect a mob for tea;
Such fun, but I must fly—
You dine, I think, with me?
Till then, my dear, good-bye!'

Mrs. Hwfa Williams
Twirled and furled her parasol,
Lightly stepped into her carriage,
Thinking it was all such fun—
Life, and May, and marriage.

Such a pretty moment—
How were they to figure
Fate in ambush, taking aim,
Finger on the trigger?

Later in a tea-gown talking
Over twinkling tea-things on a tray
(Hwfa in the Park still walking)
She was heard to say:

'When my husband and I gave it out
We should move to Great Cumberland Place

My sister-in-law gave a shriek—
"My dears, you'll be lost without trace!"
    And she said it with such a grimace!

"It's so utterly out of the world!
So fearfully wide of the mark!
A Robinson Crusoe existence will pall
On that unexplored side of the Park—
    Not a soul will be likely to call!"

Disparaging all one adores,
Relations are such a disgrace;
They gossip, as bluebottles buzz,
They deplore what one is and one does—
    But they call at Great Cumberland Place!'

                2
At home the tea-time tittle-tattle; in the Mall
Two different orbits about to intersect.
That a poor clerk and Mr. Hwfa Williams
Should there converge nobody could expect
And only a clairvoyant could foretell.

Gravely conferring with a crony, Hwfa
On one side saunters; on the other glares
A young man, seemingly a loafer,
Whose small brain, infinitely busier than theirs,
Has been inflamed by Post Office affairs.

He sends the telegrams that other people write;
From overwork a breakdown now impends;
Abrupt, elliptic phrases day and night he sends,
Recurring in his fevered brain all day
To be reiterated in his brain all night.

Now all's confused, things are not what they seem,
He stands bemused, as if he had been drinking;

Life is a cryptic, an intolerable dream—
RETURN TONIGHT AUNT HENRIETTA SINKING:
CONGRATULATIONS DEAR FROM ALL AT CHEAM.

GLOXINIA WILTING ORDER PINK GERANIUM:
TEN THOUSAND OFFERED SILLY NOT TO SELL:
Telegraphese tattoos upon his eardrums,
Like red-hot tintacks drives into his cranium
The public syntax of his private hell—

THANK YOU BOTH ENCHANTED:
OIL CONCESSION GRANTED:
HOPE ARRIVE NUNEATON TEN TO EIGHT:
ARRIVING SEVEN MABEL STOP:
DON'T SELL REFECTORY TABLE STOP:
CAT OUT OF BAG YOUR TELEGRAM TOO LATE.

Suddenly he sees two frock-coats passing,
Two top-hats tilted in a tête-à-tête—
These are to blame! Revenge upon the senders
Of countless telegrams! He feels the uprush
Of a delayed explosive charge of hate.

He draws and points a pistol, then he shoots.
'Ouch!' cries Hwfa. Something has distressed him.
He stumbles, mutters 'Somebody has shot me!'
He falls. Blood falls upon his patent-leather boots,
And cries go up, 'A murderer! Arrest him!'

3

In the light beneath the leafage
Late that afternoon in May,
In the Mall and on the ground
Mr. Hwfa Williams lay,
Happily not dead, but wounded.

'How do you feel?' they asked.
'Injured,' he said, 'and quite astounded.'

Mr. Hwfa Williams
Was attended by a Dr. Fletcher,
And vexed, but bravely bland,
Was carried home upon a stretcher;
And
On Mr. Hwfa Williams' forehead
Mrs. Hwfa Williams laid a
Ministering angel's hand.
Later 'Hwfa', Mrs. Hwfa Williams said,
'Do you prefer the sofa to your bed?'

'My dear, I don't mind *where* I lie;
What *does* it signify
When not a living soul can tell me why,
About to cross St. James's Park
I'm picked on like a sitting pheasant
By, so they tell me, a demented clerk,
A truant from the G.P.O., Mount Pleasant?
Too many wires, they say, had turned his brain—
But why he turned on *me*—no, *that* they can't explain.'

4

'Good morning, have you heard the news?
You'll be amazed!' 'Well, what?'
'I nearly fainted when I read
That Hwfa Williams has been shot.'

'My dear, your coffee's getting cold—'
'Well, does it matter in the least?'
All over London in the morning
Breakfast was a headline feast.

'Now here is what the paper says:
A dastardly assault . . . the crime
Seems without motive . . . an arrest was made . . .
Alleged . . . admitted . . . passing at the time . . .

A grudge . . . dispatch of telegrams . . .
Pistol discarded, lying in the mud . . .
Enquiries made at Mr. Williams' home . . .
Life not in danger . . . shock and loss of blood.

No one is safe, it seems, these days:
To stroll across St. James's Park
Is to receive a bullet in the leg
From some unhinged, ferocious clerk:

A little learning, as our fathers knew,
Is certainly a dangerous thing;
The lower orders have been spoilt,
And now they mean to have their fling;

But though the world's upside down
And England hastening to decay,
Ring for the carriage; we'll enquire
How Hwfa Williams is today.'

5

'Crikey!' said the butler, Crichton,
'Blocking up the blooming street
All these callers keep on calling—
No one thinks of my poor feet!

All the toffs with all their questions,
Leaving cards you can't refuse;
These reporters, nosy parkers,
Proper sharks they are for news.

I was not engaged to answer
Bells that jangle all the time,
These enquiries well might drive a
Better man than me to crime:

How's your master? Is he better?
Is his life in danger still?

Is it true a gang attacked him?
Do you think they shot to kill?

Can you tell us why they did it?
Anarchists? A Fenian plot?
More of this and I'll go barmy,
Like the lad that fired the shot.'

Carriage after carriage crowding,
Kind enquirers choke the street:
How is Mr. Hwfa Williams?
'No one thinks of MY POOR FEET!'

6

'And so,' said Mrs. Hwfa Williams,
Telling the story after years had passed,
'It seemed that half of London came to call.
Fruit, game and flowers came crowding thick and fast,

Cards like confetti rained into the hall—
Such a great fuss, poor Hwfa was aghast
Yet pleased, I think, at such extreme concern,
More pleased than our old butler with it all—
Poor Crichton hardly knew which way to turn.

The street was jammed, the knocker and the bell
Clamoured together like two fiends in hell—
And where was Crichton? Nobody could tell!
At twelve o'clock my maid rushed in and said
"Oh, ma'am, he's drinking quarts of brandy neat—
Crichton's gone mad! I'll see to the front door!"
Not mad but drunk I found him. Bursting into song
With *Home Sweet Home*, he lurched and hit the floor.

Abject when sober, Crichton said his feet
Had driven him off his head, nor had he known

That Hwfa's best old brandy was so strong . . .
Hwfa forgave him, he had been with us so long.

He stayed for years . . . Poor man, his race is run . . .
I also soon shall hear the sunset gun—
But in between times life has been *such fun!*'

EZRA POUND, *born October 30, 1885, in
Hailey, Idaho, lives with his wife, the former
Dorothy Shakespeare, in Rapallo, Italy. He
attended the University of Pennsylvania and
Hamilton College, taught Romance languages for
a brief time at Pennsylvania and at Wabash
College in Indiana, and then went to Europe to
begin a long and famous career as an expatriate.
He first settled in London, where his skill as an
editor and his zeal as a promoter of new forces
in literature were given wide exercise. In 1924
he went to live in Italy and eventually became a
propagandist for the Fascist regime, an activity
that led to his being brought back to the United
States in 1945 as a prisoner of the American Army
on a charge of treason. When psychiatrists declared
him mentally incompetent to stand trial, he was
committed to St. Elizabeth's Hospital, in Washington, where he continued to work on his magnum
opus,* The Cantos. *On the intercession of Robert
Frost and others, he was released in 1958 and
allowed to return to Italy. His dramatic history
has been given wide publicity; yet he will most
likely be remembered, not for his personal aber-
rations, but for his widely felt influence as a
great craftsman on the course of poetry and the
history of language.*

Come, my songs, let us express our baser passions,
Let us express our envy of the man with a steady job and no worry
    about the future.
You are very idle, my songs.
I fear you will come to a bad end.
You stand about in the streets,
You loiter at the corners and bus-stops,
You do next to nothing at all.

You do not even express our inner nobilities,
You will come to a very bad end.

And I?
I have gone half cracked,
I have talked to you so much that
                            I almost see you about me,
Insolent little beasts, shameless, devoid of clothing!

But you, newest song of the lot,
You are not old enough to have done much mischief,
I will get you a green coat out of China
With dragons worked upon it,
I will get you the scarlet silk trousers
From the statue of the infant Christ in Santa Maria Novella,
Lest they say we are lacking in taste,
Or that there is no caste in this family.

Go, my songs, to the lonely and the unsatisfied,
Go also to the nerve-racked, go to the enslaved-by-convention,
Bear to them my contempt for their oppressors.

Go as a great wave of cool water,
Bear my contempt of oppressors.

Speak against unconscious oppression,
Speak against the tyranny of the unimaginative,
Speak against bonds.
Go to the bourgeoise who is dying of her ennuis,
Go to the women in suburbs.
Go to the hideously wedded,
Go to them whose failure is concealed,
Go to the unluckily mated,
Go to the bought wife,
Go to the woman entailed.

Go to those who have delicate lust,
Go to those whose delicate desires are thwarted,
Go like a blight upon the dullness of the world;
Go with your edge against this,
Strengthen the subtle cords,
Bring confidence upon the algae and the tentacles of the soul.

Go in a friendly manner,
Go with an open speech.
Be eager to find new evils and new good,
Be against all forms of oppression.
Go to those who are thickened with middle age,
To those who have lost their interest.

Go to the adolescent who are smothered in family—
Oh how hideous it is
To see three generations of one house gathered together!
It is like an old tree with shoots,
And with some branches rotted and falling.

Go out and defy opinion,
Go against this vegetable bondage of the blood.
Be against all sorts of mortmain.

THE GARDEN

En robe de parade.—Samain

Like a skein of loose silk blown against a wall
She walks by the railing of a path in Kensington Gardens,
And she is dying piece-meal
              of a sort of emotional anaemia.

And round about there is a rabble
Of the filthy, sturdy, unkillable infants of the very poor.
They shall inherit the earth.

In her is the end of breeding.
Her boredom is exquisite and excessive.
She would like some one to speak to her,
And is almost afraid that I
              will commit that indiscretion.

> *The Sargasso Sea, an area in the Atlantic Ocean*
> *stretching northeast from the West Indies to the*
> *Azores, cradles the wreckage of thousands of*
> *ships that have sunk there as well as wreckage*
> *carried there by its far-ranging currents. This*
> *poem is based on one extended metaphor—a*
> *detailed comparison of the Sargasso Sea with*
> *the character and behavior of a London hostess.*

PORTRAIT D'UNE FEMME

Your mind and you are our Sargasso Sea,
London has swept about you this score years
And bright ships left you this or that in fee:
Ideas, old gossip, oddments of all things,

Strange spars of knowledge and dimmed wares of price.
Great minds have sought you—lacking someone else.
You have been second always. Tragical?
No. You preferred it to the usual thing:
One dull man, dulling and uxorious,
One average mind—with one thought less, each year.
Oh, you are patient, I have seen you sit
Hours, where something might have floated up.
And now you pay one. Yes, you richly pay.
You are a person of some interest, one comes to you
And takes strange gain away:
Trophies fished up; some curious suggestion;
Fact that leads nowhere; and a tale or two,
Pregnant with mandrakes, or with something else
That might prove useful and yet never proves,
That never fits a corner or shows use,
Or finds its hour upon the loom of days:
The tarnished, gaudy, wonderful old work;
Idols and ambergris and rare inlays,
These are your riches, your great store; and yet
For all this sea-hoard of deciduous things,
Strange woods half sodden, and new brighter stuff:
In the slow float of differing light and deep,
No! there is nothing! In the whole and all,
Nothing that's quite your own.
                    Yet this is you.

THE RIVER-MERCHANT'S WIFE: A LETTER

WHILE my hair was still cut straight across my forehead
I played about the front gate, pulling flowers.
You came by on bamboo stilts, playing horse,

You walked about my seat, playing with blue plums.
And we went on living in the village of Chokan:
Two small people, without dislike or suspicion.

At fourteen I married My Lord you.
I never laughed, being bashful.
Lowering my head, I looked at the wall.
Called to, a thousand times, I never looked back.

At fifteen I stopped scowling,
I desired my dust to be mingled with yours
Forever and forever and forever.
Why should I climb the look out?

At sixteen you departed.
You went into far Ku-to-yen, by the river of swirling eddies,
And you have been gone five months.
The monkeys make sorrowful noise overhead.

You dragged your feet when you went out.
By the gate now, the moss is grown, the different mosses,
Too deep to clear them away!
The leaves fall early this autumn, in wind.
The paired butterflies are already yellow with August
Over the grass in the West garden;
They hurt me. I grow older.
If you are coming down through the narrows of the river Kiang,
Please let me know beforehand,
And I will come out to meet you
                    As far as Cho-fu-sa.

By Rihaku

JOHN CROWE RANSOM, *born April 30, 1888, in Pulaski, Tennessee, lives in Gambier, Ohio, where he has for many years been professor of English at Kenyon College and editor of the* Kenyon Review. *He was educated at Vanderbilt University, where he was one of the group of poets who became known as the "Fugitives," and at Oxford, to which he went as a Rhodes scholar. His several books of criticism have been widely influential, and he has been mentor to many distinguished young poets, among them Robert Lowell, Randall Jarrell, and the late Edgar Bogardus.*

IN all the good Greek of Plato
I lack my roastbeef and potato.

A better man was Aristotle,
Pulling steady on the bottle.

I dip my hat to Chaucer,
Swilling soup from his saucer,

And to Master Shakespeare
Who wrote big on small beer.

The abstemious Wordsworth
Subsisted on a curd's-worth,

But a slick one was Tennyson,
Putting gravy on his venison.

What these men had to eat and drink
Is what we say and what we think.

The influence of Milton
Came wry out of Stilton.

Sing a song for Percy Shelley,
Drowned in pale lemon jelly,

And for precious John Keats,
Dripping blood of pickled beets.

Then there was poor Willie Blake,
He foundered on sweet cake.

God have mercy on the sinner
Who must write with no dinner,

No gravy and no grub,
No pewter and no pub,

No belly and no bowels,
Only consonants and vowels.

THE little cousin is dead, by foul subtraction,
A green bough from Virginia's aged tree,
And none of the county kin like the transaction,
Nor some of the world of outer dark, like me.

A boy not beautiful, nor good, nor clever,
A black cloud full of storms too hot for keeping,
A sword beneath his mother's heart—yet never
Woman bewept her babe as this is weeping.

A pig with a pasty face, so I had said,
Squealing for cookies, kinned by poor pretense
With a noble house. But the little man quite dead,
I see the forebears' antique lineaments.

The elder men have strode by the box of death
To the wide flag porch, and muttering low send round
The bruit of the day. O friendly waste of breath!
Their hearts are hurt with a deep dynastic wound.

He was pale and little, the foolish neighbors say;
The first-fruits, saith the Preacher, the Lord hath taken;
But this was the old tree's late branch wrenched away,
Grieving the sapless limbs, the shorn and shaken.

CAPTAIN Carpenter rose up in his prime
Put on his pistols and went riding out
But had got wellnigh nowhere at that time
Till he fell in with ladies in a rout.

It was a pretty lady and all her train
That played with him so sweetly but before
An hour she'd taken a sword with all her main
And twined him of his nose for evermore.

Captain Carpenter mounted up one day
And rode straightway into a stranger rogue
That looked unchristian but be that as may
The Captain did not wait upon prologue.

But drew upon him out of his great heart
The other swung against him with a club
And cracked his two legs at the shinny part
And let him roll and stick like any tub.

Captain Carpenter rode many a time
From male and female took he sundry harms
He met the wife of Satan crying "I'm
The she-wolf bids you shall bear no more arms."

Their strokes and counters whistled in the wind
I wish he had delivered half his blows
But where she should have made off like a hind
The bitch bit off his arms at the elbows.

And Captain Carpenter parted with his ears
To a black devil that used him in this wise
O Jesus ere his threescore and ten years
Another had plucked out his sweet blue eyes.

Captain Carpenter got up on his roan
And sallied from the gate in hell's despite
I heard him asking in the grimmest tone
If any enemy yet there was to fight?

"To any adversary it is fame
If he risk to be wounded by my tongue
Or burnt in two beneath my red heart's flame
Such are the perils he is cast among.

"But if he can he has a pretty choice
From an anatomy with little to lose
Whether he cut my tongue and take my voice
Or whether it be my round red heart he choose."

It was the neatest knave that ever was seen
Stepping in perfume from his lady's bower
Who at this word put in his merry mien
And fell on Captain Carpenter like a tower.

I would not knock old fellows in the dust
But there lay Captain Carpenter on his back
His weapons were the old heart in his bust
And a blade shook between rotten teeth alack.

The rogue in scarlet and grey soon knew his mind
He wished to get his trophy and depart
With gentle apology and touch refined
He pierced him and produced the Captain's heart.

God's mercy rest on Captain Carpenter now
I thought him Sirs an honest gentleman
Citizen husband soldier and scholar enow
Let jangling kites eat of him if they can.

But God's deep curses follow after those
That shore him of his goodly nose and ears

His legs and strong arms at the two elbows
And eyes that had not watered seventy years

The curse of hell upon the sleek upstart
That got the Captain finally on his back
And took the red red vitals of his heart
And made the kites to whet their beaks clack clack.

HENRY REED, *born Febru-*
ary 22, 1914, in Birmingham,
England, lives in London, where
he does free-lance work for news-
papers and magazines as well as
for radio and television. Al-
though he is well known as a
poet, he has published only one
volume, A Map of Verona.

*To read this poem properly, one must imagine the
brusque voice of a drill sergeant as it is heard by a
new recruit who is having difficulty in keeping his
mind on instructions. Toward the end of the fourth
line of every stanza but the last, the drill sergeant's
voice abruptly gives way to the unspoken comments
of the new soldier. In the fifth stanza, the recruit
speaks for himself and rounds off his inner monologue.*

NAMING OF PARTS

Today we have naming of parts. Yesterday,
We had daily cleaning. And tomorrow morning,
We shall have what to do after firing. But today,
Today we have naming of parts. Japonica
Glistens like coral in all of the neighboring gardens,
    And today we have naming of parts.

This is the lower sling swivel. And this
Is the upper sling swivel, whose use you will see,
When you are given your slings. And this is the piling swivel,
Which in your case you have not got. The branches
Hold in the gardens their silent, eloquent gestures,
    Which in our case we have not got.

This is the safety-catch, which is always released
With an easy flick of the thumb. And please do not let me
See anyone using his finger. You can do it quite easy
If you have any strength in your thumb. The blossoms
Are fragile and motionless, never letting anyone see
    Any of them using their finger.

And this you can see is the bolt. The purpose of this
Is to open the breech, as you see. We can slide it
Rapidly backwards and forwards: we call this

Easing the spring. And rapidly backwards and forwards
The early bees are assaulting and fumbling the flowers:
          They call it easing the Spring.

They call it easing the Spring: it is perfectly easy
If you have any strength in your thumb: like the bolt,
And the breech, and the cocking-piece, and the point of balance,
Which in our case we have not got, and the almond-blossom
Silent in all of the gardens, the bees going backwards and forwards,
          For today we have naming of parts.

ALASTAIR REID, *born March 22, 1926, in Whithorn, Scotland, lives in a Spanish village near the French border. He spent his childhood in a fishing village on the island of Arran, attended the University of St. Andrews, and then served with the British Navy in World War II, mainly in the East Indies. After the war, he lived for several years in the United States, teaching at Sarah Lawrence College. His first book was published here, and in 1952 he returned to Europe. He published an account of life in contemporary Spain in* The New Yorker.

On the crooked arm of Columbus, on his cloak,
they mimic his blind and statuary stare,
and the chipped profiles of his handmaidens
they adorn with droppings. Over the loud square,
from all the arms and ledges of their rest,
only a bread crust or a bell unshelves them.
Adding to Atlas' globe, they dispose themselves
with a fat propriety, and pose as garlands
importantly about his burdened shoulders.
Occasionally a lift of wind uncarves them.

Stone becomes them; they, in their turn, become it.
Their opal eyes have a monumental cast.
And, in a maze of noise,
their quiet *croomb croomb* dignifies the spaces,
suggesting the sound of silence. On cobbled islands,
marooned in tantrums of traffic, they know their place,
faithful and anonymous, like servants,
and never beg, but properly receive.

Arriving in rainbows of oil-and-water feathers,
they fountain down from buttresses and outcrops,
from Fontainebleau and London,
and, squat on the margins of roofs, with a gargoyle look,
they note, from an edge of air, with hooded eyes,
the city slowly lessening the sky.

All praise to them who nightly in the parks
keep peace for us; who, cosmopolitan,
patrol and people all cathedral places,
and easily, lazily haunt and inhabit
St. Paul's, St. Peter's, or the Madeleine,
the paved courts of the past, pompous as keepers—

a sober race of messengers and custodians,
neat in their international uniforms,
alighting with a word perhaps from Rome.
Permanence is their business, space and time
their special preservations; and wherever
the great stone men we save from death are stationed,
appropriately on the head of each is perched,
as though forever, his appointed pigeon.

ANNE RIDLER, *born July 30, 1912, in Rugby,*
England, lives in Oxford with her husband,
Vivian Ridler, printer to the university, and their
four children. She was educated at King's College,
in London, has published many volumes of poetry
and poetic drama, and now divides her time
between housekeeping, gardening, and literary
work.

I DID not see the iris move,
I did not feel the unfurling of my love.

This was the sequence of the flower:
First the leaf from which the bud would swell,
No prison, but a cell,
A rolled rainbow;
Then the sheath that enclosed the blow
Pale and close
Giving no hint of the blaze within,
A tender skin with violet vein.
Then the first unfurling petal
As if a hand that held a jewel
Curled back a finger, let the light wink
Narrowly through the chink,
Or like the rays before the sunrise
Promising glory.

And while my back is turned, the flower has blown.
Impossible to tell
How this opulent blossom from that spick bud has grown.
The chrysalis curled tight,
The flower poised for flight—
Corolla with lolling porphyry wings
And yellow tiger markings
A chasing-place for shade and light:
Between these two, the explosion
Soundless, with no duration.
        (I did not see the iris move,
        I did not feel my love unfurl.)
The most tremendous change takes place in silence,
Unseen, however you mark the sequence,
Unheard, whatever the din of exploding stars.

Down the porphyry stair
Headlong into the air
The boy has come: he crouches there
A tender startled creature
With a fawn's ears and hair-spring poise
Alert to every danger
Aghast at every noise.
A blue blink
From under squeezed-up lids
As mauve as iris buds
Is gone as quickly as a bird's bright wink.
Gone—but as if his soul had looked an instant through the chink.
And perfect as his shell-like nails,
Close as are to the flower its petals,
My love unfolded with him.
Yet till this moment what was he to me?
Conjecture and analogy;
Conceived, and yet unknown;
Behind this narrow barrier of bone
Distant as any foreign land could be.

> *I have seen the light of day,*
> *Was it sight or taste or smell?*
> *What I have been, who can tell?*
> *What I shall be, who can say?*

He floats in life as a lily in the pool
Free and yet rooted;
And strong though seeming frail,
Like the ghost fritillary
That trails its first-appearing bud
As though too weak to raise it from the mud,
But is stronger than you dream,
And soon will lift its paper lantern
High upon an arched and sinewy stem.

His smiles are all largesse,
Need ask for no return,
Since give and take are meaningless
To one who gives by needing
And takes our love for granted
And grants a favour even by his greed.
The ballet of his twirling hands
His chirping and his loving sounds,
Perpetual expectation
Perpetual surprise—
Not a lifetime satisfies
For watching, every thing he does
We wish him to do always.

> *Only in a lover's eyes*
> *Shall I be so approved again;*
> *Only the other side of pain*
> *Can truth again be all I speak,*
> *Or I again possess*
> *A saint's hilarious carelessness.*

He rows about his ocean
With its leaning cliffs and towers,
A horizontal being,
Straddled by walking people
By table-legs and chairs;
And sees the world as you can see
Upside-down in water
The wavering heights of trees
Whose roots hang from your eyes.
Then Time begins to trail
In vanishing smoke behind him,
A vertical creature now
With a pocket full of nails,
One of a gang of urchin boys
Who proves his sex by robber noise—

Roar of the sucking dove
And thunder of the wren.
Terror waits in the woods
But in the sun he is brazen
Because our love is his
No matter what he does;
His very weakness claims a share
In the larger strength of others,
And perfect in our eyes
He is only vulnerable there.

But not immortal there, alas.
We cannot keep, and see. The shapes of clouds
Which alter as we gaze
Are not more transient than these living forms
Which we so long to hold
For ever in the moment's mould.
The figures frozen in the camera's record
And carried with us from the past
Are like those objects buried with the dead—
Temporal treasures irrelevant to their need.
Yes, this is the worst:
The living truth is lost,
And is supplanted by these album smiles.

> *What you desire to keep, you slay:*
> *While you watch me, I am going.*
> *Wiser than you, I would not stay*
> *Even if I could: my hope's in growing.*
> *My form as a dapple of sun that flies*
> *On the brook, is changed; my earliest word*
> *Is the call you learnt to recognize*
> *And now forget, of a strange bird.*

Yet, as the calyx contains the life of the bud
So the bud is contained within the flower

Though past in time:
The end is not more true than the beginning,
Nor is the promise cancelled by the prime.
Not only what he was, and is, but what he might have been,
In each is rolled within.
Our life depends on that:
What other claim have we to resurrection?
For now that we can contemplate perfection
We have lost the knack of being it. What should be saved
Of these distorted lives?
All we can pray is
                Save us from Nothingness.
Nothingness, which all men dread;
Which makes us feel an irrational pity for the dead,
And fight the anodyne
Even while we long for deliverance from pain.

So, I have read,
When a man gave his darling in grief to the grave
About her neck in a locket tied
He set this urgent word—
Not to drink Lethe, at all costs not to forget.
And this is truth to us, even yet.
For if life is eternal
All must be held, though all must be redeemed.
But what can ever restore
To these sad and short-coming lives of ours
The lovely jocund creatures that we were
And did not know we were?
What can give us at once
The being and the sense?

Why, each within
Has kept his secret for some Resurrection:
The wonder that he was

And can be, which is his
Not by merit, only by grace.
It comes to light, as love is born with a child,
Neither with help nor herald
(I did not see the iris move);
Neither by sight nor sound—
I did not feel the unfurling of my love.

THEODORE ROETHKE, *born May 25, 1908, in Saginaw, Michigan, lives with his wife in Seattle, where he is professor of English at the University of Washington. He grew up in and around a greenhouse owned by his father and his uncle, a circumstance strongly reflected in the many poems in which he dramatizes the consciousness of childhood. He was educated at the University of Michigan and at Harvard, and his teaching career has included positions at Lafayette, Penn State, where he was also coach of tennis, and Bennington, where his wife was then a student. He worked on his first book of poems,* **Open** House, *for ten years; since then his output has been comparatively prolific and the range of his style and subject matter greatly extended as he has passed through several distinct phases of development. His fourth volume of poems,* The Waking, *was awarded the Pulitzer Prize in 1954.*

I KNEW a woman, lovely in her bones,
When small birds sighed, she would sigh back at them;
Ah, when she moved, she moved more ways than one:
The shapes a bright container can contain!
Of her choice virtues only gods should speak,
Or English poets who grew up on Greek
(I'd have them sing in chorus, cheek to cheek).

How well her wishes went! She stroked my chin,
She taught me Turn, and Counter-turn, and Stand;
She taught me Touch, that undulant white skin;
I nibbled meekly from her proffered hand;
She was the sickle; I, poor I, the rake,
Coming behind her for her pretty sake
(But what prodigious mowing we did make).

Loves like a gander, and adores a goose:
Her full lips pursed, the errant note to seize;
She played it quick, she played it light and loose;
My eyes, they dazzled at her flowing knees;
Her several parts could keep a pure repose,
Or one hip quiver with a mobile nose
(She moved in circles, and those circles moved).

Let seed be grass, and grass turn into hay:
I'm martyr to a motion not my own;
What's freedom for? To know eternity.
I swear she cast a shadow white as stone.
But who would count eternity in days?
These old bones live to learn her wanton ways:
(I measure time by how a body sways).

If I must of my Senses lose,
I pray Thee, Lord, that I may choose
Which of the Five I shall retain
Before oblivion clouds the brain.
My Tongue is generations dead,
My Nose defiles a comely head;
For hearkening to carnal evils
My Ears have been the very devil's.
And some have held the Eye to be
The instrument of lechery,
More furtive than the Hand in low
And vicious venery—Not so!
Its rape is gentle, never more
Violent than a metaphor.
In truth, the Eye's the abettor of
The holiest platonic love:
Lip, Breast and Thigh cannot possess
So singular a blessedness.
Therefore, O Lord, let me preserve
The Sense that does so fitly serve,
Take Tongue and Ear—all else I have—
Let Light attend me to the grave!

*This poem, written from the point of view of a child
as he encounters the world of nature, has the air of
an epiphany—a showing forth of things of a divine
order. Emphasis is placed strictly upon the reality,
the particularity, of things observed, and in the process
a sense of curiosity gives way to a sense of harmony.*

A FIELD OF LIGHT

1

CAME to lakes; came to dead water,
Ponds with moss and leaves floating,
Planks sunk in the sand.

A log turned at the touch of a foot;
A long weed floated upward;
An eye tilted.

> Small winds made
> A chilly noise;
> The softest cove
> Cried for sound.

> Reached for a grape
> And the leaves changed;
> A stone's shape
> Became a clam.

> A fine rain fell
> On fat leaves;
> I was there alone
> In a watery drowse.

2

Angel within me, I asked,
Did I ever curse the sun?
Speak and abide.

Under, under the sheaves,
Under the blackened leaves,
Behind the green viscid trellis,
In the deep grass at the edge of a field,
Along the low ground dry only in August,—

Was it dust I was kissing?
A sigh came far.
Alone, I kissed the skin of a stone;
Marrow-soft, danced in the sand.

3

The dirt left my hand, visitor.
I could feel the mare's nose.
A path went walking.
The sun glittered on a small rapids.
Some morning thing came, beating its wings.
The great elm filled with birds.

Listen, love,
The fat lark sang in the field;
I touched the ground, the ground warmed by the killdeer,
The salt laughed and the stones;
The ferns had their ways, and the pulsing lizards,
And the new plants, still awkward in their soil,
The lovely diminutives.

I could watch! I could watch!
I saw the separateness of all things!
My heart lifted up with the great grasses;
The weeds believed me, and the nesting birds.
There were clouds making a rout of shapes crossing a windbreak of
  cedars,
And a bee shaking drops from a rain-soaked honeysuckle.
The worms were delighted as wrens.
And I walked, I walked through the light air;
I moved with the morning.

ELEGY FOR JANE

My Student, Thrown by a Horse

I REMEMBER the neckcurls, limp and damp as tendrils;
And her quick look, a sidelong pickerel smile;
And how, once startled into talk, the light syllables leaped for her,
And she balanced in the delight of her thought,
A wren, happy, tail into the wind,
Her song trembling the twigs and small branches.
The shade sang with her;
The leaves, their whispers turned to kissing;
And the mould sang in the bleached valleys under the rose.

Oh, when she was sad, she cast herself down into such a pure depth,
Even a father could not find her:
Scraping her cheek against straw;
Stirring the clearest water.

My sparrow, you are not here,
Waiting like a fern, making a spiney shadow.
The sides of wet stones cannot console me,
Nor the moss, wound with the last light.

If only I could nudge you from this sleep,
My maimed darling, my skittery pigeon.
Over this damp grave I speak the words of my love:
I, with no rights in this matter,
Neither father nor lover.

THE WAKING

I WAKE to sleep, and take my waking slow.
I feel my fate in what I cannot fear.
I learn by going where I have to go.

We think by feeling. What is there to know?
I hear my being dance from ear to ear.
I wake to sleep, and take my waking slow.

Of those so close beside me, which are you?
God bless the Ground! I shall walk softly there,
And learn by going where I have to go.

Light takes the Tree; but who can tell us how?
The lowly worm climbs up a winding stair;
I wake to sleep, and take my waking slow.

Great Nature has another thing to do
To you and me; so take the lively air,
And, lovely, learn by going where to go.

This shaking keeps me steady. I should know.
What falls away is always. And is near.
I wake to sleep, and take my waking slow.
I learn by going where I have to go.

MURIEL RUKEYSER, *born December 15, 1913, in New York, lives in her native city with her teen-age son. She studied at Vassar College and later taught there and at other colleges for brief periods as lecturer or as poet-in-residence. She was in Spain as a reporter at the outbreak of the Civil War, and her experiences then have been recorded in a number of her poems. Her first book of poems,* Theory of Flight, *was written after she had completed a ground course at Roosevelt Aviation School. Her subsequent writings include, besides poetry, biographical studies of the scientist Willard Gibbs and the Republican political leader Wendell Willkie. Most of her early work reflects a deep interest in problems involving labor unionism and racial relations; in her later writings these concerns have been relaxed in favor of a more personal emphasis.*

Sunday shuts down on this twentieth-century evening.
The L passes. Twilight and bulb define
the brown room, the overstuffed plum sofa,
the boy, and the girl's thin hands above his head.
A neighbor's radio sings stocks, news, serenade.

He sits at the table, head down, the young clear neck exposed,
watching the drugstore sign from the tail of his eye;
tattoo, neon, until the eye blears, while his
solicitous tall sister, simple in blue, bending
behind him, cuts his hair with her cheap shears.

The arrow's electric red always reaches its mark,
successful neon! He coughs, impressed by that precision.
His child's forehead, forever protected by his cap,
is bleached against the lamplight as he turns head
and steadies to let the snippets drop.

Erasing the failure of weeks with level fingers,
she sleeks the fine hair, combing: "You'll look fine tomorrow!
You'll surely find something, they can't keep turning you down;
the finest gentleman's not so trim as you!" Smiling, he raises
the adolescent forehead wrinkling ironic now.

He sees his decent suit laid out, new-pressed,
his carfare on the shelf. He lets his head fall, meeting
her earnest hopeless look, seeing the sharp blades splitting,
the darkened room, the impersonal sign, her motion,
the blue vein, bright on her temple, pitifully beating.

: Speak to me.   Take my hand.   What are you now?
I will tell you all.   I will conceal nothing.
When I was three, a little child read a story about a rabbit
who died, in the story, and I crawled under a chair   :
a pink rabbit   :   it was my birthday, and a candle
burnt a sore spot on my finger, and I was told to be happy.

: Oh, grow to know me.   I am not happy.   I will be open:
Now I am thinking of white sails against a sky like music,
like glad horns blowing, and birds tilting, and an arm about me.
There was one I loved, who wanted to live, sailing.

: Speak to me.   Take my hand.   What are you now?
When I was nine, I was fruitily sentimental,
fluid   :   and my widowed aunt played Chopin,
and I bent my head on the painted woodwork, and wept.
I want now to be close to you.   I would
link the minutes of my days close, somehow, to your days.

: I am not happy.   I will be open.
I have liked lamps in evening corners, and quiet poems.
There has been fear in my life.   Sometimes I speculate
on what a tragedy his life was, really.

: Take my hand.   First my mind in your hand.   What are
    you now?
When I was fourteen, I had dreams of suicide,
and I stood at a steep window, at sunset, hoping toward death   :
if the light had not melted clouds and plains to beauty,
if light had not transformed that day, I would have leapt.
I am unhappy.   I am lonely.   Speak to me.

: I will be open.   I think he never loved me:
he loved the bright beaches, the little lips of foam

that ride small waves, he loved the veer of gulls:
he said with a gay mouth: I love you.   Grow to know me.

What are you now?   If we could touch one another,
if these our separate entities could come to grips,
clenched like a Chinese puzzle . . . yesterday
I stood in a crowded street that was live with people,
and no one spoke a word, and the morning shone.
Everyone silent, moving. . . . Take my hand.   Speak to me.

DELMORE SCHWARTZ, *born December 8, 1913, in Brooklyn, lives in New York City. He was educated at the University of Wisconsin, New York University, and Harvard University, where from 1940 to 1947 he taught in the English department as a Briggs-Copeland fellow. From 1943 to 1955 he was an editor of the* Partisan Review. *Besides poetry, his writings include many influential essays on literary themes and a number of short stories, some of which are gathered in a volume entitled* The World is a Wedding.

Where the sea gulls sleep or indeed where they fly
Is a place of different traffic. Although I
Consider the fishing bay (where I see them dip and curve
And purely glide) a place that weakens the nerve
Of will, and closes my eyes, as they should not be
(They should burn like the street-light all night quietly,
So that whatever is present will be known to me),
Nevertheless the gulls and the imagination
Of where they sleep, which comes to creation
In strict shape and color, from their dallying
Their wings slowly, and suddenly rallying
Over, up, down the arabesque of descent,
Is an old act enacted, my fabulous intent
When I skated, afraid of policemen, five years old,
In the winter sunset, sorrowful and cold,
Hardly attained to thought, but old enough to know
Such grace, so self-contained, was the best escape to know.

THE HEAVY BEAR WHO GOES WITH ME

"the withness of the body"—Whitehead

The heavy bear who goes with me,
A manifold honey to smear his face,
Clumsy and lumbering here and there,
The central ton of every place,
The hungry beating brutish one
In love with candy, anger, and sleep,
Crazy factotum, dishevelling all,
Climbs the building, kicks the football,
Boxes his brother in the hate-ridden city.

Breathing at my side, that heavy animal,
That heavy bear who sleeps with me,
Howls in his sleep for a world of sugar,
A sweetness intimate as the water's clasp,
Howls in his sleep because the tight-rope
Trembles and shows the darkness beneath.
—The strutting show-off is terrified,
Dressed in his dress-suit, bulging his pants,
Trembles to think that his quivering meat
Must finally wince to nothing at all.

That inescapable animal walks with me,
Has followed me since the black womb held,
Moves where I move, distorting my gesture,
A caricature, a swollen shadow,
A stupid clown of the spirit's motive,
Perplexes and affronts with his own darkness,
The secret life of belly and bone,
Opaque, too near, my private, yet unknown,
Stretches to embrace the very dear
With whom I would walk without him near,
Touches her grossly, although a word
Would bare my heart and make me clear,
Stumbles, flounders, and strives to be fed
Dragging me with him in his mouthing care,
Amid the hundred million of his kind,
The scrimmage of appetite everywhere.

BAUDELAIRE

WHEN I fall asleep, and even during sleep,
I hear, quite distinctly, voices speaking
Whole phrases, commonplace and trivial,
Having no relation to my affairs.

Dear Mother, is any time left to us
In which to be happy? My debts are immense.
My bank account is subject to the court's judgment.
I know nothing. I cannot know anything.
I have lost the ability to make an effort.
But now as before my love for you increases.
You are always armed to stone me, always:
It is true. It dates from childhood.

For the first time in my long life
I am almost happy. The book, almost finished,
Almost seems good. It will endure, a monument
To my obsessions, my hatred, my disgust.

Debts and inquietude persist and weaken me.
Satan glides before me, saying sweetly:
"Rest for a day! You can rest and play today.
Tonight you will work." When night comes,
My mind, terrified by the arrears,
Bored by sadness, paralyzed by impotence,
Promises: "Tomorrow: I will tomorrow."
Tomorrow the same comedy enacts itself
With the same resolution, the same weakness.

I am sick of this life of furnished rooms.
I am sick of having colds and headaches:
You know my strange life. Every day brings
Its quota of wrath. You little know
A poet's life, dear Mother: I must write poems,
The most fatiguing of occupations.

I am sad this morning. Do not reproach me.
I write from a café near the post office,
Amid the click of billiard balls, the clatter of dishes,
The pounding of my heart. I have been asked to write
"A History of Caricature." I have been asked to write

"A History of Sculpture." Shall I write a history
Of the caricatures of the sculptures of you in my heart?

Although it costs you countless agony,
Although you cannot believe it necessary,
And doubt that the sum is accurate,
Please send me money enough for at least three weeks.

WINFIELD TOWNLEY SCOTT, *born 1910, in Haverhill, Massachusetts, lives with his wife and two children in Santa Fe, New Mexico. From 1931 to 1951 he was a member of the staff of the* Providence (Rhode Island) Journal. *He is also widely known as a reviewer and essayist.*

Having banged the piano too hard
Traman turned and looked around
And seeing his friends assembled said
'To hell with that Almighty sound.

It is,' he said,—with something still
Resembling an enlarging air—
'My *Fish Sonata:* oversoul
Voyaging an underworld despair.

While less than panoramic zeal
Eliminated vaster plans,
I found myself intrigued between
The tadpoles and leviathans;—

Then plumped for giants. And you've heard:
A mackerel music round the whales.
There's nothing drier than dried fish.
Drink up, and I will practise scales.'

And Traman thereupon swung back
And found the keys as clean and fair;
And, thinking over what he'd said,
Wished his friends were really there.

BLUE SLEIGH

Blue sleigh that fifty winters gone
Swan-breasted heavier snows than ours,
Arrested on your summer lawn
Stands filled with earth and planted flowers.

WINFIELD TOWNLEY SCOTT *309*

Its shafts slant empty to the ground
As if they'd never held a horse;
Its runners make the breathless sound
Allotted rust and ghosts, of course.

The flowers are white geranium.
Stuck in June grass it looks as though
Somehow the sleigh had tunneled home
Through one immortal drift of snow.

Present preservative of past?
That what it raced through it contains?
But your illusion will not last:
Here's white geranium and it stains.

You lover of the incongruous:
Better to have your blue sleigh drawn
Through all those daisy fields across
The hills to time's malignant sun.

JAMES SCULLY, *born February 23, 1937, in New Haven, lives with his wife and infant daughter in Coventry, Connecticut. He is a graduate student at the University of Connecticut, completing work toward a doctorate degree in English. He has not yet published a volume, but his poems have appeared in* The New Yorker *and in a number of literary magazines, including* Poetry *and the* Wormwood Review, *of which he was an editor.*

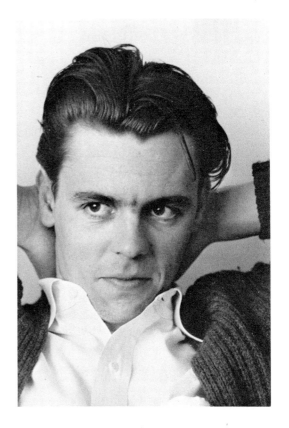

THAT the high sheen of death could blot
this green away, or life survive
the great ice age, is almost not

to be believed. Clearly, today's
raw sunlight ripens into grass
and grazing cows, as though always

it has been so. Still, glacial rock,
like giant bone, breaks through the earth
and weighs the age-old walls that block

these fields, the livestock locked within.
a herd of clear-cut whites and blacks,
the cows browse in oblivion,

their muscles ruffling under veils
of gaudy, violet-winged black flies
aswarm their hides—and swish their tails—

thickset, but limber as bullwhips
perpetually in motion, long
quick lengths unravelled at the tips,

from side to side. Nearby, a brace
of mules tethered to buried stakes
stand stock-still. And out through space,

at times, too far away to hear,
a flashing Sabre-jet transcends
the mules, the massive cows—a mere

slow-motioned slip of silver light—
and wakes a ghostly rainbow arc
flatly across far hills, its slight

exhaustion burning through the blue
useless sky, trailing away,
its destination out of view.

The glacier's gone. The cows assent
grassward, earmarked with metal tags,
delicacies of ornament

that glint and tick away the sun
as their ears twitch, as they remain
one pulsing mass—as if each one

had undergone the bull, the calf,
the frost-bit rains, and now held out
for nothing less than life itself:

such middle-aging gaiety
as knows not what it was, nor is,
nor what it is about to be,

nor cares that space thins out, goes dumb,
that time may cease to come—as if,
rockbound, this were the kingdom come,

and the hunched fields were crystal-clear
Jerusalem, and life was judged
vibration in the summer air.

THE GLASS BLOWER

CANARIES were his hobby.
Upstairs in the attic, with his knobby
hands, he put up small-gauge wire stalls;
copper gauze, from the slant roof to the floor,
huddled the birdflock in their drowsy ark.

There were a hundred or more
that sat on crusted bars, their claws locked tight—
upright albino bats, until the night-
time came. When he groped up the stairs, the light
blazed and they awoke.
The hungry bodies quickened.
A few flew at the screen, but every dark
reflection glided skillfully on the walls
behind the gold wheelings—wheels of a clock
chirping every second on the second.

  Gradually it unwound.
And going to work, a Jonah's underground,
he'd disappear into a warehouse: punch in,
check orders, stir a batch of sand, start
the wheel grinding out his daily payload
of undistracted art—
and shape a universe, a toy glass ball
one shakes, seeing the plastic snowflakes fall
within a pool, upon a parasol
of plastic (underneath,
a woman and a man
were frozen in their strolling). And the haloed,
high-stooled glass blower, leaning over a Bunsen
burner, at a wooden bench, would breathe
glass straws into strings of glass balloons.

  They were sold—the rare
canaries, then pigeons, chickens, and a pair
of guinea pigs. Experiments, they arrived
and left, like courses in their covered dish.
He even bred, in an aquarium,
rainbow-colored fish:
then, streaked with orange scars, the slim swordtails
cut a wakeless way, and the milky sails

of angelfish, razor-thin, edged trails
of tendril over rock;
the snails neither sank
nor swam, but stuffed their pinkish horns with scum.
He also stocked black mollies. Short-lived,
their bulbous heads and tapering bodies, black
tear-shapes, cruised the bottom of the tank.

    Lightheaded bubbles swirled
surfacewise. Wound in a filmy world,
a fetus feeding on its inmost part,
he'd circle bar to bar each night, without
going far, but staggering home stone blind,
his pockets inside-out.
Fleeced, he made the cellar workshop a cage
of pipes and copper coils, trying to gauge
the distillation and advancing age
of alcohol. Ferment-
ing, dribbling from the lips,
he would sit wall-eyed with his wheeling mind
among odd junk. Near a dog-eared sea chart,
a bottle made a toppled monument
preserving remnants of a model ship.

ANNE SEXTON, *born November 9, 1928, in Newton, Massachusetts, lives with her husband and two daughters in Newton Lower Falls, not far from her birthplace. She attended local schools, lived for periods in Baltimore and San Francisco, and was a student of Robert Lowell during the years he was at Boston University. She has spent many summers on Cape Cod and in Maine at her ancestral home.*

I AM surprised to see
that the ocean is still going on.
Now I am going back
and I have ripped my hand
from your hand as I said I would
and I have made it this far
as I said I would
and I am on the top deck now,
holding my wallet, my cigarettes,
and my car keys
at two o'clock on a Tuesday
in August of 1960.

Dearest,
although everything has happened,
nothing has happened.
The sea is very old.
The sea is the face of Mary,
without miracles or rage
or unusual hope,
grown rough and wrinkled
with incurable age.

Still,
I have eyes.
These are my eyes:
the orange letters that spell
"ORIENT" on the life preserver
that hangs by my knees,
the cement lifeboat that wears
its dirty canvas coat,
the faded sign that sits on its shelf
saying "KEEP OFF."

Oh, all right, I say,
I'll save myself.

Over my right shoulder
I see four nuns
who sit like a bridge club,
their faces poked out
from under their habits,
as good as good babies who
have sunk into their carriages.
Without discrimination,
the wind pulls the skirts
of their arms.
Almost undressed,
I see what remains:
that holy wrist,
that ankle,
that chain.

Oh, God,
although I am very sad,
could you please
let these four nuns
loosen from their leather boots
and their wooden chairs
to rise out
over this greasy deck,
out over this iron rail,
nodding their pink heads to one side,
flying four abreast
in the old-fashioned side stroke,
each mouth open and round,
breathing together
as fish do,
singing without sound.

Dearest,
see how my dark girls sally forth,
over the passing lighthouse of Plum Gut,
its shell as rusty
as a camp dish,
as fragile as a pagoda
on a stone,
out over the little lighthouse
that warns me of drowning winds
that rub over its blind bottom
and its blue cover—
winds that will take the toes
and the ears of the rider
or the lover.

There go my dark girls;
their dresses puff
in the leeward air.
Oh, they are lighter than flying dogs
or the breath of dolphins;
each mouth opens gratefully,
wider than a milk cup.
My dark girls sing for this:
They are going up.

Here are my four dark girls.
See them rise
on black wings, drinking
the sky, without smiles
or hands
or shoes.
They call back to us
from the gauzy edge of paradise,
good news, good news.

I HAVE gone out, a possessed witch,
haunting the black air, braver at night;
dreaming evil, I have done my hitch
over the plain houses, light by light:
lonely thing, twelve-fingered, out of mind.
A woman like that is not a woman, quite.
I have been her kind.

I have found the warm caves in the woods,
filled them with skillets, carvings, shelves,
closets, silks, innumerable goods;
fixed the suppers for the worms and the elves:
whining, rearranging the disaligned.
A woman like that is misunderstood.
I have been her kind.

I have ridden in your cart, driver,
waved my nude arms at villages going by,
learning the last bright routes, survivor
where your flames still bite my thigh
and my ribs crack where your wheels wind.
A woman like that is not ashamed to die.
I have been her kind.

KARL SHAPIRO, *born November 10, 1913 in Baltimore, Maryland, lives with his wife and three children in Lincoln, Nebraska, where he is professor of English at the University of Nebraska. He attended the University of Virginia for a brief and unhappy period and graduated from Johns Hopkins University. He served with the Army in the South Pacific for four years in World War II, during which his first books were published, and on his return was appointed Consultant in Poetry at the Library of Congress. Before going to Nebraska, he taught at Johns Hopkins for several years and then moved to Chicago when he was appointed editor of* Poetry: A Magazine of Verse. *His critical attitudes are stated in a volume of poetry,* Essay on Rime, *and in a volume of essays,* In Defense of Ignorance.

*World War II took hundreds of thousands of American
soldiers to the other side of the world. This poem,
written in 1942, when its author was on military
duty in the Indian Ocean, makes particular use of
geography and time to suggest the topsy-turvy
quality of a life interrupted by global conflict.*

NOSTALGIA

Mᴙ soul stands at the window of my room,
      And I ten thousand miles away;
My days are filled with Ocean's sound of doom,
      Salt and cloud and the bitter spray.
Let the wind blow, for many a man shall die.

My selfish youth, my books with gilded edge,
      Knowledge and all gaze down the street;
The potted plants upon the window ledge
      Gaze down with selfish lives and sweet.
Let the wind blow, for many a man shall die.

My night is now her day, my day her night,
      So I lie down, and so I rise;
The sun burns close, the star is losing height,
      The clock is hunted down the skies.
Let the wind blow, for many a man shall die.

Truly a pin can make the memory bleed,
      A world explode the inward mind
And turn the skulls and flowers never freed
      Into the air, no longer blind.
Let the wind blow, for many a man shall die.

Laughter and grief join hands. Always the heart
      Clumps in the breast with heavy stride;

The face grows lined and wrinkled like a chart,
   The eyes bloodshot with tears and tide.
Let the wind blow, for many a man shall die.

O WONDERFUL nonsense of lotions of Lucky Tiger,
Of savory soaps and oils of bottle-bright green,
The gold of liqueurs, the unguents of Newark and Niger,
Powders and balms and waters washing me clean,

In mirrors of marble and silver I see us forever
Increasing, decreasing the puzzles of luminous spaces
As I turn, am revolved and am pumped in the air on a lever,
With the backs of my heads in chorus with all of my faces.

Scissors and comb are mowing my hair into neatness,
Now pruning my ears, now smoothing my neck like a plain;
In the harvest of hair and the chaff of powdery sweetness
My snow-covered slopes grow dark with the wooly rain.

And the little boy cries, for it hurts to sever the curl,
And we too are quietly bleating to part with our coat.
Does the barber want blood in a dish? I am weak as a girl,
I desire my pendants, the fatherly chin of a goat.

I desire the pants of a bear, the nap of a monkey
Which trousers of friction have blighted down to my skin.
I am bare as a tusk, as jacketed up as a flunkey,
With the chest of a moth-eaten camel growing within.

But in death we shall flourish, you summer-dark leaves of my head,
While the flesh of the jaw ebbs away from the shores of my teeth;
You shall cover my sockets and soften the boards of my bed
And lie on the flat of my temples as proud as a wreath.

I do remember an apothecary,
And hereabouts 'a dwells

Iᴛ baffles the foreigner like an idiom,
And he is right to adopt it as a form
Less serious than the living-room or bar;
     For it disestablishes the cafe,
Is a collective, and on basic country.

Not that it praises hygiene and corrupts
The ice-cream parlor and the tobacconist's
Is it a center; but that the attractive symbols
     Watch over puberty and leer
Like rubber bottles waiting for sick-use.

Youth comes to jingle nickels and crack wise;
The baseball scores are his, the magazines
Devoted to lust, the jazz, the Coca-Cola,
     The lending-library of love's latest.
He is the customer; he is heroized.

And every nook and cranny of the flesh
Is spoken to by packages with wiles.
"Buy me, buy me," they whimper and cajole;
     The hectic range of lipsticks pouts,
Revealing the wicked and the simple mouth.

With scarcely any evasion in their eye
They smoke, undress their girls, exact a stance;
But only for a moment. The clock goes round;
     Crude fellowships are made and lost;
They slump in booths like rags, not even drunk.

*Allied with reason and science, the spirit of Faust—
the legendary German doctor who gained magical
powers by selling his soul to the devil—moves
stealthily through history in many disguises.
According to this poem, his latest manifes-
tation is in the collective role of the scientists
who developed the nuclear bombs.*

THE PROGRESS OF FAUST

HE was born in Deutschland, as you would suspect,
And graduated in magic from Cracow
In Fifteen Five. His portraits show a brow
Heightened by science. The eye is indirect,
As of bent light upon a crooked soul,
And that he bargained with the Prince of Shame
For pleasures intellectually foul
Is known by every court that lists his name.

His frequent disappearances are put down
To visits in the regions of the damned
And to the periodic deaths he shammed,
But, unregenerate and in Doctor's gown,
He would turn up to lecture at the fair
And do a minor miracle for a fee.
Many a life he whispered up the stair
To teach the black art of anatomy.

He was as deaf to angels as an oak
When, in the fall of Fifteen Ninety-four,
He went to London and crashed through the floor
In mock damnation of the playgoing folk.
Weekending with the scientific crowd,
He met Sir Francis Bacon and helped draft
"Colours of Good and Evil" and read aloud
An obscene sermon at which no one laughed.

He toured the Continent for a hundred years
And subsidized among the peasantry
The puppet play, his tragic history;
With a white glove he boxed the Devil's ears
And with a black his own. Tired of this,
He published penny poems about his sins,
In which he placed the heavy emphasis
On the white glove which, for a penny, wins.

Some time before the hemorrhage of the Kings
Of France, he turned respectable and taught;
Quite suddenly everything that he had thought
Seemed to grow scholars' beards and angels' wings.
It was the Overthrow. On Reason's throne
He sat with the fair Phrygian on his knees
And called all universities his own, ·
As plausible a figure as you please.

Then back to Germany as the sages' sage
To preach comparative science to the young
Who came from every land in a great throng
And knew they heard the master of the age.
When for a secret formula he paid
The Devil another fragment of his soul,
His scholars wept, and several even prayed
That Satan would restore him to them whole.

Backwardly tolerant, Faustus was expelled
From the Third Reich in Nineteen Thirty-nine.
His exit caused the breaching of the Rhine,
Except for which the frontier might have held.
Five years unknown to enemy and friend
He hid, appearing on the sixth to pose
In an American desert at war's end
Where, at his back, a dome of atoms rose.

LOUIS SIMPSON, *born March 27, 1923, in Jamaica, British West Indies, lives with his wife and three children in Berkeley, where he teaches in the English department of the University of California. He was educated in British schools in Jamaica and took his Ph.D. from Columbia University.*

A HOT midsummer night on Water Street—
The boys in jeans were combing their blond hair,
Watching the girls go by on tired feet;
And an old woman with a witch's stare
Cried "Praise the Lord!" She vanished on a bus
With hissing air brakes, like an incubus.

Three hardware stores, a barbershop, a bar,
A movie playing Westerns—where I went
To see a dream of horses called *The Star* . . . .
Some day, when this uncertain continent
Is marble, and men ask what was the good
We lived by, dust may whisper "Hollywood."

Then back along the river bank on foot
By moonlight . . . . On the West Virginia side
An owlish train began to huff and hoot;
It seemed to know of something that had died.
I didn't linger—sometimes when I travel
I think I'm being followed by the Devil.

At the newsstand in the lobby, a cigar
Was talkative: "Since I've been in this town
I've seen one likely woman, and a car
As she was crossing Main Street, knocked her down."
I was a stranger here myself, I said,
And bought the *New York Times*, and went to bed.

THE GREEN SHEPHERD

HERE sit a shepherd and a shepherdess,
He playing on his melancholy flute;

The sea wind ruffles up her simple dress
And shows the delicacy of her foot.

And there you see Constantinople's wall
With arrows and Greek fire, molten lead;
Down from a turret seven virgins fall,
Hands folded, each one praying on her head.

The shepherd yawns and puts his flute away.
It's time, she murmurs, we were going back.
He offers certain reasons she should stay—
But neither sees the dragon on their track.

A dragon like a car in a garage
Is in the wood, his long tail sticking out.
Here rides St. George, swinging his sword and targe,
And sticks the grinning dragon in the snout.

Puffing a smoke ring, like the cigarette
Over Times Square, Sir Dragon snorts his last.
St. George takes off his armor in a sweat.
The Middle Ages have been safely passed.

What is the sail that crosses the still bay,
Unnoticed by the shepherds? It could be
A caravel that's sailing to Cathay,
Westward from Palos on the unknown sea.

But the green shepherd travels in her eye
And whispers nothings in his lady's ear,
And sings a little song, that roses die,
Carpe diem, which she seems pleased to hear.

The vessel they ignored still sails away
So bravely on the water, Westward Ho!
And murdering, in a religious way,
Brings Jesus to the Gulf of Mexico.

Now Portugal is fading, and the state
Of Castile rising purple on Peru;
Now England, now America grows great—
With which these lovers have nothing to do.

What do they care if time, uncompassed, drift
To China, and the crew is a baboon?
But let him whisper always, and her lift
The oceans in her eyelids to the moon.

The dragon rises crackling in the air,
And who is god but Dagon? Wings careen,
Rejoicing, on the Russian hemisphere.
Meanwhile, the shepherd dotes upon her skin.

Old Aristotle, having seen this pass,
From where he studied in the giant's cave,
Went in and shut his book and locked the brass
And lay down with a shudder in his grave.

The groaning pole had gone more than a mile;
These shepherds did not feel it where they loved,
For time was sympathetic all the while
And on the magic mountain nothing moved.

MY FATHER IN THE NIGHT COMMANDING NO

My father in the night commanding No
Has work to do. Smoke issues from his lips;
    He reads in silence.
The frogs are croaking and the street lamps glow.

And then my mother winds the gramophone—
The Bride of Lammermoor begins to shriek—

Or reads a story
About a prince, a castle, and a dragon.

The moon is glittering above the hill.
I stand before the gateposts of the King—
        So runs the story—
Of Thule, at midnight when the mice are still.

And I have been in Thule! It has come true—
The journey and the danger of the world,
        All that there is
To bear and to enjoy, endure and do.

Landscapes, seascapes . . . Where have I been led?
The names of cities—Paris, Venice, Rome—
        Held out their arms.
A feathered god, seductive, went ahead.

Here is my house. Under a red rose tree
A child is swinging; another gravely plays.
        They are not surprised
That I am here; they were expecting me.

And yet my father sits and reads in silence,
My mother sheds a tear, the moon is still,
        And the dark wind
Is murmuring that nothing ever happens.

Beyond his jurisdiction as I move,
Do I not prove him wrong? And yet, it's true
        They will not change
There, on the stage of terror and of love.

The actors in that playhouse always sit
In fixed positions—father, mother, child
        With painted eyes.
How sad it is to be a little puppet!

Their heads are wooden. And you once pretended
To understand them! Shake them as you will,
    They cannot speak.
Do what you will, the comedy is ended.

Father, why did you work? Why did you weep,
Mother? Was the story so important?
    "Listen!" the wind
Said to the children, and they fell asleep.

EDITH SITWELL, *born September 7, 1887, in Scarborough, Yorkshire, lives in London and at her ancestral home, Renishaw, Derbyshire, and usually spends part of each year at the castle of her brother, Sir Osbert, in Montegufoni, near Florence. The three Sitwells—Dame Edith, Sir Osbert, and Sacheverell—are the most famous family of writers in the contemporary world. She is known for her distinctive mode of costume, which often suggests the medieval. Her interest in English literary and social history has led to the writing of such books as* Bath, Alexander Pope, The English Eccentrics, *and a biography of Elizabeth I. She has made a number of reading tours of the United States.*

Said the Lion to the Lioness—'When you are amber dust—
No more a raging fire like the heat of the Sun
(No liking but all lust)—
Remember still the flowering of the amber blood and bone,
The rippling of bright muscles like a sea,
Remember the rose-prickles of bright paws,
Though we shall mate no more
Till the fire of that sun the heart and the moon-cold bone are one.'

Said the Skeleton lying upon the sands of Time—
'The great gold planet that is the mourning heat of the Sun
Is greater than all gold, more powerful
Than the tawny body of a Lion that fire consumes
Like all that grows or leaps . . . so is the heart
More powerful than all dust. Once I was Hercules
Or Samson, strong as the pillars of the seas:
But the flames of the heart consumed me, and the mind
Is but a foolish wind.'

Said the Sun to the Moon—'When you are but a lonely white crone,
And I, a dead King in my golden armor somewhere in a dark wood,
Remember only this of our hopeless love:
That never till Time is done
Will the fire of the heart and the fire of the mind be one.'

STILL FALLS THE RAIN

The Raids, 1940. Night and Dawn

STILL falls the Rain—
Dark as the world of man, black as our loss—
Blind as the nineteen hundred and forty nails
Upon the Cross.

Still falls the Rain
With a sound like the pulse of the heart that is changed to the hammer-
  beat
In the Potter's Field, and the sound of the impious feet

On the Tomb:
   Still falls the Rain
In the Field of Blood where the small hopes breed and the human brain
Nurtures its greed, that worm with the brow of Cain.

Still falls the Rain
At the feet of the Starved Man hung upon the Cross.
Christ that each day, each night, nails there, have mercy on us—

On Dives and on Lazarus:
Under the Rain the sore and the gold are as one.

Still falls the Rain—
Still falls the Blood from the Starved Man's wounded Side:
He bears in His Heart all wounds—those of the light that died,
The last faint spark
In the self-murdered heart, the wounds of the sad uncomprehending
    dark,
The wounds of the baited bear—
The blind and weeping bear whom the keepers beat
On his helpless flesh . . . the tears of the hunted hare.

Still falls the Rain—
Then—O Ile leape up to my God: who pulles me doune—
See, see where Christ's blood streames in the firmament:
It flows from the Brow we nailed upon the tree
Deep to the dying, to the thirsting heart
That holds the fires of the world—dark-smirched with pain
As Caesar's laurel crown.

Then sounds the voice of One who like the heart of man
Was once a child who among beasts has lain—
'Still do I love, still shed my innocent light, my Blood, for thee.'

SCOTCH RHAPSODY

'Do not take a bath in Jordan,
              Gordon,
On the holy Sabbath, on the peaceful day!'
Said the huntsman, playing on his old bagpipe,
Boring to death the pheasant and the snipe—
Boring the ptarmigan and grouse for fun—
Boring them worse than a nine-bore gun.

Till the flaxen leaves where the prunes are ripe
Heard the tartan wind a-droning in the pipe,
And they heard MacPherson say:
'Where do the waves go? What hotels
Hide their bustles and their gay ombrelles?
And would there be room?—Would there be *room*?
　　Would there be room for me?'
There is a hotel at Ostend
Cold as the wind, without an end,
Haunted by ghostly poor relations
Of Bostonian conversations
(Bagpipes rotting through the walls).
And there the pearl-ropes fall like shawls
With a noise like marine waterfalls.
And 'Another little drink wouldn't do us any harm'
Pierces through the Sabbatical calm.
And that is the place for me!
So do not take a bath in Jordan,
　　　　　　Gordon,
On the holy Sabbath, on the peaceful day—
Or you'll never go to heaven, Gordon MacPherson,
And speaking purely as a private person
That is the place—*that* is the place—that is the *place* for me!

WILLIAM JAY SMITH, *born
1918, in Winnfield, Louisiana, lives
with his wife, the poet Barbara
Howes, and their two sons in the
village of North Pownal, Vermont.
He was educated at Washington
University, Columbia, and Oxford,
which he attended as a Rhodes
scholar. During World War II he
was Navy personnel officer of a
Pacific air base and, for two years,
liaison officer aboard a French war
vessel in the Atlantic and the
Pacific. He has taught at Wesleyan
University, Columbia, and Williams
College and is now an active member of the Vermont Legislature.
Besides poetry, he has published
books for children—*Laughing Time
and Boy Blue's Book of Beasts, *as
well as translations of the poems of
Laforgue and Larbaud, and* The
Spectra Hoax.

Look at him there in his stovepipe hat,
His high-top shoes, and his handsome collar;
Only my Daddy could look like that,
And I love my Daddy like he loves his Dollar.

The screen door bangs, and it sounds so funny—
There he is in a shower of gold;
His pockets are stuffed with folding money,
His lips are blue, and his hands feel cold.

He hangs in the hall by his black cravat,
The ladies faint, and the children holler:
Only my Daddy could look like that,
And I love my Daddy like he loves his Dollar.

Life is inadequate, but there are many real
    Things of beauty here: the flower peddler's cart
Adrift like an island in the city streets,
    The peddler's mare, lifting her mighty hoof
Aware of all that beauty. And the slate
    Where the schoolboy draws his forty-eight
States, ready to make room for the world.
    The sea's enormous wealth; societies
Commemorating blizzards in the North; the small
    White birds in the South where trees are tall
And the hoopsnake bounces downhill like a wagon wheel.

There are real things of beauty; all
    These things were yours. The shadowy

And fabulous quality of the imaginary
	Is presumed; we know it shall
One day take the world. Now the sea
	Has but poor mimic in the shell; a bell
Must free itself of sound, must break with freedom
	To be free. And so you broke, and so you waved
Farewell to us, and turned away
	To a mirror of completion and of certainty,
To clocks that tick, and have no time to tell.

Poems are praise, and poems cannot end.
	There is no answer for we do not ask.
Upon a cliff of sadness the trees bend
	Strangely toward the sea; the end
Is in oneself. O our unsuffering, suffering
	Sick friend, so life is adequate
And you are whole? There are real things of beauty
	Here, and sorrow is our praise. The day
Is bright, the cloud bank white with gulls.
	And while we lie, and watch the ocean roll,
The wind, an Indian paintbrush, sweeps the sky.

THE CLOSING OF THE RODEO

The lariat snaps; the cowboy rolls
	His pack, and mounts and rides away.
Back to the land the cowboy goes.

Plumes of smoke from the factory sway
	In the setting sun. The curtain falls,
A train in the darkness pulls away.

Goodbye, says the rain on the iron roofs.
	Goodbye, say the barber poles.
Dark drum the vanishing horses' hooves.

W. D. SNODGRASS, *born January 5, 1926, in Wilkinsburg, Pennsylvania, lives with his second wife and his two children in Detroit, where he teaches in the creative-writing program of Wayne State University. He attended Geneva College for a year, joined the Navy as an apprentice seaman and, three years later, entered the University of Iowa, from which he graduated. He has taught at Cornell and the University of Rochester. The first book he published,* Heart's Needle, *was awarded the Pulitzer Prize in 1960.*

Up the reputable walks of old established trees
They stalk, children of the *nouveaux riches;* chimes
Of the tall Clock Tower drench their heads in blessing:
"I don't wanna play at your house;
I don't like you any more."
My house stands opposite, on the other hill,
Among meadows, with the orchard fences down and falling;
Deer come almost to the door.
You cannot see it, even in this clearest morning.
White birds hang in the air between
Over the garbage landfill and those homes thereto adjacent,
Hovering slowly, turning, settling down
Like the flakes sifting imperceptibly onto the little town
In a waterball of glass.
And yet, this morning, beyond this quiet scene,
The floating birds, the backyards of the poor,
Beyond the shopping plaza, the dead canal, the hillside
        lying tilted in the air,
Tomorrow has broken out today:
Riot in Algeria, in Cyprus, in Alabama;
Aged in wrong, the empires are declining,
And China gathers, soundlessly, like evidence.
What shall I say to the young on such a morning?—
Mind is the one salvation?—also grammar?—
No; my little ones lean not toward revolt. They
Are the Whites, the vaguely furiously driven, who resist
Their souls with such passivity
As would make Quakers swear. All day, dear Lord, all day
They wear their godhead lightly.
They look out from their hill and say,
To themselves, "We have nowhere to go but down;
The great destination is to stay."

Surely the nations will be reasonable;
They look at the world—don't they?—the world's way?
The clock just now has nothing more to say.

THE green catalpa tree has turned
All white; the cherry blooms once more.
In one whole year I haven't learned
A blessed thing they pay you for.
The blossoms snow down in my hair;
The trees and I will soon be bare.

The trees have more than I to spare.
The sleek, expensive girls I teach,
Younger and pinker every year,
Bloom gradually out of reach.
The pear tree lets its petals drop
Like dandruff on a tabletop.

The girls have grown so young by now
I have to nudge myself to stare.
This year they smile and mind me how
My teeth are falling with my hair.
In thirty years I may not get
Younger, shrewder, or out of debt.

The tenth time, just a year ago,
I made myself a little list
Of all the things I'd ought to know,
Then told my parents, analyst,
And everyone who's trusted me
I'd be substantial, presently.

I haven't read one book about
A book or memorized one plot.
Or found a mind I did not doubt.
I learned one date. And then forgot.
And one by one the solid scholars
Get the degrees, the jobs, the dollars.

And smile above their starchy collars.
I taught my classes Whitehead's notions;
One lovely girl, a song of Mahler's.
Lacking a source-book or promotions,
I showed one child the colors of
A luna moth and how to love.

I taught myself to name my name,
To bark back, loosen love and crying;
To ease my woman so she came,
To ease an old man who was dying.
I have not learned how often I
Can win, can love, but choose to die.

I have not learned there is a lie
Love shall be blonder, slimmer, younger;
That my equivocating eye
Loves only by my body's hunger;
That I have forces, true to feel,
Or that the lovely world is real.

While scholars speak authority
And wear their ulcers on their sleeves,
My eyes in spectacles shall see
These trees procure and spend their leaves.
There is a value underneath
The gold and silver in my teeth.

Though trees turn bare and girls turn wives,
We shall afford our costly seasons;

There is a gentleness survives
That will outspeak and has its reasons.
There is a loveliness exists,
Preserves us, not for specialists.

STEPHEN SPENDER *was born February 28, 1909, in London, where he now lives with his wife, the pianist Natasha Litvin, and his two children. He was educated at Oxford, where he became a friend of W. H. Auden and with whom he was popularly associated as joint leader of the "English Group," whose other members were Cecil Day Lewis and Louis MacNeice. He is often regarded as a sort of roving ambassador of modern letters, an honorary title attendant upon his lifelong editorial and political activities and his wide travels as lecturer and cultural representative in America, Europe, and Asia. He is a frequent lecturer and visiting professor at American universities. Since 1953, he has been a coeditor of* Encounter, *an international monthly magazine sponsored by the Congress for Cultural Freedom.*

AFTER the first powerful plain manifesto
The black statement of pistons, without more fuss
But gliding like a queen, she leaves the station.
Without bowing and with restrained unconcern
She passes the houses which humbly crowd outside,
The gasworks and at last the heavy page
Of death, printed by gravestones in the cemetery.
Beyond the town there lies the open country
Where, gathering speed, she acquires mystery,
The luminous self-possession of ships on ocean.
It is now she begins to sing—at first quite low
Then loud, and at last with a jazzy madness—
The song of her whistle screaming at curves,
Of deafening tunnels, brakes, innumerable bolts.
And always light, aerial, underneath
Goes the elate metre of her wheels.
Steaming through metal landscape on her lines
She plunges new eras of wild happiness
Where speed throws up strange shapes, broad curves
And parallels clean like the steel of guns.
At last, further than Edinburgh or Rome,
Beyond the crest of the world, she reaches night
Where only a low streamline brightness
Of phosphorus on the tossing hills is white.
Ah, like a comet through flame she moves entranced
Wrapt in her music no bird song, no, nor bough
Breaking with honey buds, shall ever equal.

Far far from gusty waves, these children's faces.
Like rootless weeds the torn hair round their paleness.
The tall girl with her weighed-down head. The paper-seeming boy with
    rat's eyes. The stunted unlucky heir
Of twisted bones, reciting a father's gnarled disease,
His lesson from his desk. At back of the dim class,
One unnoted, sweet and young: his eyes live in a dream
Of squirrels' game, in tree room, other than this.

On sour cream walls, donations. Shakespeare's head
Cloudless at dawn, civilized dome riding all cities.
Belled, flowery, Tyrolese valley. Open-handed map
Awarding the world its world. And yet, for these
Children, these windows, not this world, are world,
Where all their future's painted with a fog,
A narrow street sealed in with a lead sky,
Far far from rivers, capes, and stars of words.

Surely Shakespeare is wicked, the map a bad example
With ships and sun and love tempting them to steal—
For lives that slyly turn in their cramped holes
From fog to endless night? On their slag heap, these children
Wear skins peeped through by bones and spectacles of steel
With mended glass, like bottle bits on stones.
All of their time and space are foggy slum
So blot their maps with slums as big as doom.

Unless, governor, teacher, inspector, visitor,
This map becomes their window and these windows
That open on their lives like crouching tombs
Break, O break open, till they break the town
And show the children to the fields and all their world
Azure on their sands, to let their tongues

Run naked into books, the white and green leaves open
The history theirs whose language is the sun.

During the Spanish Civil War, Port Bou was a main
point of entry into Spain from France. This poem is
the meditation of a sympathetic stranger, enisled in a
remote seaside village, as he encounters the forces of
the peasant militia and observes, first with detach-
ment, finally with a grotesque sense of physical
involvement, their practice for war.

PORT BOU

As a child holds a pet
Arms clutching but with hands that do not join
And the coiled animal watches the gap
To outer freedom in animal air,
So the earth-and-rock flesh arms of this harbour
Embrace but do not enclose the sea
Which, through a gap, vibrates to the open sea
Where ships and dolphins swim and above is the sun.
In the bright winter sunlight I sit on the stone parapet
Of a bridge; my circling arms rest on a newspaper
Empty in my mind as the glittering stone
Because I search for an image
And seeing an image I count out the coined words
To remember the childish headlands of this harbour.
A lorry halts beside me with creaking brakes
And I look up at warm waving flag-like faces
Of militiamen staring down at my French newspaper.
'How do they speak of our struggle, over the frontier?'
I hold out the paper, but they refuse,

They did not ask for anything so precious
But only for friendly words and to offer me cigarettes.
In their smiling faces the war finds peace, the famished mouths
Of the rusty carbines brush against their trousers
Almost as fragilely as reeds;
And wrapped in a cloth—old mother in a shawl—
The terrible machine-gun rests.
They shout, salute back as the truck jerks forward
Over the vigorous hill, beyond the headland.
An old man passes, his running mouth,
With three teeth like bullets, spits out 'pom-pom-pom.'
The children run after; and, more slowly, the women
Clutching their clothes, follow over the hill;
Till the village is empty, for the firing practice,
And I am left alone on the bridge at the exact centre
Where the cleaving river trickles like saliva.
At the exact centre, solitary as a target,
Where nothing moves against a background of cardboard houses
Except the disgraceful skirring dogs; and the firing begins,
Across the harbour mouth from headland to headland,
White flecks of foam gashed by lead in the sea;
And the echo trails over its iron lash
Whipping the flanks of the surrounding hills.
My circling arms rest on the newspaper,
My mind seems paper where dust and ink fall,
I tell myself the shooting is only for practice,
And my body seems a cloth which the machine-gun stitches
Like a sewing machine, neatly, with cotton from a reel;
And the solitary, irregular, thin 'paffs' from the carbines
Draw on long needles white threads through my navel.

GEORGE STARBUCK, *born 1931, in Columbus, Ohio, studied at the California Institute of Technology, the University of Chicago, and Harvard. After the publication of his first book,* Bone Thoughts, *he spent a year in Europe as winner of the* Prix de Rome *and now lives with his second wife in Italy.*

WALKING *to the museum*
over the Outer Drive,
I think, before I see them
dead, of the bones alive.

How perfectly the snake smooths over the fact
he strings sharp beads around that charmer's neck.

Bird bone may be breakable, but
have you ever held a cat's jaw shut?
Brittle as ice.

Take mice:
the mouse is a berry, his bones mere seeds:
step on him once and see.

You mustn't think that the fish
choke on those bones, or that chickens wish.

The wise old bat
hangs his bones in a bag.

Two chicks ride a bike,
unlike
that legless swinger of crutches, the ostrich.

Only the skull of a man is much of an ashtray.

Each owl
turns on a dowel.

When all the other tents are struck, an old
elephant pitches himself on his own poles.

But as for my bones—
tug of a toe, blunt-bowed barge of a thighbone,
gondola-squadron of ribs, and the jaw scow—

they weather the swing and storm of the flesh they plow,
out of conjecture of shore, one jolt from land.

I climb the museum steps like a beach.
There, on squared stone, some cast-up keels bleach.
Here, a dark sea speaks with white hands.

NEW STRAIN

You should see these musical mice.
    When we start the device
they rise on their haunches and sniff
    the air as if
they remembered all about dancing.
    Soon they are chancing
a step or two, and a turn.
    How quickly they learn
The rest, and with leaps and spins
    master the ins
and outs of it, round and round
    and round. We found
the loudest music best
    and now we test
with a kind of electric bell
    which works as well.

In two to two-and-a-quarter
    minutes, a shorter
rhythm captures the front
    legs, and they stunt
in somersaults until
    they become still

and seem to have lost their breath.
    But the sign of death
is later: the ears, which have been
    flat, like a skin
skullcap, relax and flare
    as if the air
might hold some further thing
    for the listening.

WALLACE STEVENS, *born October 2, 1879, in Reading, Pennsylvania, died in 1955. He was educated at Harvard and the New York Law School and, in 1904, began to practice law in New York City. From 1916 until his death, he lived with his wife and daughter in Hartford, Connecticut, where he was associated with the Hartford Accident and Indemnity Company, of which he became vice-president in 1934. He did not publish his first book of poems,* Harmonium, *until he was forty years old. As a businessman, he kept his writing career a strictly private preoccupation and lived wholly apart from literary society.*

*The central issue of this poem is the contrast between
the radiant simplicity of a bowl of carnations and
the restlessness of the mind that observes it. The issue
is closely examined and then resolved in one forthright
statement. The true and final paradise for modern
man is not the static perfection of a still life,
however beautiful it may be, however per-
suasively it may invite him to emulation,
because "The imperfect is our paradise."*

THE POEMS OF OUR CLIMATE

I

CLEAR water in a brilliant bowl,
Pink and white carnations. The light
In the room more like a snowy air,
Reflecting snow. A newly-fallen snow
At the end of winter when afternoons return.
Pink and white carnations—one desires
So much more than that. The day itself
Is simplified: a bowl of white,
Cold, a cold porcelain, low and round,
With nothing more than the carnations there.

II

Say even that this complete simplicity
Stripped one of all one's torments, concealed
The evilly compounded, vital I
And made it fresh in a world of white,
A world of clear water, brilliant-edged,
Still one would want more, one would need more,
More than a world of white and snowy scents.

III

There would still remain the never-resting mind,
So that one would want to escape, come back
To what had been so long composed.

WALLACE STEVENS *357*

The imperfect is our paradise.
Note that, in this bitterness, delight,
Since the imperfect is so hot in us,
Lies in flawed words and stubborn sounds.

*Beginning with random notations on any man's emo-
tions and on a variety of natural phenomena, the
speaker delights in the accidents by which the mind
and the natural world are made congruent. This
sense of participation, he implies, is not dependent
upon myths, gods, religions, but is open to everyone
since "ignorant man, alone" has the capacity to see
metaphors in nature and to feel that his life is one
with the energy that flows through all things.*

THE SENSE OF THE SLEIGHT-OF-HAND MAN

ONE's grand flights, one's Sunday baths,
One's tootings at the weddings of the soul
Occur as they occur. So bluish clouds
Occurred above the empty house and the leaves
Of the rhododendrons rattled their gold,
As if someone lived there. Such floods of white
Came bursting from the clouds. So the wind
Threw its contorted strength around the sky.

Could you have said the bluejay suddenly
Would swoop to earth? It is a wheel, the rays
Around the sun. The wheel survives the myths.
The fire eye in the clouds survives the gods.

To think of a dove with an eye of grenadine
And pines that are cornets, so it occurs,
And a little island full of geese and stars:

It may be that the ignorant man, alone,
Has any chance to mate his life with life
That is the sensual, pearly spouse, the life
That is fluent in even the wintriest bronze.

*A grand, well-upholstered, dowager-like lady on a
bored donkey rides laboriously upward through the
moonlight of imagination to reach the summit of
reality; a poor figure of a knight on horseback goes
clattering downhill, seeking the sun and the magical
realm of the imagination. The lady's mission is hopeless: she already possesses as much reality as her
limited mind can accommodate. The man on horseback
is more capable. By directing his search into life
instead of away from it, he achieves the victory denied
her—"The ultimate elegance: the imagined land."*

MRS. ALFRED URUGUAY

So what said the others and the sun went down
And, in the brown blues of evening, the lady said,
In the donkey's ear, "I fear that elegance
Must struggle like the rest." She climbed until
The moonlight in her lap, mewing her velvet,
And her dress were one and she said, "I have said no
To everything, in order to get at myself.
I have wiped away moonlight like mud. Your innocent ear
And I, if I rode naked, are what remain."

The moonlight crumbled to degenerate forms,
While she approached the real, upon her mountain,
With lofty darkness. The donkey was there to ride,
To hold by the ear, even though it wished for a bell,
Wished faithfully for a falsifying bell.

Neither the moonlight could change it. And for her,
To be, regardless of velvet, could never be more
Than to be, she could never differently be,
Her no and no made yes impossible.

Who was it passed her there on a horse all will,
What figure of capable imagination?
Whose horse clattered on the road on which she rose,
As it descended, blind to her velvet and
The moonlight? Was it a rider intent on the sun,
A youth, a lover with phosphorescent hair,
Dressed poorly, arrogant of his streaming forces,
Lost in an integration of the martyrs' bones,
Rushing from what was real; and capable?

The villages slept as the capable man went down,
Time swished on the village clocks and dreams were alive,
The enormous gongs gave edges to their sounds,
As the rider, no chevalere and poorly dressed,
Impatient of the bells and midnight forms,
Rode over the picket rocks, rode down the road,
And, capable, created in his mind,
Eventual victor, out of the martyrs' bones,
The ultimate elegance: the imagined land.

*This poem is a poetic retelling of a story from the
Apocrypha: Susanna, the beautiful wife of Joachim,
was spied upon by two Hebrew elders as she bathed.
When they attempted to seduce her, she drove them
off and soon brought charges against them. They,
in turn, charged that it was she who had attempted
to seduce them. Their word was accepted against hers
and Susanna was condemned to death. But just as
she was about to be executed, the prophet Daniel
proved her innocence, and the elders were put to
death instead. Peter Quince is a fictitious name given
to an individual who, moved by passion for a woman
who is absent, recreates the story of Susanna
in terms of a musical composition played
on a clavier, a delicate forerunner of the piano.*

PETER QUINCE AT THE CLAVIER

I

JUST as my fingers on these keys
Make music, so the selfsame sounds
On my spirit make a music, too.

Music is feeling, then, not sound;
And thus it is that what I feel,
Here in this room, desiring you,

Thinking of your blue-shadowed silk,
Is music. It is like the strain
Waked in the elders by Susanna.

Of a green evening, clear and warm,
She bathed in her still garden, while
The red-eyed elders watching, felt

The basses of their beings throb
In witching chords, and their thin blood
Pulse pizzicati of Hosanna.

II

In the green water, clear and warm,
Susanna lay.

She searched
The touch of springs,
And found
Concealed imaginings.
She sighed,
For so much melody.

Upon the bank, she stood
In the cool
Of spent emotions.
She felt, among the leaves,
The dew
Of old devotions.

She walked upon the grass,
Still quavering.
The winds were like her maids,
On timid feet,
Fetching her woven scarves,
Yet wavering.

A breath upon her hand
Muted the night.
She turned—
A cymbal crashed,
And roaring horns.

III

Soon, with a noise like tambourines,
Came her attendant Byzantines.

They wondered why Susanna cried
Against the elders by her side;

And as they whispered, the refrain
Was like a willow swept by rain.

Anon, their lamps' uplifted flame
Revealed Susanna and her shame.

And then, the simpering Byzantines
Fled, with a noise like tambourines.

IV

Beauty is momentary in the mind—
The fitful tracing of a portal;
But in the flesh it is immortal.

The body dies; the body's beauty lives.
So evenings die, in their green going,
A wave, interminably flowing.
So gardens die, their meek breath scenting
The cowl of winter, done repenting.

So maidens die, to the auroral
Celebration of a maiden's choral.

Susanna's music touched the bawdy strings
Of those white elders; but, escaping,
Left only Death's ironic scraping.
Now, in its immortality, it plays
On the clear viol of her memory,
And makes a constant sacrament of praise.

MAY SWENSON, *born 1927, in Utah, lives in New York City, where she is an editor of the publishing house New Directions. She attended Utah State Agricultural College and then worked for a year as a reporter on the Salt Lake* Deseret News *before going to New York.*

THE summer that I was ten—
Can it be there was only one
summer that I was ten? It must

have been a long one then—
each day I'd go out to choose
a fresh horse from my stable

which was a willow grove
down by the old canal.
I'd go on my two bare feet.

But when, with my brother's jack-knife,
I had cut me a long limber horse
with a good thick knob for a head,

and peeled him slick and clean
except a few leaves for the tail,
and cinched my brother's belt

around his head for a rein,
I'd straddle and canter him fast
up the grass bank to the path,

trot along in the lovely dust
that talcumed over his hoofs,
hiding my toes, and turning

his feet to swift half-moons.
The willow knob with the strap
jouncing between my thighs

was the pommel and yet the poll
of my nickering pony's head.
My head and my neck were mine,

yet they were shaped like a horse.
My hair flopped to the side
like the mane of a horse in the wind.

My forelock swung in my eyes,
my neck arched and I snorted.
I shied and skittered and reared,

stopped and raised my knees,
pawed at the ground and quivered.
My teeth bared as we wheeled

and swished through the dust again.
I was the horse and the rider,
and the leather I slapped to his rump

spanked my own behind.
Doubled, my two hoofs beat
a gallop along the bank,

the wind twanged in my mane,
my mouth squared to the bit.
And yet I sat on my steed

quiet, negligent riding,
my toes standing the stirrups,
my thighs hugging his ribs.

At a walk we drew up to the porch.
I tethered him to a paling.
Dismounting, I smoothed my skirt

and entered the dusky hall.
My feet on the clean linoleum
left ghostly toes in the hall.

Where have you been? said my mother.
Been riding, I said from the sink,
and filled me a glass of water.

What's that in your pocket? she said.
Just my knife. It weighted my pocket
and stretched my dress awry.

Go tie back your hair, said my mother,
and *Why is your mouth all green?*
*Rob Roy, he pulled some clover
as we crossed the field,* I told her.

ALLEN TATE, *born November 19, 1899, in*
Winchester, Kentucky, lives with his second wife,
the poet Isabella Gardner, in Minneapolis, where
he is professor of English at the University of
Minnesota. He is a graduate of Vanderbilt Uni-
versity, where he was one of the founders of
The Fugitive, *the magazine which served as the*
mouthpiece of a movement in Southern letters
that deeply influenced the careers of a number
of writers identified with the "new criticism."
One of America's leading literary critics, he has
published highly regarded studies of modern
literature and has otherwise contributed his talents
to a number of editorial and academic positions.

WHEN Alexander Pope strolled in the city
Strict was the glint of pearl and gold sedans.
Ladies leaned out more out of fear than pity
For Pope's tight back was rather a goat's than man's.

Often one thinks the urn should have more bones
Than skeletons provide for speedy dust,
The urn gets hollow, cobwebs brittle as stones
Weave to the funeral shell a frivolous rust.

And he who dribbled couplets like a snake
Coiled to a lithe precision in the sun
Is missing. The jar is empty; you may break
It only to find that Mr. Pope is gone.

What requisitions of a verity
Prompted the wit and rage between his teeth
One cannot say. Around a crooked tree
A moral climbs whose name should be a wreath.

DEATH OF LITTLE BOYS

WHEN little boys grown patient at last, weary,
Surrender their eyes immeasurably to the night,
The event will rage terrific as the sea;
Their bodies fill a crumbling room with light.

Then you will touch at the bedside, torn in two,
Gold curls now deftly intricate with gray
As the windowpane extends a fear to you
From one peeled aster drenched with the wind all day.

And over his chest the covers in an ultimate dream
Will mount to the teeth, ascend the eyes, press back
The locks—while round his sturdy belly gleam
The suspended breaths, white spars above the wreck:

Till all the guests, come in to look, turn down
Their palms, and delirium assails the cliff
Of Norway where you ponder, and your little town
Reels like a sailor drunk in his rotten skiff.

The bleak sunshine shrieks its chipped music then
Out to the milkweed amid the fields of wheat.
There is a calm for you where men and women
Unroll the chill precision of moving feet.

DYLAN THOMAS, *born October 22, 1914,*
in Swansea, Wales, died in New York City on
November 9, 1953. He received no formal educa-
tion beyond secondary school, and his first pro-
fessional writing was done as a journalist in his
native town. Until his death, which occurred during
the fourth of the extensive reading tours he made
in the United States, he lived with his wife and
three children in the village of Laugharne, on the
southwest coast of Wales. His "play for voices,"
Under Milk Wood, *has been widely produced in*
the United States and in Europe, and his recorded
readings of his own poems have had an unpar-
alleled success with a large public.

The hunchback in the park
A solitary mister
Propped between trees and water
From the opening of the garden lock
That lets the trees and water enter
Until the Sunday sombre bell at dark

Eating bread from a newspaper
Drinking water from the chained cup
That the children filled with gravel
In the fountain basin where I sailed my ship
Slept at night in a dog kennel
But nobody chained him up.

Like the park birds he came early
Like the water he sat down
And Mister they called Hey mister
The truant boys from the town
Running when he had heard them clearly
On out of sound

Past lake and rockery
Laughing when he shook his paper
Hunchbacked in mockery
Through the loud zoo of the willow groves
Dodging the park keeper
With his stick that picked up leaves.

And the old dog sleeper
Alone between nurses and swans
While the boys among willows
Made the tigers jump out of their eyes
To roar on the rockery stones
And the groves were blue with sailors

Made all day until bell time
A woman figure without fault
Straight as a young elm
Straight and tall from his crooked bones
That she might stand in the night
After the locks and chains

All night in the unmade park
After the railings and shrubberies
The birds the grass the trees the lake
And the wild boys innocent as strawberries
Had followed the hunchback
To his kennel in the dark.

*This poem, one of a number that reflect Dylan
Thomas's experience when he served as a fire warden
during the bombings of London, is based upon a
solemn irony. Whereas its title states a firm reluctance
to honor the child's death with an elegy, the poem
proceeds to do precisely that. To celebrate the event
with an elegy, the poet implies, would be to accept
it, and this he refuses to do. "I shall not murder/
The mankind of her going with a grave truth," he
says, since grave truths are the same old homilies and
clichés that have always been spoken at burial ceremonies. He would prefer to honor this death by re-
fusing to see it, not as a single tragedy, but as another
frightful reminder of the murderous history of mankind.*

A REFUSAL TO MOURN THE DEATH, BY FIRE, OF A CHILD IN LONDON

NEVER until the mankind making
Bird beast and flower
Fathering and all humbling darkness

Tells with silence the last light breaking
And the still hour
Is come of the sea tumbling in harness

And I must enter again the round
Zion of the water bead
And the synagogue of the ear of corn
Shall I let pray the shadow of a sound
Or sow my salt seed
In the least valley of sackcloth to mourn

The majesty and burning of the child's death.
I shall not murder
The mankind of her going with a grave truth
Nor blaspheme down the stations of the breath
With any further
Elegy of innocence and youth.

Deep with the first dead lies London's daughter,
Robed in the long friends,
The grains beyond age, the dark veins of her mother,
Secret by the unmourning water
Of the riding Thames.
After the first death, there is no other.

*David Thomas, a quiet, gentle, dignified man, was for
many years a dedicated schoolteacher who, in his
youth, had hoped to become a poet. This poem, written
as a tribute by his son as he watched the progress
of his father's fatal illness, was completed barely
a year before the death of Dylan Thomas himself.*

DO NOT GO GENTLE INTO THAT GOOD NIGHT

Do not go gentle into that good night,
Old age should burn and rave at close of day;
Rage, rage against the dying of the light.

Though wise men at their end know dark is right,
Because their words had forked no lightning they
Do not go gentle into that good night.

Good men, the last wave by, crying how bright
Their frail deeds might have danced in a green bay,
Rage, rage against the dying of the light.

Wild men who caught and sang the sun in flight,
And learn, too late, they grieved it on its way,
Do not go gentle into that good night.

Grave men, near death, who see with blinding sight
Blind eyes could blaze like meteors and be gay,
Rage, rage against the dying of the light.

And you, my father, there on the sad height,
Curse, bless, me now with your fierce tears, I pray.
Do not go gentle into that good night.
Rage, rage against the dying of the light.

On the map, Fern Hill is located near the village of
Laugharne (pronounced larn), in southwestern Wales,
where Dylan Thomas lived. In this poem, he gives
the name to another location—a hillside farm where,
as a child, he spent many summers with his aunt
and uncle. This farm has pasture lands overlooking
the estuary of the river Towy. The old whitewashed
house is surrounded by a number of barns, high
mounds of hay, and an apple orchard of great age.

FERN HILL

Now as I was young and easy under the apple boughs
About the lilting house and happy as the grass was green,
    The night above the dingle starry,
        Time let me hail and climb
      Golden in the heydays of his eyes,
And honoured among wagons I was prince of the apple towns
And once below a time I lordly had the trees and leaves
       Trail with daisies and barley
      Down the rivers of the windfall light.

And as I was green and carefree, famous among the barns
About the happy yard and singing as the farm was home,
    In the sun that is young once only,
        Time let me play and be
      Golden in the mercy of his means,
And green and golden I was huntsman and herdsman, the calves
Sang to my horn, the foxes on the hills barked clear and cold,
      And the sabbath rang slowly
    In the pebbles of the holy streams.

All the sun long it was running, it was lovely, the hay
Fields high as the house, the tunes from the chimneys, it was air
    And playing, lovely and watery
      And fire green as grass.

And nightly under the simple stars
As I rode to sleep the owls were bearing the farm away,
All the moon long I heard, blessed among stables, the nightjars
    Flying with the ricks, and the horses
        Flashing into the dark.

And then to awake, and the farm, like a wanderer white
With the dew, come back, the cock on his shoulder: it was all
    Shining, it was Adam and maiden,
        The sky gathered again
    And the sun grew round that very day.
So it must have been after the birth of the simple light
In the first, spinning place, the spellbound horses walking warm
    Out of the whinnying green stable
        On to the fields of praise.

And honoured among foxes and pheasants by the gay house
Under the new made clouds and happy as the heart was long,
    In the sun born over and over,
        I ran my heedless ways,
    My wishes raced through the house high hay
And nothing I cared, at my sky blue trades, that time allows
In all his tuneful turning so few and such morning songs
    Before the children green and golden
        Follow him out of grace.

Nothing I cared, in the lamb white days, that time would take me
Up to the swallow thronged loft by the shadow of my hand,
    In the moon that is always rising,
        Nor that riding to sleep
    I should hear him fly with the high fields
And wake to the farm forever fled from the childless land.
Oh as I was young and easy in the mercy of his means,
        Time held me green and dying
    Though I sang in my chains like the sea.

JOHN WAIN, *born March 14, 1925, in Stoke-on-Trent, Staffordshire, England, lives with his second wife and their son in London. He was educated at St. John's College, Oxford, and then taught at Reading University before resigning to devote his time to writing. His works include novels, short stories, and volumes of criticism and essays, and he has lectured widely in the United States and in India.*

The January sky is deep and calm.
The mountain sprawls in comfort, and the sea
Sleeps in the crook of that enormous arm.

And Nature from a simple recipe—
Rocks, water, mist, a sunlit winter's day—
Has brewed a cup whose strength has dizzied me.

So little beauty is enough to pay;
The heart so soon yields up its store of love,
And where you love you cannot break away.

So sages never found it hard to prove
Nor prophets to declare in metaphor
That God and Nature must be hand in glove.

And this became the basis of their lore.
Then later poets found it easy going
To give the public what they bargained for,

And like a spectacled curator showing
The wares of his museum to the crowd,
They yearly waxed more eloquent and knowing,

More slick, more photographic, and more proud:
From Tennyson with notebook in his hand
(His truth to Nature fits him like a shroud)

To moderns who devoutly hymn the land.
So be it: each is welcome to his voice;
They are a gentle, if a useless, band.

But leave me free to make a sterner choice;
Content, without embellishment, to note
How little beauty bids the heart rejoice,

How little beauty catches at the throat.
Simply, I love this mountain and this bay
With love that I can never speak by rote,

And where you love you cannot break away.

THESE are my thoughts on realizing
That I am the same age as my father was
On the day I was born.

As a little scarlet howling mammal,
Crumpled and unformed, I depended entirely on someone
Not very different from what I am to-day.

When I think this over,
I feel more crumpled and unformed than ever:
I ask myself what I have done to compare with that.

It also makes me aware, inescapably,
Of having entered upon the high table-land,
The broad flat life of a mature man.

Where everything is seen from its actual distance,
E.g. childhood not so remote as to seem a boring myth,
Nor senility as something that awaits other people.

But deeper than that,
It is like entering a dark cone,
The shadow thrown across my life it derives from.

And deeper than that still,
It is the knowledge that life is the one communicable thing.
I called, I heard it from where I slept in seed and liquid.

The patterns of seed and brine coalesced in a solemn dance,
Whence my life arose in the form of a crest,
And has carried itself blindly forward until now.

In ignorance of its uniqueness until now,
Until I stumbled over these thoughts solid as bricks,
And like bricks fearsome in their everyday squareness.

ROBERT PENN WARREN, *born April 24, 1905, in Todd County, Kentucky, lives with his second wife, the writer Eleanor Clark, and their son and daughter in Fairfield, Connecticut. Currently a member of the Yale faculty, he was educated at Vanderbilt, California, and Yale and was a Rhodes scholar at Oxford. He has taught at Vanderbilt, at Louisiana State, where, with Cleanth Brooks, he edited the* Southern Review, *at the University of Minnesota, and at Yale. The wide public success of his novels, among them* All the King's Men *and* World Enough and Time, *has at times obscured the fact that he is one of the most accomplished of American poets.*

The oaks, how subtle and marine,
Bearded, and all the layered light
Above them swims; and thus the scene,
Recessed, awaits the positive night.

So, waiting, we in the grass now lie
Beneath the languorous tread of light:
The grasses, kelp-like, satisfy
The nameless motions of the air.

Upon the floor of light, and time,
Unmurmuring, of polyp made,
We rest; we are, as light withdraws,
Twin atolls on a shelf of shade.

Ages to our construction went,
Dim architecture, hour by hour:
And violence, forgot now, lent
The present stillness all its power.

The storm of noon above us rolled,
Of light the fury, furious gold,
The long drag troubling us, the depth:
Dark is unrocking, unrippling, still.

Passion and slaughter, ruth, decay
Descend, minutely whispering down,
Silted down swaying streams, to lay
Foundation for our voicelessness.

All our debate is voiceless here,
As all our rage, the rage of stone;
If hope is hopeless, then fearless fear,
And history is thus undone.

Our feet once wrought the hollow street
With echo when the lamps were dead
At windows, once our headlight glare
Disturbed the doe that, leaping, fled.

I do not love you less that now
The caged heart makes iron stroke,
Or less that all that light once gave
The graduate dark should now revoke.

We live in time so little time
And we learn all so painfully,
That we may spare this hour's term
To practice for eternity.

The "you" in this poem is anyone who seeks some
answer to his nameless sense of guilt, some explana-
tion for a malady no one can diagnose. He tries the
clinic, the past, and a rest cure in Florida, but nothing
works. He suffers and does not know why. Guilt
pursues him as he pursues blindly some solution to a burden as heavy as original sin.

PURSUIT

THE hunchback on the corner, with gum and shoelaces,
Has his own wisdom and pleasures, and may not be lured
To divulge them to you, for he has merely endured
Your appeal for his sympathy and your kind purchases;
And wears infirmity but as the general who turns
Apart, in his famous old greatcoat there on the hill
At dusk when the rapture and cannonade are still,
To muse withdrawn from the dead, from his gorgeous subalterns;

Or stares from the thicket of his familiar pain, like a fawn
That meets you a moment, wheels, in imperious innocence is gone.

Go to the clinic. Wait in the outer room
Where like an old possum the snag-nailed hand will hump
On its knee in murderous patience, and the pomp
Of pain swells like the Indies, or a plum.
And there you will stand, as on the Roman hill,
Stunned by each withdrawn gaze and severe shape,
The first barbarian victor stood to gape
At the sacrificial fathers, white-robed, still;
And even the feverish old Jew stares stern with authority
Till you feel like one who has come too late, or improperly clothed, to a
    party.

The doctor will take you now. He is burly and clean;
Listening, like lover or worshiper, bends at your heart;
But cannot make out just what it tries to impart;
So smiles; says you simply need a change of scene.
Of scene, of solace: therefore Florida,
Where Ponce de León clanked among the lilies,
Where white sails skit on blue and cavort like fillies,
And the shoulder gleams in the moonlit corridor.
A change of love: if love is a groping Godward, though blind,
No matter what crevice, cranny, chink, bright in dark, the pale tentacle
    find.

In Florida consider the flamingo
Its color passion but its neck a question;
Consider even that girl the other guests shun
On beach, at bar, in bed, for she may know
The secret you are seeking, after all;
Or the child you humbly sit by, excited and curly,
That screams on the shore at the sea's sunlit hurlyburly,
Till the mother calls its name, toward nightfall.

Till you sit alone: in the dire meridians, off Ireland, in fury
Of spume-tooth and dawnless sea-heave, salt rimes the lookout's devout
   eye.

Till you sit alone—which is the beginning of error—
Behind you the music and lights of the great hotel:
Solution, perhaps, is public, despair personal,
But history held to your breath clouds like a mirror.
There are many states, and towns in them, and faces,
But meanwhile, the little old lady in black, by the wall,
Who admires all the dancers, and tells you how just last fall
Her husband died in Ohio, and damp mists her glasses;
She blinks and croaks, like a toad or a Norn, in the horrible light,
And rattles her crutch, which may put forth a small bloom, perhaps white.

VERNON WATKINS, *born June 27, 1906, in Maesteg, South Wales, lives near Swansea with his wife and three children. He studied modern languages at Magdalene College, Cambridge, and then worked for a time as a clerk in Lloyds Bank. During World War II he served in the Royal Air Force, first as a police-man and then on special duties, eventually becoming a flight sergeant. He was a close friend and poetic mentor to Dylan Thomas, a relationship docu-mented in* Letters to Vernon Watkins, *published in 1957.*

THE cloud-backed heron will not move:
He stares into the stream.
He stands unfaltering while the gulls
And oyster-catchers scream.
He does not hear, he cannot see
The great white horses of the sea,
But fixes eyes on stillness
Below their flying team.

How long will he remain, how long
Have the grey woods been green?
The sky and the reflected sky,
Their glass he has not seen,
But silent as a speck of sand
Interpreting the sea and land,
His fall pulls down the fabric
Of all that windy scene.

Sailing with clouds and woods behind,
Pausing in leisured flight,
He stepped, alighting on a stone,
Dropped from the stars of night.
He stood there unconcerned with day,
Deaf to the tumult of the bay,
Watching a stone in water,
A fish's hidden light.

Sharp rocks drive back the breaking waves,
Confusing sea with air.
Bundles of spray blown mountain-high
Have left the shingle bare.
A shipwrecked anchor wedged by rocks,
Loosed by the thundering equinox,

Divides the herded waters,
The stallion and his mare.

Yet no distraction breaks the watch
Of that time-killing bird.
He stands unmoving on the stone;
Since dawn he has not stirred.
Calamity about him cries,
But he has fixed his golden eyes
On water's crooked tablet,
On light's reflected word.

This poem takes its title from the famous set of six tapestries (1509–1513) now in the Cluny Museum, in Paris. The first five panels deal with the senses of sight, hearing, smell, touch, and taste, and the sixth is "à mon seul désir."

THE LADY WITH THE UNICORN

ABOUT this lady many fruitful trees.
There the chaste unicorn before her knees
Stares in a glass to purify her sight.
At her right hand a lion sits,
And through the foliage, in and out, there flits
Many a bird; then hounds, with deer in flight:
Light is her element; her tapestry is light.

There is her mediaeval music met.
On the high table-top, with damask set
To charm, between the chaste beast and the strong,
An organ which her fingers play

Rests, and her pretty servant's hands obey
Those pipes with bellows to sustain their song
Attuned to distant stars, making their short life long.

This ended, gathered from some leafy way,
That servant brings her flowers upon a tray.
She lifts them to inhale their magic breath.
Caught in that breath's elusive maze,
She marvels. On a stool a monkey plays
With flowers from wicker trailing, strewn beneath,
A heaven of fragrance breathing through their mask of death.

Next, her right hand upholds that coat-of-arms
Seeming love's guardian against war's alarms,
And with her left she grips the upright horn.
This touch, while birds through branches peer,
Consecrates all the beasts as they appear,
Frisking among dark foliage to adorn
Her fingers that caress the constant unicorn.

A lion rampant grips the upright pole.
Her serving-maid now proffers her a bowl
Of peaches, damsons, almonds, grapes, and sweets.
This lady savours one, and sees
How white of almonds, red of mulberries,
Is each a praise no other tree repeats,
Now strangely on love's tree engrafted while she eats.

The senses leave a chain upon her tongue.
That place is hushed, from which the light is sprung.
Curtains are hung, embroidered with strange art.
The letters 'TO MY SOLE DESIRE'
Crown that pavilion with a band of fire
Whose folds the unicorn and lion part,
Revealing in their midst her love-awakened heart.

O sovereign balm to heal all mortal illness:
Long let him look, and still he will find stillness,
Her one betrothed, who sees her museful face.
This lady, with her flowers and hounds,
Woven in light, in air, in wooded grounds,
Transmits a glory wrought about her grace,
Caught in a sacred bond within the encircling space.

Let him look softly, with some seventh sense
Breaking that circle's hushed magnificence,
And see what universe her love controls,
Moving with hushed, divine intent
Through the five senses to their sacrament
Whose Eden turns between two silent poles,
Creating with pure speed that harmony of souls.

Where is the heart of mathematic space?
Throned on a mystery in that leafy place,
This lady's fingers hold, where distance flies,
The Past and Future like a skein
For her betrothed to wind, and loose again.
Lion and unicorn forbid disguise.
He looks, and she looks forth: there are no other eyes.

RICHARD WILBUR, *born March 1, 1921, in New York City, lives with his wife and four children in Portland, Connecticut. He is a graduate of Amherst College and has taught English literature at Harvard, Wellesley, and Wesleyan University, where he is now professor of English. In World War II he served in the infantry, mainly in Italy, and later spent long periods of residence with his family there and in France, New Mexico, and Texas. He wrote most of the lyrics for the Lillian Hellman-Leonard Bernstein musical* Candide; *his translation of Molière's* Le Misanthrope *was given an off-Broadway production in 1959.*

"Far enough down is China," somebody said.
"Dig deep enough and you might see the sky
As clear as at the bottom of a well.
Except it would be real—a different sky.
Then you could burrow down until you came
To China! Oh, it's nothing like New Jersey.
There's people, trees, and houses, and all that,
But much, much different. Nothing looks the same."

I went and got the trowel out of the shed
And sweated like a coolie all that morning,
Digging a hole beside the lilac-bush,
Down on my hands and knees. It was a sort
Of praying, I suspect. I watched my hand
Dig deep and darker, and I tried and tried
To dream a place where nothing was the same.
The trowel never did break through to blue.

Before the dream could weary of itself
My eyes were tired of looking into darkness,
My sunbaked head of hanging down a hole.
I stood up in a place I had forgotten,
Blinking and staggering while the earth went round
And showed me silver barns, the fields dozing
In palls of brightness, patens growing and gone
In the tides of leaves, and the whole sky china blue.
Until I got my balance back again
All that I saw was China, China, China.

Beasts in their major freedom
Slumber in peace tonight. The gull on his ledge
Dreams in the guts of himself the moon-plucked waves below,
And the sunfish leans on a stone, slept
By the lyric water,

In which the spotless feet
Of deer make dulcet splashes, and to which
The ripped mouse, safe in the owl's talon, cries
Concordance. Here there is no such harm
And no such darkness

As the selfsame moon observes
Where, warped in window-glass, it sponsors now
The werewolf's painful change. Turning his head away
On the sweaty bolster, he tries to remember
The mood of manhood,

But lies at last, as always,
Letting it happen, the fierce fur soft to his face,
Hearing with sharper ears the wind's exciting minors,
The leaves' panic, and the degradation
Of the heavy streams.

Meantime, at high windows
Far from thicket and pad-fall, suitors of excellence
Sigh and turn from their work to construe again the painful
Beauty of heaven, the lucid moon
And the risen hunter,

Making such dreams for men
As told will break their hearts as always, bringing
Monsters into the city, crows on the public statues,
Navies fed to the fish in the dark
Unbridled waters.

Spilling language and minute observations from stanza to stanza, this poem imitates an elaborate fountain that spills water in fixed yet constantly varied patterns. A trefoil is a tripartite design. A reticulum is a network. Areté is a Greek word roughly meaning virtue. *In Chapter V of the* Life of St. Francis, *there is mention of Francis's often lying or sleeping in the snow and cold, and, in Chapter VIII of the* Little Flowers of St. Francis, *the saint tells Friar Leo that perfect joy might come of patiently suffering exclusion by a doorkeeper who ". . . maketh us stay outside hungry and cold all night in the rain and snow."*

A BAROQUE WALL-FOUNTAIN IN THE VILLA SCIARRA

Under the bronze crown
Too big for the head of the stone cherub whose feet
  A serpent has begun to eat,
Sweet water brims a cockle and braids down

    Past spattered mosses, breaks
On the tipped edge of a second shell, and fills
  The massive third below. It spills
In threads then from the scalloped rim, and makes

    A scrim or summery tent
For a faun-ménage and their familiar goose.
  Happy in all that ragged, loose
Collapse of water, its effortless descent

    And flatteries of spray,
The stocky god upholds the shell with ease,
  Watching, about his shaggy knees,
The goatish innocence of his babes at play;

    His fauness all the while
Leans forward, slightly, into a clambering mesh

Of water-lights, her sparkling flesh
In a saecular ecstasy, her blinded smile

     Bent on the sand floor
Of the trefoil pool, where ripple-shadows come
    And go in swift reticulum,
More addling to the eye than wine, and more

     Interminable to thought
Than pleasure's calculus. Yet since this all
    Is pleasure, flash, and waterfall,
Must it not be too simple? Are we not

     More intricately expressed
In the plain fountains that Maderna set
    Before St. Peter's—the main jet
Struggling aloft until it seems at rest

     In the act of rising, until
The very wish of water is reversed,
    That heaviness borne up to burst
In a clear, high, cavorting head, to fill

     With blaze, and then in gauze
Delays, in a gnatlike shimmering, in a fine
    Illumined version of itself, decline,
And patter on the stones its own applause?

     If that is what men are
Or should be, if those water-saints display
    The pattern of our areté,
What of these showered fauns in their bizarre,

     Spangled, and plunging house?
They are at rest in fulness of desire
    For what is given, they do not tire
Of the smart of the sun, the pleasant water-douse

And riddled pool below,
Reproving our disgust and our ennui
  With humble insatiety.
Francis, perhaps, who lay in sister snow

    Before the wealthy gate
Freezing and praising, might have seen in this
  No trifle, but a shade of bliss—
That land of tolerable flowers, that state

    As near and far as grass
Where eyes become the sunlight, and the hand
  Is worthy of water: the dreamt land
Toward which all hungers leap, all pleasures pass.

*The prophet in this poem is a contemporary in whose
vision the world is laid waste by a nuclear holo-
caust. Xanthus is the river, also known as
Scamander, which, according to Homer, was
scalded by Hephaestus, the fire bringer.*

ADVICE TO A PROPHET

WHEN you come, as you soon must, to the streets of our city,
Mad-eyed from stating the obvious,
Not proclaiming our fall but begging us
In God's name to have self-pity,

Spare us all word of the weapons, their force and range,
The long numbers that rocket the mind;
Our slow, unreckoning hearts will be left behind,
Unable to fear what is too strange.

Nor shall you scare us with talk of the death of the race.
How should we dream of this place without us?—
The sun mere fire, the leaves untroubled about us,
A stone look on the stone's face?

Speak of the world's own change. Though we cannot conceive
Of an undreamt thing, we know to our cost
How the dreamt cloud crumbles, the vines are blackened by frost,
How the view alters. We could believe,

If you told us so, that the white-tailed deer will slip
Into perfect shade, grown perfectly shy,
The lark avoid the reaches of our eye,
The jack-pine lose its knuckled grip

On the cold ledge, and every torrent burn
As Xanthus once, its gliding trout
Stunned in a twinkling. What should we be without
The dolphin's arc, the dove's return,

These things in which we have seen ourselves and spoken?
Ask us, prophet, how we shall call
Our natures forth when that live tongue is all
Dispelled, that glass obscured or broken

In which we have said the rose of our love and the clean
Horse of our courage, in which beheld
The singing locust of the soul unshelled,
And all we mean or wish to mean.

Ask us, ask us whether with the worldless rose
Our hearts shall fail us; come demanding
Whether there shall be lofty or long standing
When the bronze annals of the oak-tree close.

WILLIAM CARLOS WILLIAMS, *born September 17, 1883, in Rutherford, New Jersey, was until a few years ago a practicing pediatrician in his native town. He was educated at the University of Pennsylvania, where he took his degree in medicine and where he was acquainted with Ezra Pound and the imagist poet H.D. He has published scores of books which, besides poetry, include his autobiography, short stories, novels, and plays, some of which have been given productions here and abroad. As the leading promoter of a distinctly American idiom in poetry, he has taken as protégés many young writers whose work departs from the English metrical tradition.*

THE little sparrows
hop ingenuously
about the pavement
quarreling
with sharp voices
over those things
that interest them.
But we who are wiser
shut ourselves in
on either hand
and no one knows
whether we think good
or evil.
         Meanwhile,
the old man who goes about
gathering dog-lime
walks in the gutter
without looking up
and his tread
is more majestic than
that of the Episcopal minister
approaching the pulpit
of a Sunday.
         These things
astonish me beyond words.

Like the contemporary painter Edward Hopper, who is famous for many paintings that illustrate a just-under-the-surface seam of loneliness in American life, Dr. Williams often takes for his subject some small everyday occurrence that evokes pathos, nostalgia, or a sense of isolation. Both poet and painter present these scenes in terms of simple realism, withholding any comment not implicit in the scene itself.

THE LONELY STREET

SCHOOL is over. It is too hot
to walk at ease. At ease
in light frocks they walk the streets
to while the time away.
They have grown tall. They hold
pink flames in their right hands.
In white from head to foot,
with sidelong, idle look—
in yellow, floating stuff,
black sash and stockings—
touching their avid mouths
with pink sugar on a stick—
like a carnation each holds in her hand—
they mount the lonely street.

Ostensibly a preachment to fellow citizens on the vir-
tues of simplicity in regard to a funeral, this
poem, in the light of the author's long crusade for
the use of the native rhythms and natural accents
of American speech in literature, may also be
read as Dr. Williams's advice to his fellow poets.

TRACT

I WILL teach you my townspeople
how to perform a funeral—
for you have it over a troop
of artists—
unless one should scour the world—
you have the ground sense necessary.

See! the hearse leads.
I begin with a design for a hearse.
For Christ's sake not black—
nor white either—and not polished!
Let it be weathered—like a farm wagon—
with gilt wheels (this could be
applied fresh at small expense)
or no wheels at all:
a rough dray to drag over the ground.

Knock the glass out!
My God—glass, my townspeople!
For what purpose? Is it for the dead
to look out or for us to see
how well he is housed or to see
the flowers or the lack of them—
or what?
To keep the rain and snow from him?
He will have a heavier rain soon:
pebbles and dirt and what not.

Let there be no glass—
and no upholstery, phew!
and no little brass rollers
and small easy wheels on the bottom—
my townspeople what are you thinking of?

A rough plain hearse then
with gilt wheels and no top at all.
On this the coffin lies
by its own weight.

          No wreaths please—
especially no hot house flowers.
Some common memento is better,
something he prized and is known by:
his old clothes—a few books perhaps—
God knows what! You realize
how we are about these things
my townspeople—
something will be found—anything
even flowers if he had come to that.
So much for the hearse.

For heaven's sake though see to the driver!
Take off the silk hat! In fact
that's no place at all for him—
up there unceremoniously
dragging our friend out to his own dignity!
Bring him down—bring him down!
Low and inconspicuous! I'd not have him ride
on the wagon at all—damn him—
the undertaker's understrapper!
Let him hold the reins
and walk at the side
and inconspicuously too!

Then briefly as to yourselves:
Walk behind—as they do in France,
seventh class, or if you ride
Hell take curtains! Go with some show
of inconvenience; sit openly—
to the weather as to grief.
Or do you think you can shut grief in?
What—from us? We who have perhaps
nothing to lose? Share with us
share with us—it will be money
in your pockets.
                    Go now
I think you are ready.

THE BULL

It is in captivity—
ringed, haltered, chained
to a drag
the bull is godlike

Unlike the cows
he lives alone, nozzles
the sweet grass gingerly
to pass the time away

He kneels, lies down
and stretching out
a foreleg licks himself
about the hoof

then stays
with half-closed eyes,

Olympian commentary on
the bright passage of days.

—The round sun
smooths his lacquer
through
the glossy pinetrees

his substance hard
as ivory or glass—
through which the wind
yet plays—
                    milkless

he nods
the hair between his horns
and eyes matted
with hyacinthine curls.

DAVID WRIGHT, *born February 23, 1920, in Johannesburg, South Africa, lives with his wife in London. Becoming deaf after having contracted scarlet fever when he was seven years old, he was edu-*

cated at the Northampton School for the Deaf and later at Oriel College, Oxford. He has been widely active as an editor of anthologies (on some of which he collaborated with John Heath-Stubbs) and of literary magazines.

Composed at thirty, my funeral oration: Here lies
David John Murray Wright, 6′2″, myopic blue eyes;
Hair grey (very distinguished looking, so I am told);
Shabbily dressed as a rule; susceptible to cold;
Acquainted with what are known as the normal vices;
Perpetually short of cash; useless in a crisis;
Preferring cats, hated dogs; drank (when he could) too much;
Was deaf as a tombstone; and extremely hard to touch.
Academic achievements: B.A., Oxon (2nd class);
Poetic: the publication of one volume of verse,
Which in his thirtieth year attained him no fame at all
Except among intractable poets, and a small
Lunatic fringe congregating in Soho pubs.
He could roll himself cigarettes from discarded stubs,
Assume the first position of Yoga; sail, row, swim;
And though deaf, in church appear to be joining a hymn.
Often arrested for being without a permit,
Starved on his talents as much as he dined on his wit,
Born in a dominion to which he hoped not to go back
Since predisposed to imagine white possibly black:
His life, like his times, was appalling; his conduct odd;
He hoped to write one good line; died believing in God.

MONOLOGUE OF A DEAF MAN

'Et lui comprit trop bien, n'ayant pas entendu.'—Tristan Corbière

It is a good plan, and began with childhood
As my fortune discovered, only to hear
How much it is necessary to have said.
Oh silence, independent of a stopped ear,
You observe birds, flying, sing with wings instead.

Then do you console yourself? You are consoled
If you are, as all are. So easy a youth
Still unconcerned with the concern of the world
Where, masked and legible, a moment of truth
Manifests what, gagged, a tongue should have told;

Still observer of vanity and courage
And of these mirror as well; that is something
More than a sound of violin to assuage
What the human being most dies of: boredom
Which makes hedgebirds clamour in their blackthorn cage.

But did the brushless fox die of eloquence?
No, but talked himself, it seems, into a tale.
The injury, dominated, is an asset;
It is there for domination, that is all.
Else what must faith do deserted by mountains?

Talk to me then, you who have so much to say,
Spectator of the human conversation,
Reader of tongues, examiner of the eye,
And detective of clues in every action,
What could a voice, if you heard it, signify?

The tone speaks less than a twitch and a grimace.
People make to depart, do not say 'Goodbye.'
Decision, indecision, drawn on every face
As if they spoke. But what do they really say?
You are not spared, either, the banalities.

In whatever condition, whole, blind, dumb,
One-legged or leprous, the human being is,
I affirm the human condition is the same,
The heart half broken in ashes and in lies,
But sustained by the immensity of the divine.

Thus I too must praise out of a quiet ear
The great creation to which I owe I am
My grief and my love. O hear me if I cry
Among the din of birds deaf to their acclaim
Involved like them in the not unhearing air.

BIBLIOGRAPHY *The following lists do not pretend to be comprehensive: broadsides, single poems published as pamphlets, volumes intended for children, and other minor works have been omitted; plays in verse and volumes of selected poems have generally been included. When a particular volume has been published both in England and in America, the earlier publication date has been preferred. Thus, while the lists are not exhaustive, it is hoped that no major work by an author named has been omitted.*

DANNIE ABSE

After Every Green Thing (*1949*)

Walking under Water (*1952*)

Tenants of the House: Poems 1951–1956 (*1957*)

Poems: Golders Green (*1962*)

CONRAD AIKEN

Earth Triumphant and Other Tales in Verse (*1914*)

A Jig of Forslin (*1916*)

Turns and Movies, and Other Tales in Verse (*1916*)

The Charnel Rose, Senlin: A Biography, and Other Poems (*1918*)

Priapus and the Pool (*1922*)

The Pilgrimage of Festus (*1923*)

Priapus and the Pool and Other Poems (*1925*)

Senlin: A Biography (*1925*)

Prelude (*1929*)

Selected Poems (*1929*)

John Deth: A Metaphysical Legend and Other Poems (*1930*)

Preludes for Memnon (*1931*)

The Coming Forth by Day of Osiris Jones (*1931*)

Selected Poems (*1933*)

Landscape West of Eden (*1934*)

Time in the Rock: Preludes to Definition (*1936*)

And in the Human Heart (*1940*)

Brownstone Eclogues and Other Poems (*1942*)

The Soldier: A Poem (*1944*)

The Kid (*1947*)

Skylight One: Fifteen Poems (*1949*)

Collected Poems (*1953*)

A Letter from Li Po and Other Poems (*1955*)

Sheepfold Hill: Fifteen Poems (*1958*)

Selected Poems (*1961*)

KINGSLEY AMIS

Bright November (*1947*)

A Frame of Mind: Eighteen Poems (*1953*)

Poems (*1954*)

A Case of Samples: Poems 1946–1956 (*1956*)

W. H. AUDEN

Poems (*1930*)

The Orators: An English Study (*1932*)

The Dance of Death (*1933*)

The Witnesses (*1933*)

Poems (2d ed., *1934*)

W. H. AUDEN (CONTINUED)

The Dog Beneath the Skin; or Where is Francis? (*1935*, with Christopher Isherwood)

Look, Stranger (*1935*; published in New York in *1937* as On This Island)

The Ascent of F6: A Tragedy in Two Acts (*1936*, with Christopher Isherwood)

Letters from Iceland (*1937*, with Louis MacNeice)

On the Frontier: A Melodrama in Three Acts (*1938*, with Christopher Isherwood)

Selected Poems (*1938*)

Journey to a War (*1939*, with Christopher Isherwood)

Another Time (*1940*)

Some Poems (*1940*)

The Double Man (*1941*; published in London as New Year Letter)

For the Time Being (*1944*)

The Collected Poetry of W. H. Auden (*1945*)

The Age of Anxiety: A Baroque Eclogue (*1947*)

Collected Shorter Poems, 1930–1944 (*1950*)

Nones (*1951*)

The Shield of Achilles (*1955*)

Selected Poetry of W. H. Auden (*1958*)

W. H. Auden: A Selection by the Author (*1958*)

Homage to Clio (*1960*)

ROBERT BAGG

Madonna of the Cello: Poems (*1961*)

GEORGE BARKER

Thirty Preliminary Poems (*1933*)

Poems (*1935*)

Calamiterror (*1937*)

Lament and Triumph (*1940*)

Selected Poems (*1941*)

Sacred and Secular Elegies (*1943*)

Eros in Dogma (*1944*)

Love Poems (*1947*)

News of the World (*1950*)

The True Confession of George Barker (*1950*)

A Vision of Beasts and Gods (*1954*)

Collected Poems, 1930–1955 (*1957*)

The View from a Blind I (*1962*)

JOHN BERRYMAN

Poems (*1942*)

The Dispossessed (*1948*)

Homage to Mistress Bradstreet (*1956*)

His Thoughts Made Pockets and the Plane Buckt (*1958*)

JOHN BETJEMAN

Mount Zion, or, In Touch with the Infinite (*1931*)

Continual Dew: A Little Book of Bourgeois Verse (*1937*)

Old Lights for New Chancels (*1940*)

New Bats in Old Belfries (*1945*)

Slick but Not Streamlined (*1947*)

Selected Poems (*1948*)

A Few Late Chrysanthemums (*1954*)

Poems in the Porch (*1954*)

Collected Poems (*1958*)

Poems (*1958*)

Summoned by Bells (*1960*)

ELIZABETH BISHOP

North and South (*1946*)

Poems: North and South, A Cold Spring (*1955*)

LOUISE BOGAN

Body of This Death (*1923*)

Dark Summer (*1929*)

The Sleeping Fury (*1937*)

LOUISE BOGAN (CONTINUED)
Poems and New Poems (*1941*)
Collected Poems 1923–1953 (*1954*)

PHILIP BOOTH
Letter from a Distant Land (*1957*)
The Islanders (*1961*)

JOHN MALCOLM BRINNIN
The Lincoln Lyrics (*1942*)
The Garden Is Political (*1942*)
No Arch, No Triumph (*1945*)
The Sorrows of Cold Stone: Poems 1940–1950 (*1951*)
Selected Poems (*1963*)

JOHN CIARDI
Homeward to America (*1940*)
Other Skies (*1947*)
Live Another Day (*1949*)
From Time to Time (*1951*)
As If: Poems New and Selected (*1955*)
I Marry You: A Sheaf of Love Poems (*1958*)
Thirty-nine Poems (*1959*)
The Reason for the Pelican (*1959*)
In the Stoneworks (*1961*)
In Fact (*1962*)

TRAM COMBS
Pilgrim's Terrace (*1957*)
Ceremonies in Mind (*1959*)
But Never Mind: Poems etc., 1946–50 (*1961*)

HILARY CORKE
The Early Drowned and Other Poems (*1961*)

E. E. CUMMINGS
Tulips and Chimneys (*1923*)
XLI Poems (*1925*)

& (*1925*)
is 5 (*1926*)
Him (*1927*; a play)
W (Viva) (*1931*)
no thanks (*1935*)
Tom (*1935*)
One Over Twenty (*1936*)
Collected Poems (*1938*)
50 POEMS (*1940*)
I x I (*1944*)
Santa Claus: A Morality (*1946*)
XAIPE: 71 poems (*1950*)
Poems, 1923–1954 (*1954*)
95 Poems (*1958*)
100 Selected Poems (*1959*)

ALAN DUGAN
Poems (*1961*)

RICHARD EBERHART
A Bravery of Earth (*1930*)
Reading the Spirit (*1936*)
Song and Idea (*1940*)
Poems: New and Selected (*1944*)
Burr Oaks (*1947*)
Rumination (*1947*)
Brotherhood of Men (*1949*)
An Herb Basket (*1950*)
Selected Poems (*1951*)
Undercliff: Poems, 1946–1953 (*1953*)
The Oak (*1957*)
Great Praises (*1957*)
Collected Poems 1930–1960 (*1960*)

T. S. ELIOT
Prufrock and Other Observations (*1917*)
Poems (*1919*)
The Waste Land (*1922*)
Poems, 1909–25 (*1925*)
Poems (*1927*)
Ash-Wednesday (*1930*)
Sweeney Agonistes (*1932*)

T. S. ELIOT (CONTINUED)

The Rock: A Pageant Play (*1934*)
Murder in the Cathedral (*1935*)
Collected Poems, 1909–1935 (*1936*)
Old Possum's Book of Practical Cats
   (*1939*)
The Family Reunion: A Play (*1939*)
East Coker (*1940*)
Dry Salvages (*1941*)
Burnt Norton (*1941*)
Later Poems, 1925–1935 (*1941*)
Little Gidding (*1942*)
Four Quartets (*1943*)
Selected Poems (*1948*)
The Cocktail Party: A Comedy (*1950*)
The Complete Poems and Plays,
   1909–1950 (*1952*)
Selected Poems (*1954; 1961*)
The Confidential Clerk: A Play (*1954*)
The Elder Statesman (*1959*)

D. J. ENRIGHT

Season Ticket (*1948*)
The Laughing Hyena, and Other Poems
   (*1953*)
Bread Rather than Blossoms (*1956*)
Some Men Are Brothers (*1960*)

IRVING FELDMAN

Works and Days (*1961*)

ROBERT FITZGERALD

Poems (*1935*)
A Wreath for the Sea (*1943*)
In the Rose of Time: Poems 1931–1956
   (*1956*)

ROBERT FROST

A Boy's Will (*1913*)
North of Boston (*1914*)
Mountain Interval (*1916*)
New Hampshire: A Poem (*1923*)

Selected Poems (*1923, 1928, 1934, 1936*)
West-running Brook (*1928*)
Collected Poems (*1930, 1939, 1943*)
A Further Range (*1936*)
A Witness Tree (*1942*)
Come In and Other Poems (*1943*)
A Masque of Reason (*1945*)
Poems (*1946*)
Steeple Bush (*1947*)
A Masque of Mercy (*1947*)
Complete Poems of Robert Frost, 1949
   (*1949*)
Selected Poems (*1955*)
You Come Too (*1959*)
In the Clearing (*1962*)

JEAN GARRIGUE

The Ego and the Centaur (*1947*)
The Monument Rose (*1953*)
A Water Walk by Villa d'Este (*1959*)

DAVID GASCOYNE

Roman Balcony and Other Poems (*1932*)
Man's Life Is This Meat (*1936*)
Poems, 1937–1942 (*1943*)
A Vagrant and Other Poems (*1950*)
Night Thoughts (*1956*)

W. S. GRAHAM

Cage without Grievance (*1942*)
The Seven Journies (*1944*)
Second Poems (*1945*)
The White Threshold (*1949*)
The Nightfishing (*1955*)

ROBERT GRAVES

Fairies and Fusiliers (*1917*)
Country Sentiment (*1920*)
The Pier Glass (*1921*)
Welchman's Hose (*1925*)
Poems 1914–1926 (*1927*)
Ten Poems (*1930*)

ROBERT GRAVES (CONTINUED)
Poems 1926–1930 (*1931*)
Poems 1930–1933 (*1933*)
Collected Poems (*1938*)
No More Ghosts: Selected Poems (*1940*)
Poems (*1943*)
Poems 1938–1945 (*1946*)
Collected Poems 1914–1947 (*1948*)
Poems and Satires (*1951*)
Poems, 1953 (*1953*)
Collected Poems (*1955*)
Poems: Selected by Himself (*1957*)
Collected Poems, 1959 (*1959*)
Food for Centaurs (*1960*)
More Poems, 1961 (*1961*)
New Poems: 1962 (*1962*)

THOM GUNN
Poems (*1953*)
Fighting Terms (*1954*)
The Sense of Movement (*1957*)
My Sad Captains (*1961*)
Selected Poems (*1962*, with Ted Hughes)

DONALD HALL
To the Loud Wind, and Other Poems
(*1955*)
Exiles and Marriages (*1955*)
The Dark Houses (*1958*)

MICHAEL HAMBURGER
Flowering Cactus: Poems, 1942–49
(*1950*)
Poems, 1950–1951 (*1952*)
The Dual Site (*1958*)

JOHN HEATH-STUBBS
Wounded Thammuz (*1942*)
Beauty and the Beast (*1943*)
The Divided Ways (*1946*)
The Charity of the Stars (*1949*)
The Swarming of the Bees (*1950*)

A Charm against the Toothache (*1954*)
The Triumph of the Muse, and Other
Poems (*1958*)
Helen in Egypt and Other Plays (*1958*)
The Blue-fly in His Head (*1962*)

ANTHONY HECHT
A Summoning of Stones (*1954*)
The Seven Deadly Sins (*1958*)

DANIEL G. HOFFMAN
An Armada of Thirty Whales (*1954*)
A Little Geste, and Other Poems (*1960*)

JOHN HOLLANDER
A Crackling of Thorns (*1958*)
Movie-going and Other Poems (*1962*)

BARBARA HOWES
The Undersea Farmer (*1948*)
In the Cold Country (*1954*)
Light and Dark (*1959*)

TED HUGHES
The Hawk in the Rain (*1957*)
Lupercal (*1960*)
Selected Poems (*1962*, with Thom Gunn)

RANDALL JARRELL
Blood for a Stranger (*1942*)
Little Friend, Little Friend (*1945*)
Losses (*1948*)
The Seven-league Crutches (*1951*)
Selected Poems (*1955*)
The Woman at the Washington Zoo:
Poems and Translations (*1960*)

ELIZABETH JENNINGS
Poems (*1953*)
A Way of Looking (*1955*)
A Sense of the World (*1958*)
Song for a Birth or a Death (*1961*)

GALWAY KINNELL
What a Kingdom It Was (*1960*)

STANLEY KUNITZ
Intellectual Things (*1930*)
Passport to the War: A Selection of Poems (*1944*)
Selected Poems, 1928–1958 (*1958*)

JOSEPH LANGLAND
"The Green Town: Poems" in *Poets of Today III* (*1956*)

PHILIP LARKIN
The North Ship (*1945*)
Poems (*1954*)
The Less Deceived (*1955*)

JOHN LEHMANN
A Garden Revisited, and Other Poems (*1931*)
Forty Poems (*1942*)
The Sphere of Glass and Other Poems (*1944*)
The Age of the Dragon: Poems 1930–1951 (*1951*)

CECIL DAY LEWIS
Beechen Vigil and Other Poems (*1925*)
Bank Holiday (*1926*)
Country Comets (*1928*)
Transitional Poem (*1929*)
From Feathers to Iron (*1931*)
The Magnetic Mountain (*1933*)
A Time to Dance and Other Poems (*1935*)
Collected Poems, 1929–1933 (*1935*)
Noah and the Waters (*1936*)
Overtures to Death and Other Poems (*1938*)
Selected Poems (*1940*)
Poems (*1943*)

Word over All (*1943*)
Collected Poems (*1945*)
Short Is the Time: Poems 1936–1943 (*1945*)
Collected Poems, 1929–1936 (*1948*)
Poems, 1943–1947 (*1948*)
Selected Poems (*1951*)
An Italian Visit (*1953*)
Collected Poems (*1954*)
Pegasus and Other Poems (*1957*)
The Gate (*1962*)

ROBERT LOWELL
Land of Unlikeness (*1944*)
Lord Weary's Castle (*1946;* with changes, *1947*)
Poems, 1938–1949 (*1950*)
The Mills of the Kavanaughs (*1951*)
Life Studies (*1959*)
Imitations (*1961*)

ARCHIBALD MACLEISH
Songs for a Summer's Day: A Sonnet Cycle (*1915*)
Tower of Ivory (*1917*)
The Happy Marriage and Other Poems (*1924*)
The Pot of Earth (*1925*)
Streets in the Moon (*1926*)
The Hamlet of A. MacLeish (*1928*)
New Found Land: Fourteen Poems (*1930*)
Conquistador (*1932*)
Poems 1924–1933 (*1933*)
Frescoes for Mr. Rockefeller's City (*1933*)
Panic: A Play in Verse (*1935*)
Public Speech (*1936*)
The Fall of the City: A Verse Play for Radio (*1937*)
Air Raid: A Verse Play for Radio (*1938*)
Land of the Free (*1938*)

ARCHIBALD MACLEISH (CONTINUED)
America Was Promises (*1939*)
Poems (*1943*)
Actfive and Other Poems (*1948*)
Collected Poems, 1917–1952 (*1952*)
Songs for Eve (*1954*)
J.B. (*1958*)

LOUIS MACNEICE
Blind Fireworks (*1929*)
Poems (*1935*)
Letters from Iceland (*1937*, with W. H. Auden)
Poems (*1937*)
The Earth Compels (*1938*)
Out of the Picture (*1938*)
Autumn Journal (*1939*)
The Last Ditch (*1940*)
Poems, 1925–1940 (*1940*)
Selected Poems (*1940*)
Plant and Phantom (*1941*)
Springboard: Poems 1941–1944 (*1944*)
The Dark Tower and Other Radio Scripts (*1947*)
Holes in the Sky: Poems 1944–1947 (*1948*)
Collected Poems, 1925–1948 (*1949*)
Ten Burnt Offerings (*1952*)
Autumn Sequel: A Rhetorical Poem in XXVI Cantos (*1954*)
Visitations (*1957*)
Eighty-five Poems (*1959*)
Solstices (*1961*)

JAMES MERRILL
The Black Swan and Other Poems (*1946*)
First Poems (*1951*)
The Country of a Thousand Years of Peace and Other Poems (*1959*)
Selected Poems (*1961*)
Water Street (*1962*)

W. S. MERWIN
A Mask for Janus (*1952*)
The Dancing Bears (*1954*)
Green with Beasts (*1956*)
The Drunk in the Furnace (*1960*)

MARIANNE MOORE
Poems (*1921*)
Observations (*1924*)
Selected Poems (*1935*)
The Pangolin and Other Verse (*1936*)
What Are Years (*1941*)
Nevertheless (*1944*)
Collected Poems (*1951*)
Like a Bulwark (*1956*)
O To Be a Dragon (*1959*)

HOWARD MOSS
The Wound and the Weather (*1946*)
The Toy Fair (*1954*)
A Swimmer in the Air (*1957*)
A Winter Come, a Summer Gone: Poems, 1946–1960 (*1960*)

HOWARD NEMEROV
The Image and the Law (*1947*)
Guide to the Ruins (*1950*)
The Salt Garden (*1955*)
Mirrors and Windows (*1958*)
New and Selected Poems (*1960*)

SYLVIA PLATH
The Colossus (*1960*)

WILLIAM PLOMER
Notes for Poems (*1927*)
The Family Tree (*1929*)
The Fivefold Screen (*1932*)
Visiting the Caves (*1936*)
Selected Poems (*1940*)
The Dorking Thigh and Other Satires (*1945*)

WILLIAM PLOMER (CONTINUED)
Borderline Ballads (*1955*)
A Shot in the Park (*1955*)
Collected Poems (*1960*)

EZRA POUND
A Lume Spento (*1908*)
Personae (*1909*)
Exultations (*1909*)
Provenca: Poems Selected from Personae, Exultations, and Canzonieri (*1910*)
Canzoni (*1911*)
Ripostes (*1912*)
Canzoni and Ripostes (*1913*)
Personae and Exultations (*1913*)
Cathay: Translations by Ezra Pound (*1915*)
Lustra (*1916*)
Lustra with Earlier Poems (*1917*)
Pavannes and Divagations (*1918*)
The Fourth Canto (*1919*)
Quia Pauper Amavi (*1919*)
Hugh Selwyn Mauberley (*1920*)
Umbra: The Early Poems (*1920*)
Poems 1918–1921 (including Three Portraits and Four Cantos) (*1921*)
A Draft of XVI Cantos (*1925*)
Personae: The Collected Poems of Ezra Pound (*1926*)
A Draft of the Cantos 17–27 of Ezra Pound (*1928*)
Selected Poems (*1928*)
A Draft of XXX Cantos (*1930*)
Selected Poems (*1933*)
Homage to Sextus Propertius (*1934*)
Eleven New Cantos: XXXI–XLI (*1934*; English title: A Draft of Cantos XXXI–XLI)
The Fifth Decad of Cantos (*1937*)
A Selection of Poems (*1940*)
Cantos LII–LXXI (*1940*)
The Pisan Cantos (*1948*)

The Cantos of Ezra Pound (*1948*)
Selected Poems (*1949*)
Seventy Cantos (*1950*)
Personae: Collected Shorter Poems (*1950*)
Cantos 1–84 (*1954*)
Section: Rock-drill: 85–95 de los Cantares (*1955*)
Personae: Collected Poems (*1956*)
Selected Poems (*1956*)
Diptych: Rome-London (*1958*)
Thrones 96–109 de los Cantares (*1959*)
Love Poems of Ancient Egypt (*1962*)

JOHN CROWE RANSOM
Poems about God (*1919*)
Armageddon (*1923*)
Chills and Fever: Poems (*1924*)
Grace after Meat (*1924*)
Two Gentlemen in Bonds (*1927*)
Selected Poems (*1945*)
Selected Poems (*1952*)
Poems and Essays (*1955*)

HENRY REED
A Map of Verona and Other Poems (*1947*)

ALASTAIR REID
To Lighten My House (*1953*)
Oddments, Inklings, Omens, Moments (*1959*)

ANNE RIDLER
Poems (*1939*)
A Dream Observed and Other Poems (*1941*)
The Nine Bright Shiners (*1943*)
Cain: A Play in Two Acts (*1943*)
The Shadow Factory (*1946*)
Henry Bly and Other Plays (*1950*)
The Golden Bird and Other Poems (*1951*)
The Trial of Thomas Cranmer (*1956*)

ANNE RIDLER (CONTINUED)
A Matter of Life and Death (*1959*)
Selected Poems (*1961*)

THEODORE ROETHKE
Open House (*1941*)
The Lost Son and Other Poems (*1948*)
Praise to the End! (*1951*)
The Waking: Poems 1933–1953 (*1953*)
Words for the Wind (*1958*)
I Am! Says the Lamb (*1961*)

MURIEL RUKEYSER
Theory of Flight (*1935*)
U. S. 1 (*1938*)
A Turning Wind (*1939*)
The Soul and Body of John Brown (*1940*)
Wake Island (*1942*)
Beast in View (*1944*)
The Green Wave (*1948*)
Elegies (*1949*)
Orpheus (*1949*)
Selected Poems (*1951*)
Body of Waking (*1958*)

DELMORE SCHWARTZ
In Dreams Begin Responsibilities (*1938*)
Shenandoah (*1941*)
Genesis: Book I (*1943*)
Vaudeville for a Princess and Other
    Poems (*1950*)
Summer Knowledge: New and Selected
    Poems, 1938–1958 (*1959*)

WINFIELD TOWNLEY SCOTT
Biography for Traman (*1937*)
Wind the Clock (*1941*)
The Sword on the Table (*1942*)
To Marry Strangers (*1945*)
Mr. Whittier and Other Poems (*1948*)
The Dark Sister (*1958*)
Scrimshaw (*1959*)
Collected Poems (*1962*)

JAMES SCULLY
(book forthcoming)

ANNE SEXTON
To Bedlam and Part Way Back (*1960*)
All My Pretty Ones (*1962*)

KARL SHAPIRO
Poems (*1935*)
Person Place and Thing (*1942*)
V-Letter and Other Poems (*1944*)
Essay on Rime (*1945*)
Trial of a Poet and Other Poems (*1947*)
Poems, 1940–1953 (*1953*)
Poems of a Jew (*1958*)

LOUIS SIMPSON
The Arrivistes: Poems, 1940–1948 (*1949*)
"Good News of Death and Other Poems"
    in *Poets of Today II* (*1955*)
A Dream of Governors (*1959*)

EDITH SITWELL
Clowns' Houses (*1918*)
The Wooden Pegasus (*1920*)
Facade (*1922*)
Bucolic Comedies (*1923*)
The Sleeping Beauty (*1924*)
Troy Park (*1925*)
Elegy on Dead Fashion (*1926*)
Rustic Elegies (*1927*)
Five Poems (*1928*)
Gold Coast Customs (*1929*)
The Collected Poems of Edith Sitwell
    (*1930*)
Selected Poems, with an Essay on Her
    Own Poetry (*1936*)
Poems New and Old (*1940*)
Street Songs (*1942*)
Green Song and Other Poems (*1944*)
The Song of the Cold (*1945*)
The Shadow of Cain (*1947*)

EDITH SITWELL (CONTINUED)

The Canticle of the Rose: Selected Poems, 1920–1947 (*1949*)

The Canticle of the Rose: Poems 1917–1949 (*1949*)

Facade and Other Poems, 1920–1935 (*1950*)

Poor Men's Music (*1950*)

Selected Poems (*1952*)

Gardeners and Astronomers: New Poems (*1953*)

Collected Poems (*1954*)

WILLIAM JAY SMITH

Poems (*1947*)

Celebration at Dark (*1950*)

Poems, 1947–1957 (*1957*)

W. D. SNODGRASS

Heart's Needle (*1959*)

STEPHEN SPENDER

Twenty Poems (*1930*)

Poems (*1933*)

Vienna (*1934*)

Trial of a Judge: A Tragedy in Five Acts (*1938*)

The Still Centre (*1939*)

Selected Poems (*1940*)

Ruins and Visions: Poems 1934–1942 (*1942*)

Poems of Dedication (*1946*)

Returning to Vienna 1947: Nine Sketches (*1947*)

The Edge of Being (*1949*)

Collected Poems, 1928–1953 (*1955*)

Inscriptions (*1958*)

GEORGE STARBUCK

Bone Thoughts (*1960*)

WALLACE STEVENS

Harmonium (*1923*; enlarged ed., *1931*)

Ideas of Order (*1935*)

Owl's Clover (*1936*)

The Man with the Blue Guitar and Other Poems (*1937*)

Parts of a World (*1942*)

Notes toward a Supreme Fiction (*1942*)

Esthétique du Mal (*1945*)

Three Academic Pieces (*1947*)

Transport to Summer (*1947*)

The Auroras of Autumn (*1950*)

The Man with the Blue Guitar, including Ideas of Order (*1952*)

Selected Poems (*1953*)

Collected Poems (*1954*)

Opus Posthumous (*1957*)

Poems: Selected with Introduction by Samuel French Morse (*1959*)

MAY SWENSON

"Another Animal, Poems" in *Poets of Today I* (*1954*)

A Cage of Spines (*1958*)

ALLEN TATE

The Golden Mean, and Other Poems (*1923*, with Ridley Wills)

Mr. Pope and Other Poems (*1928*)

Ode to the Confederate Dead (*1930*)

Poems, 1928–1931 (*1932*)

The Mediterranean and Other Poems (*1936*)

Selected Poems (*1937*)

Sonnets at Christmas (*1941*)

The Winter Sea (*1944*)

Poems, 1920–1945: A Selection (*1947*)

Poems, 1922–1947 (*1948*)

Poems (*1960*)

DYLAN THOMAS

18 Poems (*1934*)

Twenty-five Poems (*1936*)

DYLAN THOMAS (CONTINUED)

The World I Breathe (*1939*)

The Map of Love: Verse and Prose (*1939*)

New Poems (*1943*)

Deaths and Entrances (*1946*)

Selected Writings of Dylan Thomas, edited, with introduction, by John L. Sweeney (*1946*)

Twenty-six Poems (*1950*)

Poems (*1950*)

In Country Sleep and Other Poems (*1951*)

Collected Poems 1934–1952 (*1952*)

Under Milk Wood (*1957*)

JOHN WAIN

Mixed Feelings: Nineteen Poems (*1951*)

A Word Carved on a Sill (*1956*)

Weep before God (*1961*)

ROBERT PENN WARREN

Thirty-six Poems (*1935*)

Eleven Poems on the Same Theme (*1942*)

Selected Poems, 1923–1943 (*1944*)

Brother to Dragons (*1953*)

Promises: Poems 1954–1956 (*1957*)

You, Emperors, and Others: Poems, 1957–1960 (*1960*)

VERNON WATKINS

Ballad of the Mari Lwyd and Other Poems (*1941*)

The Lamp and the Veil (*1945*)

The Lady with the Unicorn (*1948*)

Selected Poems (*1948*)

The Death Bell: Poems and Ballads (*1954*)

Cypress and Acacia (*1959*)

Affinities (*1962*)

RICHARD WILBUR

The Beautiful Changes and Other Poems (*1947*)

Ceremony and Other Poems (*1950*)

Things of This World (*1956*)

Poems, 1943–1956 (*1957*)

Advice to a Prophet (*1961*)

WILLIAM CARLOS WILLIAMS

Poems (*1909*)

The Tempers (*1913*)

A Book of Poems: Al Que Quiere! (*1917*)

Kora in Hell: Improvisations (*1920*)

Sour Grapes: A Book of Poems (*1921*)

Spring and All (*1923*)

Collected Poems, 1921–1931 (*1934*)

An Early Martyr and Other Poems (*1935*)

Adam and Eve and the City (*1936*)

The Complete Collected Poems, 1906–1938 (*1938*)

The Broken Span (*1941*)

The Wedge (*1944*)

Paterson (Book One, *1946*; Book Two, *1948*; Book Three, *1949*; Book Four, *1951*; Book Five, *1958*)

The Pink Church (*1948*)

Selected Poems (*1949*)

William Carlos Williams: Selected Poems (*1949*)

The Collected Later Poems (*1950*)

The Collected Earlier Poems (*1951*)

The Desert Music and Other Poems (*1954*)

Journey to Love (*1955*)

DAVID WRIGHT

Poems (*1949*)

Moral Stories (*1952*)

Moral Stories (with additional poems) (*1954*)

Monologue of a Deaf Man (*1958*)